ISLAMIC PERIL

for Rosie, Imran, and Irshad

ISLAMIC PERIL

Media and Global Violence

Karim H. Karim

Montréal/New York
London

Black Rose Books No. FF312

Hardcover ISBN: 1-55164-227-1 (bound)

Paperback ISBN: 1-55164-226-3 (pbk.)

Canadian Cataloguing in Publication Data

Karim, Karim H. (Karim Haiderali), 1956

The Islamic Peril : media and global violence, updated edition

Includes bibliographical references.

1. Islam in mass media. 2. Islam and world politics. 3. Islamic countries--Relations--Europe. 4. Europe--Relations--Islamic countries. I. Title.

BP52.K37 2000   909'.0976710829   C99-901586-9

Cover design: Associés libres

BLACK ROSE BOOKS

C.P. 1258	2250 Military Road	99 Wallis Road
Succ. Place du Parc	Tonawanda, NY	London, E9 5LN
Montréal, H2X 4A7	14150	England
Canada	USA	UK

To order books:

In Canada: (phone) 1-800-565-9523 (fax) 1-800-221-9985
email: utpbooks@utpress.utoronto.ca

In United States: (phone) 1-800-283-3572 (fax) 1-651-917-6406

In the UK & Europe: (phone) London 44 (0)20 8986-4854 (fax) 44 (0)20 8533-5821
email: order@centralbooks.com

Our Web Site address: http://www.web.net/blackrosebooks

A publication of the Institute of Policy Alternatives of Montréal (IPAM)

Printed in Canada

The Canada Council | Le Conseil des Arts
for the Arts | du Canada

CONTENTS

List of Illustrations, Tables and Figures

Tables

PREFACE TO THE SECOND EDITION

The perpetrators of September 11, 2001's attacks against U.S. targets most likely intended their actions to obtain maximum media coverage. America's own airliners were turned into weapons against its symbols of economic and military power. Two of the tallest structures on the planet were demolished in minutes. Thousands of people were killed. The most powerful government in the world had been unable to prevent a few dozen individuals from carrying out the mayhem. The horrendous event and its aftermath occupied the attention of television, radio, newspapers, magazines and online media for months. Despite all this exposure we have learnt very little from the mainstream media about the fundamental reasons underlying one of the deadliest terrorist attacks in history.

"The world has changed forever," we were told repeatedly. But despite the radically unusual events, the responses of the authorities and the media have been largely predictable. Whenever the state comes under threat, its primary instinct is to ensure the continuation of its own power. Various governments set about establishing new laws and bureaucratic structures, enhancing their security and surveillance capabilities, incarcerating suspects without due process, curtailing the rights of prisoners, expanding propaganda activities, carrying out war, and discouraging criticism of these actions. The "world's greatest democracy" and "the land of freedom" is even encouraging citizens to spy on each other under its Terrorism Information and Prevention System (TIPS).

Media coverage has not been completely uncritical of the abuses of power and the infringement of civil liberties. However, the dominant news discourses largely reflect government perspectives on "the war against terrorism," which, besides completely disregarding the violence committed by states, also generally exclude terrorism carried out by various groups in countries such as Ireland, Spain, and Sri Lanka. The coverage within this frame seems to imply that once the elimination of Osama bin Laden and Al-Qaeda is accomplished the war against terrorism will have been won once and for all. Quite apart from the difficulty in eradicating all forms of terrorism from the world, the task of even identifying and locating the cells or the individual members of Al-Qaeda has proved to be immensely arduous.

That the Israeli state's increasingly vicious attempts to crush Palestinian resistence for over half a century have actually led to its exacerbation seems to be lost as a lesson on the governments seeking to eliminate terrorism with brute force. As the media focus on the day-to-day attacks and counter-attacks in "the war against terrorism," they fail to comprehend the bigger picture that a historical perspective would provide. Many mainstream journalists tend to act as cheerleaders of state militarism, shunning the effort to analyse critically the on-going violence and its long-term consequences. There are some who seek to explore the nature of both "retail" and "wholesale" terrorism and propose other ways of resolving antagonisms; but they are few and far between.

The enormity of the attack on the World Trade Centre and the Pentagon building shook the cognitive foundations of reality. Scenes of the twin towers crumbling to the ground had been unimaginable and seemed to come out of some dark, nightmarish fantasy. Received wisdom provides few clues as to what would motivate anyone to plan and carry out an act of cruelty on such an immense scale. This rupture in the flow of normative patterns of thinking actually provided the opportunity to consider other perspectives of looking at the world. Policymakers, journalists and citizens could have set in motion novel ways of comprehending the fundamental reasons why human beings engage in terrorist activity.

The single-minded discipline and the self-sacrifice required in the suicidal acts of the September 11 terrorists and those attacking Israeli targets need to be understood if we are to be able to deal with this form of violence. What is the source of the ice-cold determination of a pilot as he rushes to crash into a building that will result in his own death and that of many others? Is it anger, fear, humiliation, self-righteousness, psychosis? What prompts people to dedicate their skills and their lives to carefully plotting mass destruction? Is it of relevance that most terrorists who kill in the name of Islam tend to have scientific but not theological training? Why are America and Israel their primary targets? What can we learn from the relationship between Northern powers and Muslim societies over the last two centuries? Is a better understanding of universal human needs and tendencies the necessary first step on the path to resolving, or even mitigating, the problem of terrorism?

Opinion leaders in government, academia and media could have initiated a genuine search for answers to these and other questions. The rupture had opened a up space for innovative ways to understand the relationship between Northern and Muslim societies. Unfortunately, the opportunity was lost and integration propagandists shepherded people back to the set patterns of thinking about "us and them."

Enormous harm had been done to America, and the country was grieving. Many Americans were angry and vengeful. The most powerful government in the world did not want to acknowledge its failure to protect the nation—nor did it want to show defeat. American elites sought to ensure that no fingers were pointed at them. Criticism about any possible blame on U.S. political and military actions abroad as even remotely being the causes for the attacks was strongly discouraged. The perennial theme of America the Innocent came into play; on the other hand, President George W. Bush consistently described Al-Qaeda as "evil." Having created the bi-polar cognitive frame of the good Self and the evil Other, no further explanation was necessary in order to understand the reasons for the attacks. Most media proceeded to conduct their reporting within the broad parameters of this discourse. As with Ronald Reagan's singular characterization of the Soviet Union as "the evil empire" in the 1980s, there was no need to address the existence of any evil that may exist within the Self.

Primary stereotypes of Muslims that have been existence of hundreds of years were pressed into service. The term "Islamic" was used indiscriminately to describe acts of murder and destruction. Discussions of jihad frequently implied that the religion of Islam is endemically violent, disregarding similar behaviour by adherents of other faiths or the centuries-long debate about jihad among Muslims. Decontextualized quotations from the Koran were used to support the view of Islam as a perverted creed. The medieval European tale of the "Assassins" was unearthed by several Northern media organizations to construct the Muslim genealogy of the September 11 terrorists. Journalistic images of disaster, heroism and grief draw on dramatistic and ritualistic modes of narrative.

All this is not to imply that the coverage of the September 11 attacks and their aftermath have been monolithic. There were three distinct phases of reporting. On the day of the attacks, broadcasters were generally reluctant to identify Muslims as the possible perpetrators. (The media had been criticized for immediately blaming Muslims for the bombing of U.S. federal buildings in Oklahoma in 1995, which was carried out by anti-government terrorists with Christian fundamentalist leanings.) Once the U.S. government pointed the finger at Al-Qaeda, there began intense speculation about "Islamic terrorism" by journalists—most of whom had little or no understanding of the phenomenon. The third phase was characterized by a greater diversity of voices, including those of Muslims who were given the opportunity to discuss their religion and distinguish its principles from the worldview of the terrorists who claimed to act in the name of Islam.

Nevertheless, the dominant discourse continued to determine the overall media narrative and governmental behaviour towards Muslims: at the very time that the U.S. president was meeting with a group of American Muslim leaders the FBI was conducting a search of a delegation member's residence. Racial and religious profiling has become the norm in the treatment of Muslims or "Muslim-looking" individuals by airport security personnel and immigration officials. The death of dozens of Muslims in the destruction of the World Trade Center has been virtually ignored by most media which use the frame of the "(non-Muslim) American Self versus the (non-American) Muslim Other." The detention without charge of hundreds of Muslims by U.S. authorities came to prominence only when judges ruled on the illegality of this practice. Whereas the international controversy over Washington's contravention of the Geneva Convention through its use of military tribunals to try suspected Al-Qaeda and Taliban members received sustained coverage in November 2001, attention to this story soon faded. The death of individual Americans, Canadians, and Europeans in Afghanistan saw vastly more reporting than that of scores of Afghans, including civilians, killed by Western forces.

A handful of correspondents have sought to present alternative discourses on "the war against terrorism." But most mainstream media have tended to accept the notion that the primarily military and security-oriented approach is the most appropriate way to deal with terrorism. Few address the much larger context of human suffering that comes from ongoing structural violence in the world.

The single-minded focus of most media and policymakers on acts of direct violence prevents them from appreciating the magnitude of the structural violence resulting from the inequitable distribution of the world's resources and the absence of social justice.

It is incumbent upon the users of media to act as citizens rather than merely as consumers of news by challenging journalists to provide reporting that questions the dominant frames. Given the failure of educational systems to provide an adequate understanding of Islam and Muslims, it behooves journalists to explore intelligently the currents that run through this religious community which is present around the world, including all Northern countries. The vast diversity of belief and practice among Muslims as well as the intellectual debates that they are conducting on modernity, ethics and the good life as well as on their engagement with the North will provide valuable insights into contemporary global affairs. Abuses of power in Muslim-majority states also need to be reported; however, they also have to be placed within the context of the networks of influence that link many of the autocratic governments around the world to Northern elites. That most Muslim terrorists happen to have had training in the contemporary sciences seems to indicate that their terrorism draws inspiration from perverted conceptions of both Islam and Northern modernity. They appear to seek the sources of power that make the North dominant in the world; they are replicating the violence that they see the North perpetrating around the planet. In order to make sense of the "Islamic peril" the North will have to look carefully at the increasingly hybrid formations of its own Self and the Other.

PREFACE TO THE FIRST EDITION

The eve of the twenty-first century saw the photographs of "Islamic terrorists" plastered on the front pages of North American newspapers. Ahmed Ressam, a man of Algerian origins living in Quebec, was caught attempting to smuggle a bomb-making kit into the U.S. on December 14, 1999. This prompted frantic searches by heavily armed counter terrorist forces of both sides of the border in places that included "Little Pakistan" in Brooklyn, New York. This led to the arrests of four others suspected of being part of a plot to carry out "millennial attacks" during New Year's celebrations. Media speculation centred around the links of these people to the Algerian GIA ("Armed Islamic Group") and to the current incarnation of global arch-terrorist, Osama bin Laden. Muslim communities were faced once again with descriptions of "Islamic terror group," "Islamic terrorists," "Islamic militants," "violent Islamic group," "Islamic fundamentalists," "Islamic extremism," "Islamic radicalism" etc., in which "Islam" is a synonym for fanaticism and senseless violence. Some overenthusiastic journalists and editors cast a wide net in identifying other accomplices, providing names and pictures. Many of these people, living quietly with their families in North American cities, were mere acquaintances of the suspects and knew nothing of the alleged plots.

Youssef Karroum, a Moroccan Canadian father of three young children, who crossed the Canada-U.S. border to buy cheaper groceries on the American side in January 2000 was detained and kept in high security isolation for a week. He was not permitted to contact his wife and was denied access to the Koran. Sniffer dogs had apparently indicated traces of explosives in the trunk of his car, a suspicion which was not borne out by rigorous testing in FBI laboratories. Karroum was released, without his car, money, passport, or an apology.

On February 1, 2000, The Ottawa Citizen carried a prominent front page headline, "Secret arrest of a Saddam ally." The article was illustrated with the reproduction of a poster which showed the stark drawing of a woman in hijab, identified as Mahnaz Samadi. She was arrested in an apartment across the street from the U.S. Embassy in Ottawa. The diminutive woman was described in the article as being a member of the civilian branch of the Mujahedeen-e Khalq, an armed organization based in Iraq whose goal is to overthrow the government of Iran. Despite such serious allegations in the media, the police did not have evidence other than that supporting a charge of violating immigration rules. Samadi, who said that she worked as a human rights worker based in the U.S., had entered Canada without a visa. She was released after being held for two months in a detention centre.

Terrorists, whether Muslims from Algeria or Christians from Oklahoma, clearly pose a danger to society. The particular task facing security agencies in democracies is ensuring public safety while upholding the civil rights of all citizens. Unfortunately, the treatment accorded to a growing number of Muslims in Western countries seems to resemble the darkest days of the "red scare" when people who did not adhere completely to the dominant ideology were harassed, imprisoned, and some even driven to suicide. Such fundamentalist approaches of ensuring loyalty to the country leaves those who are not members of the mainstream open to suspicion. The increasing humiliation of innocent Muslim men and women by Northern states can probably be attributed to the continually negative media references to Islam; this has led to the creation of a general impression that the religion promotes extremism and that a practising Muslim anywhere in the world can be none other than an "Islamic extremist."

Neither globalization nor technological advances guarantee international, inter-cultural harmony. On the contrary, it seems that the growth of communications links between Northern and Muslim societies has parallelled rising misperception of each other. Such misperceptions are fed by historical stereotypes and the ongoing manipulation of information on both sides. This book examines how Northern mass media, from the mid-1980s to the year 2000, constructed events in which the North was perceived to be in conflict with "Islam." The overwhelming communications superiority of Northern powers ensures that their world views remain dominant. In expanding their cultural, economic and military influence in developing countries, they will continue to face resistance from the latter's inhabitants, including Muslims. Judging by current trends, Northern mass media will describe them—regardless of their philosophical and tactical orientations—as "extremists." The pliability of the largely negative Northern images of "Islam" enables propagandists to press them into service to demonize significant challenges from Muslim societies.

These tendencies are in danger of being exacerbated by the growing agitation among many Muslims frustrated by the failure of their own political leaders to ensure the basic necessities of life and human rights. Potential Islamists are frequently induced into militancy by demagogues quoting scripture out of context to offer simplistic (but vengeful) solutions to life's problems. The rapid rise in the Muslim populations will also increase the probability of confrontations with inimical Northern interests. Terrorism and other atrocities will continue to be justified in the name of "Islam" by the few who carry them out—claims which many Northern journalists will generally accept at face value.

The beliefs of hundreds of millions of Muslims who view their religion as a path to harmony with fellow human beings and with nature will probably continue to be disregarded by most Northern observers. Post-Cold War fear mongers who foretell the emergence of "Islamic radicalism" as the major new threat to global stability in the 21st century possibly stand to be perversely gratified by the self-fulfilment of their prophecies. Speaking at the beginning of the new millennium, they suggest no structural alternatives—only offering apocalyptic visions of great confrontations between the righteous North and the evil Muslim. Media focus remains on the extremists on both sides as their mutual fear feeds on each others' mirror images about "the Great Satan." Nevertheless, this is not a result of an active media conspiracy against Islam; it can be understood, rather, as the adherence—mostly unconscious—of a narrow set of meanings.

In all likelihood, an Armageddon-like showdown will not take place between Northern powers and Muslims. However, the reservoir of negative Northern images of Islam will probably continue to justify the stream of individual incidents of harassment as well as military actions. This book studies the manners in which such acts have been rationalized by propagandists. It also explores ways in which journalists can attempt to avoid framing their accounts of the Other in stereotypical images and foster genuine understanding through "other ways of telling." This inquiry acknowledges the work of several reporters who attempt to rise above the usual clichés about Muslims to present information in conscientious manners. It also demonstrates how such attempts are often subverted by dominant discourses. There is an urgent need for a fundamental reassessment of the way the media operate if they are to function as a vital component of civil society.

Regarding style, I have not adopted a strict system of transliteration for words derived from Middle Eastern languages, but have instead chosen to use commonly-used English forms of such terms in order to facilitate access to a non-specialist readership. Finally, a word about the primary title of the book: it is meant to draw attention to the absurdity of turning a perception of danger into an all-encompassing, monolithic threat.

ACKNOWLEDGEMENTS

A number of individuals and institutions provided assistance during the extended period of this project. George Szanto was an invaluable source of support and advice. Gertrude Robinson and Issa Boullata were other key influences in shaping this work. I am also deeply indebted to John Sigler and Farouk Mitha for their constructive comments. Thanks also go to the many friends and students who referred me to pertinent academic and media material.

Discussions with Zayn Kassam and Amyn Sajoo, during their respective sojourns in Ottawa, provided opportunities to sound out initial ideas. Stephen Riggins's suggestions on an earlier version of a chapter that he edited for publication helped sharpen some rough edges.

My stint as a news agency journalist afforded the opportunity to understand the mechanics involved in the construction of media messages. Antoine Char, Allan Armstrong, and Gerry Loughran's guidance is much appreciated. Participation in *The Ottawa Citizen*'s Readers' Council also allowed insight into the workings of a daily newspaper.

I would like to thank the Institute of Ismaili Studies, London, and the Department of Canadian Heritage, which provided funding during different periods of the research. My gratitude also goes to Roger Butt, Ned Ellis, Ajit Mehat, Renée Joyal, and Greg Gauld for their support. They helped me see the multiplicity of discourses that exist even in government.

Farida Jamal kindly consented to read the final draft and Dina Salha the proofs. Thanks also go to Linda Barton for the care she has taken in editing. However, any shortcomings in the book, are, of course, mine.

To my children, Imran and Irshad, I offer profound apologies for the sunny days that were spent indoors, and to my wife, Rosemin, my deepest thanks for making this task much less arduous than it would have been.

Finally, I would like to acknowledge that nothing is possible without the presence of Spirit.

INTRODUCTION

Competing Discourses

The representation of Western and Muslim societies as irreconcilable enemies tends towards *mis*representation. Terrorist acts and the sometimes bloody clashes between Christian and Muslim groups in various parts of the world, while demanding serious attention, should be understood within their distinct social contexts. They are not symptomatic of a global war between Christianity and Islam. Conflicts in places such as the Balkans, the Caucasus, and the Holy Land, are driven less by religion than by territorial ambitions, ethnic differences, and political machinations. From time to time Western powers engage in military partnerships even with those Muslim-majority countries whom they have identified as terrorist states. Saddam Hussein's government was dropped from the U.S. State Department's list of terrorist regimes in the 1980s when it was at war with Iran, then America's nemesis in the Middle East; Syria, another "pariah state" according to Washington, was brought by the Bush administration into the U.S.-led UN Coalition against Iraq in 1991; Yasser Arafat, long vilified in the West as arch-terrorist, has been remodelled into peacemaker. But quite apart from these secular leaders, the Saudi family, which presides over a religiously conservative state, has been a stanch U.S. ally for decades.

Essentialist and polarized scenarios such as Samuel Huntington's "clash of civilizations" and Benjamin Barber's "jihad vs. McWorld"[1] belie complex real world realities. Nevertheless, in the wake of the Cold War there has emerged the notion of Islam as a primary Other. An ancient enemy darkens the dawn of the new millennium just as we rise from the triumph over the communist East. Despite occasional portrayals of individual Muslims in a favourable light, dominant media discourses have tended to create an overall picture of the religion as a source of planetary instability: the "Islamic peril" disrupts international order at the very time that globalization is bringing humanity together.

The view of the Muslim East as the source of danger to the West has old origins in Eurocentric discourses. Even in the Middle Ages, narratives about the alliances linking Muslim and Christian rulers was overwhelmed by the polarized construction of the relationship between Islam and Christianity. Polemical discourses produced in the centuries when Europeans fought long wars with "Saracens," "Moors" and Turks are embedded in the classic works produced by the likes of Dante, Shakespeare, Voltaire, Beethoven, Mozart, and Delacroix. Their continued consumption by post-Enlightenment generations sustains a world view in which "Mohammadens" are essentially gripped by violence, lust, greed, and barbarism. These core images are reproduced with remarkable regularity in contemporary cultural productions, like film, television programs, and websites, as well as in press accounts. Depictions of Middle Eastern terrorists by Hollywood and transnational wire services seem to bear a striking resemblance to the Muslim characters in European polemics penned a thousand years ago. Whereas Muslims also produced negative imagery about Europeans, they did not develop an overarching discourse about the West comparable to Europe's institutionalized study of the East (Orientalism), that grew in tandem with the imperialist venture.

The idea of Islam constituting a primary threat to the West was eclipsed in the latter part of the nineteenth century by the military defeat of Muslim powers. Many Muslim lands were brought under European colonial control and the Ottoman empire, which, at its height had attempted to push into western Europe, was in retreat. The First World War resulted in the triumph of the Allies over the remnants of the Muslim Caliphate, which had been in existence since the early period of Islam. Indeed, as British troops marched into Jerusalem, General Allenby remarked that the Crusades were finally over. But the Red Army proved victorious in Russia, and the communist East replaced the Muslim East as the primary enemy of the West. A short-lived alliance of Western powers with the Soviet Union during the Second World War was followed by the intensification of ideological conflict during the Cold War. Dominant discourses presented the entire world as a red and blue checkerboard in this global struggle between communism and capitalism.

Development theory propounded by the likes of Daniel Lerner (who carried out a study of the use of media in several Middle Eastern countries in the 1950s[2]) assumed that the gradual replacement of religion by westernization was inevitable and irreversible. Islam's influence on public life was seen as being on the wane. The secularly-oriented policies of twentieth century leaders such as Ataturk, Jinnah, Nasser, Suharto, and the Shah of Iran were viewed as evidence that Muslim states were "modernizing" (i.e., westernizing). However, the mid-1970s saw a growing movement to revive the role of religion in the public sphere in various Middle Eastern societies, partly due to the failure of the Eurocentric model of development. The overthrow of Shah Mohammed Reza Pahlevi of Iran in 1979 and the assassination of president Anwar Sadat of Egypt in 1981 (both major allies of the U.S.) by separate elements of Islamist revivalism signalled "the return of Islam" to Western opinion leaders.

This "return" in many ways is a continuation of the attempt by Muslims since the 18th century to understand the contingencies of contemporary life from the perspective of Koranic teachings. Its manifestations range from the profound intellectual debates with Enlightenment philosophy to the fashioning of practical strategies for development within Muslim frameworks to the militant rejection of all Western influences. Many variants of this broad "revival" have emerged in Muslim countries from western Africa to South-East Asia, leading to differing responses from their governments. These discourses have also posed a challenge to the hegemony of the post-Enlightenment world view at international fora. Several insurgencies have threatened secular systems of government in Muslim-majority countries and have launched terrorist attacks against Western targets. As the Muslim resurgence was gaining ground in the 1980s, European communism was steadily declining. The fall of the Berlin Wall in 1989 and the subsequent collapse of the Soviet Union marked the end of the Cold War.

These significant historical developments have led to the reordering of the ways in which global conflict is constructed. For most of the twentieth century, the West had been pitted against the Soviet Union. As state-based communism expanded its locus after the Second World War, Eastern Europe had come to be conceived as the primary ideological and military Other, and, in some quarters, the "Evil Empire." Vast institutional and economic infrastructures had been been built in the West and in Eastern Europe to wage the Cold War. NATO, the Warsaw Pact, national military machines, military industrial complexes, and foreign intelligence services furthered innumerable careers and created enormous wealth for armaments producers. Weapons manufacturers in the North sold billions of dollars worth of arms to Southern countries to fight many proxy wars.

However, the end of the Cold War and the resulting "threat vacuum"[3] have endangered these structures of power and wealth. Faced with the loss of their *raison d'être*, some of the military and intelligence-gathering establishments began searching for new enemies. It is in this context that a number of ideologues in both the West and in Eastern Europe now (re-)present Islam as Other. Indeed, the Cold War is reconstructed by some as a mere historical diversion from the centuries-old clash between Christians and Muslims, and old images of the Islamic threat are reinvigorated.

> With the end of the Cold War another chapter was written: numerous [American] politicians were heard to proclaim that the USA was now facing the threat of Islamic militancy, and this received partial confirmation from the Gulf conflict of 1990-91. In 1990 Vice-President Dan Quayle, in an address to cadets at the Annapolis naval academy, linked Islamic fundamentalism to Nazism and communism. The right-wing Republican candidate in the 1992 presidential campaign, Pat Buchanan, declared: 'For a millennium, the struggle for mankind's destiny was between Christianity and Islam; in the twenty-first century it may be so again.'[4]

Whereas Western propagandists had been reluctant to couch the conflict in East Timor within a religious frame during the Cold War, it is now often placed within the discursive model of "Muslims against Christians." And Moscow has constructed its war with Chechnya as a struggle against "Islamic terrorists."

The transnational mass media play a key role in these discursive constructions. Based primarily in North America and Europe, their political and cultural reference points about international relations tend mainly to be anchored in the North. This tendency was well-illustrated during the Cold War in the almost mandatory journalistic framing of Southern states as either pro-West or pro-Soviet: the significance of events in these countries were then judged according to their geopolitical placement in relation to the North. Mainstream media now tend to highlight real or alleged links of Muslims suspected of terrorism to Iran, Saddam Hussein, or Osama bin Laden. Violence committed by militant Muslims is usually placed within journalistic frameworks whose cultural roots are hundreds of years old. For example, editorial cartoons draw on images such as the bloodthirsty Saracen wielding "the sword of Islam" embedded in medieval European literature. Such depictions tend to hinder the understanding of violence as well as of Islam.

This book traces media re-constructions of Islam as a primary Other in the last two decades leading up to the twenty-first century. It does this through the analysis of the coverage of events such as the hijacking of an American airliner by a Lebanese group, the holding of Western hostages in Beirut, the *intifadah* in the West Bank, the Iran-Iraq war, the Gulf War, and various wars in the Caucasus and the Balkans. It is important to state at the outset that this study does not function according to the notion that there is a centrally-organized journalistic conspiracy against Islam—the mechanics of the mass media in liberal political systems do not favour such overt orchestrations of information. The inquiry attempts, rather, to elucidate several of the complex and contradictory processes through which dominant discourses portray Muslim societies. It applies discourse competition methodology to demonstrate how, despite a tendency among a growing number of Northern opinion leaders (including journalists) to distinguish between the vast diversity of Muslim groups, the dominant perspectives on Islam tend to subvert these alternative approaches. The collection of images about Islam is formed by history, myth, socialization, and propaganda, as well as by the political manipulation of Islamic symbols by Muslims themselves. Whereas this book views violence as an ubiquitous human phenomenon prevalent in all cultures, it does not seek to justify atrocities through cultural relativism. The violent acts against non-combatants carried out by people who see themselves acting in the name of the state, communism, democracy, Islam, Christianity, Judaism, or any other cause are all reprehensible. What this study seeks to demonstrate is how dominant media discourses simultaneously highlight and downplay specific types of violence.

Human perceptions of everyday encounters are the products of social constructions of meanings rather than the results of objective observations. Hegemonic meanings of events are developed through the engineering of societal consensus, usually by those who are able to influence dominant discourses.

Dominant discourse here does not refer only to linguistic structure, but to the broader process of communication. In so far as the bulk of a society subscribes in a particular historical period to a set of fundamental myths, one can speak of a dominant discourse that serves as a matrix for its members' discussions on various issues. The dominant discourses of a society are not manifestations of a monolithic or static set of ideological and cultural currents: their complexities, which reflect the ever-changing structures of power, are shaped by continually evolving and often contradictory combinations of the assumptions, hypotheses, and world views of socio-economic and intellectual elites. Stuart Hall tells us:

> We must remember that this is not a single, unitary, but a plurality of dominant discourses: that they are not deliberately selected by encoders to 'reproduce events within the horizon of the dominant ideology', but constitute the *field* of meanings within which they must choose. Precisely because they have become 'universalized and naturalized', they appear to be the only forms of intelligibility available; they have become sedimented as the 'only rational, universally valid ones'…that these premises embody the dominant definitions of the situation, and represent or refract the existing structures of power, wealth and domination, hence that they *structure* every event they signify, and *accent* them in a manner which reproduces the given ideological structures—this process has become unconscious, even for the encoders.[5]

There is, therefore, not a deliberate plan by the mass media to portray certain issues in particular ways, but a "naturalized" hegemonic process through which they adhere to a common field of meanings. Nor is it valid to speak of capitalist, liberal, or Zionist control over media content. It is pertinent, however, to study how certain types of media discourses manage, despite competition from other discourses, to remain dominant.

The consensus of hegemonic classes on the major issues of the day at particular junctures in time are mirrored by dominant discourses. They provide the definitions, theoretical paradigms, agendas, and frames with reference to which a society gives meaning to subjects of importance. These reference points form the bases for public discussions and integration propaganda[6] about topics such as democracy, science, culture, violence, and peace. Specific (conscious and unconscious) uses of language, visual imagery, and presentation formats by hegemonic discourses tend to reinforce the *status quo*. Preferred networks of terminology and preferred meanings of terms prevail in important discussions while alternative terminology and meanings are either disparaged or disregarded. Whereas *oppositional discourses*[7] in a society may criticize dominant discourses' specific viewpoints, they both generally subscribe to the same sets of fundamental myths and premises. *Alternative discourses*, however, provide more serious challenges to the hegemony of dominant discourses, which through their pre-eminent and ubiquitous character usually manage to overwhelm or subvert messages that do not conform to their particular ideological frameworks. One of the primary features of a dominant discourse is its power to comment on and interpret major issues and events; it maintains superiority by being dynamic, continually co-opting and transmuting the words, images, and symbols of other discursive modes that threaten its consensus-building efforts. In this way, it corresponds to the manoeuvring of elites by whom it is produced and whose positions it reinforces. This ability to reframe alternative discourses is at the heart of a dominant discourse's power to sustain its hegemony. It may be ultimately transformed through cultural, ideological, or political revolutions, which in turn give rise to consensus based on new dominant discourses.

The mainstream media, which are largely owned by the socio-economic elite or the state, are important channels for hegemonic communication and usually function as instruments of consensus-engineering. Dominant discourses reproduce themselves inter-textually, with the various media that carry them continually referring to each other. The mass media are indeed a "marketplace of ideas," but the information that supports the dominant ideas in society are usually placed in the most prominent showcases of the journalistic bazaars. Hegemonic discourses normally appear on the front and editorial pages and at the beginning of news programs, while alternative discourses that contradict the structures of societal power are relegated (in the rare instances when they do appear) to the more obscure parts of newspapers and electronic broadcasts. Mainstream journalists tend to highlight the "factual" evidence that buttresses society's dominant discourses by placing events into ideologically preferred frames. Acting as integration propagandists, the mass media primarily couch "reality" within dominant societal myths. Alternative discourses that attempt to offer different world views are generally recoded within dominant frameworks. However, it bears restating that the preferred encoding of events and issues by the mass media is not a centrally-orchestrated or precisely-directed procedure but one that operates within a hegemonic process of meaning creation.

North, South, West, Muslim, Islamic

Since the relationships between various cultures are of pertinence in this book, it is useful to outline how it uses terms such as "North," "South," "West," and "Muslim societies." Rather than being reflections of absolute geographical, political, economic, or cultural realities, these formulations are merely used as analytical tools for the study: they are denotations neither of insulated nor monolithic regions of the planet, but are broad categories that are meant to indicate certain characteristics shared by their inhabitants. While recognizing the multilayered identities of individuals and the inter-connectedness of various regions of the world, a project such as the current one has to delineate some general boundaries to distinguish specific cultural and political actors. Its focus is the relationship of the technological civilization, which is generally considered to have European origins, with long-standing Muslim societies, which are viewed as being located in lands stretching from Senegal in western Africa to Mindanao in the Philippines. Even though there are numerous overlapping features between the Northern and Muslim societies, these regions are viewed as being distinct vis-à-vis each other for purposes of the present analysis.

"The North," which is used here primarily as a geopolitical, economic, and cultural term rather than a geographical one, comprises of United States, Canada, Western Europe, Eastern Europe, Japan, Australia, New Zealand, and Israel. Following the collapse of the Soviet bloc, it is even more pertinent to speak of the North-South dichotomy than of "the three worlds." Whereas both the North and the South consist of countries with substantial differences in levels of economic development as well as a variety of distinct cultures, it is legitimate to group them into two global regions in the context of the North-South geopolitical divide. Northern societies have Eurocentric world views and Southern ones generally share the cultural subordination (which comes from being former colonies of Northern powers) and the disadvantages of global economic structures that are largely weighted in favour of the North.[8] Although the general framework of this study is the relationship between Northern and Muslim societies, it is pertinent at times to isolate "the West" as a distinct part of the North that does not include the formerly communist Eastern Europe. Like other regional categories, "the West" is not an all-encompassing term indicating a fixed geographic territory but a historical and cultural locus which has specific sets of relationships with other parts of the world. "Muslim societies" are considered part of the South, even though there are a number of indigenous and immigrant Muslim communities in the northern hemisphere.

One of the primary problem that underlies dominant Northern constructions of Muslim societies is the failure to acknowledge their diversity. The terms "Muslim world" or "Islamic world" are therefore avoided in order not to reinforce the false impression of a monolithic global Muslim entity, the self-image of a unified Muslim *ummah* (community) notwithstanding. Aziz Al-Azmeh asserts that "there are as many Islams as there are situations that support it."[9] Whereas the followers of Islam adhere to a set of beliefs in common, there remains a vast plurality that exists not only in cultural but also religious behaviour among the billion Muslims living around the world.

Bengalis, for instance, viewed the Pakistan army as a violent instrument of oppression; many Afghans accused the *jihad* of their compatriots of being funded and organized by the American CIA; many in Ayatollah Khomeini's Iran, including the Ayatollah himself, criticized General Zia's Islamization efforts in Pakistan as inadequate; in turn, many Muslims in the Middle East and South Asia condemned the Ayatollah's revolution in Iran as excessive. Critics were quick to point out the connection between military regimes and the use of Islam: to them Islam in Numeiri's Sudan and Zia's Pakistan was reduced to the chopping off of hands and whipping of petty criminals. Some scholars were cynical of colleagues who attempted to 'Islamize' knowledge, since merely appending the label 'Islamic' was no guarantee of academic quality. Sectarian champions, Shia or Sunni, denounced their rivals and proclaimed their exclusive ownership of the truth; smaller groups, like the Ismaili, Ahmadi and Baha'i, were dismissed as heretics and sometimes physically persecuted.[10]

And there are those who have considered themselves to be Muslim only in a cultural but not in a religious sense, the most well-known example being Salman Rushdie.

Mohammed Arkoun remarks that "We can no longer use the word 'Islam' without quotation marks. It has been so misused and distorted by the media, Muslims themselves, and political scientists that we need a radical reworking of the concept."[11] The core of dominant Muslim discourses, established during the three centuries after the death of the prophet Muhammad in 632, has come historically to be used by hegemonic groups within Muslim societies to maintain their respective dominance. Over time, these discourses have become part of the orthodox understanding of Muslim creed and history and are broadly subscribed to not only by the political and religious elites but even militants who oppose the hegemony of these sections of society. Whereas the positions of the Muslim militants (Islamists) do form *oppositional* Muslim discourses, they do not seem to provide viable answers for the contingencies of technological society. More profound and practical Muslim proposals for countering Eurocentric influences and ensuring a modernity that is authentically Islamic have come from the *alternative* writings in contemporary times of such scholars as Muhammad Iqbal, Ali Shariati, Fazlur Rahman, Akbar Ahmed, Fatima Mernissi, Abdullah al-Na'im, Aziz Al-Azmeh, Mohammed Arkoun, and Aziz Esmail, deriving from their familiarity with Islamic as well as Northern thought.

Illustration 1: Islam depicted as destabilizing the world

Illustration 2: "Islamic" threats in journalistic discourses

Muslim discourses often attempt to legitimize actions of certain groups of Muslims with references to "*Islamic* history," "*Islamic* peoples," "*Islamic* socialism," "*Islamic* government," "*Islamic* revolution" etc. In the absence of a singular authoritative "Church," each Muslim group, in so far as it adheres to a particular school of law (*madhhab*), can claim that its actions follow scriptural dictates. However, consensus does not exist even among Islamist groups on the legitimacy of the using terrorism as a tactic. Nevertheless, the Northern-based transnational media tend uncritically to accept the "Islamicness" of these actions without putting them into the context of the rigorous debates among Muslims on such issues. (They usually do not draw attention to the "Christianness" of extremist groups such as white supremacists or cult members who use Christian symbols and offer religious rationalization for their actions.) Unlike the consensus in the Northern polity regarding a separation of Church and State, faith (*din*) in the dominant Muslim view is not divorced from the temporal world (*dunya*). But whereas Islam may be described as a way of life, *all* that Muslims do is not necessarily Islamic.

Due to the many cases of disagreements about what is truly Islamic, it is necessary to distinguish between two dimensions in which the religion manifests itself. The adjective "Islamic" will be reserved in this study for the "metaphysical, religious, spiritual" dimension of the faith[12], limiting it to the fundamental aspects of Muhammad's message as it appears in the primary scriptural sources (the Koran and the *hadith*—the Prophet's traditions). "Muslim" will be used, in a qualified sense, for "the second level of signification, [which] is the sociohistorical space in which human existence unfolds."[13] This will help to distinguish between the theological ideals and the reality that Muslims encounter in pursuing these ideals. In this sense, there are histories of respective Muslim peoples, governments of various Muslim countries, and socialism(s) practised by Muslim peoples living in specific states, rather than "Islamic history," "Islamic peoples," "Islamic governments," or "Islamic socialism."

Edward Said notes that "the word *Muslim* is less provocative and more habitual for most Arabs; the word *Islamic* has acquired an activist, even aggressive quality that belies the more ambiguous reality."[14]

The acts of terrorism by individuals, groups, or governments professing Islam are seen here as belonging to "the socio-historical space in which human existence unfolds." These actions are willy-nilly part of the history of certain Muslims who carry them out and, by extension, of the histories of their specific (regional, national) collectivities and even the global Muslim community, in so far as significant acts carried out by members of these groupings are part of these respective histories. However, bombings and hijackings carried out by the Islamic Jihad organization in Lebanon in the 1980s and 1990s cannot be considered "Islamic" since these acts do not constitute part of the essential metaphysical, religious, or spiritual dimension of the faith. They cannot even be considered to be expressions of "Muslim *terrorism*" if this were to be posited as an essential feature of Islam. Nevertheless, the individuals who profess Islam and carry out terrorist acts could be viewed as "Muslim terrorists"—one would then similarly refer to "Christian terrorists," "Jewish terrorists," "Hindu terrorists," "Buddhist terrorists" etc. Distinguishing between the two dimensions helps to identify the ideological use of Islamic terminology in Northern and Muslim discourses. "Islamism" and "Islamist"[15] rather than "fundamentalism" and "fundamentalist" (terms whose etymological roots lie in Christian contexts)[16] are used in this study to refer to those Muslims who adopt an ideologically reformist stance which promotes a return to an imagined ideal from the Muslim past. There is not only a geographic and cultural diversity among Islamists but also in their beliefs about establishing a utopic Islamic society and in their tactics. Islamism and Islamists therefore cannot be viewed monolithically. Those Islamists who embrace the use of violence in the pursuit of their goals are referred to here as militants.

Misuse of the terms related to Islam is endemic in the transnational media. In his landmark study on *Covering Islam*, Edward Said attempted to show how Northern mass media have supported a particular perspective on Islam that is more an expression of the power relationships between Northern and majority-Muslim states than a real attempt to understand the religion's adherents.[17] The resurgence of strong religious feelings among Muslims in various parts of the world has led to a form of reporting that serves more to mystify than to explain events occurring in Muslim societies.

It has given consumers of news the sense that they have understood Islam without at the same time intimating to them that a great deal in this energetic coverage is based on far from objective material. In many instances, "Islam" has licensed not only patent inaccuracy but also expressions of unrestrained ethnocentrism, cultural and even racial hatred, deep yet paradoxically free-floating hostility. All this has taken place as part of what is presumed to be fair, balanced, responsible coverage of Islam. Aside from the fact that neither Christianity nor Judaism, both of them going through quite remarkable revivals (or "returns"), is treated in so emotional a way, there is an unquestioned assumption that Islam can be characterized limitlessly by means of a handful of recklessly general and repeatedly deployed clichés.[18]

The particular global "problem" of the challenge that some Muslims present to the Northern-dominated global order is thus named "Islam," a term that is manipulated according to the needs of the particular source discussing it. Among other things, it has come variously to refer to a religion, a culture, a civilization, a community, a religious revival, a militant cult, an ideology, a geographical region, and an historical event. Whereas a number of Northern journalists, academics, and politicians have taken pains to state that Islam is not synonymous with violence or terrorism, their alternative discourses are usually overshadowed by many other opinion leaders who continue to frame information within dominant discourses. Consequently, "Islam," "Islamic," "Muslim" "Shi'ite" etc. have largely become what Gordon Allport called "labels of primary potency," that "act like shrieking sirens, deafening us to all finer discriminations that we might otherwise perceive."[19] Such blurring of reality makes it possible to portray the performance of Islamic rituals as acts of militancy and, therefore, all practicing Muslims as fanatical militants.

Islam as Other

In analysing the coverage of Muslim societies by the Western mass media one cannot disregard the long history of inter-cultural relations between Middle Easterners and Europeans. The images that have developed of each other over millennia necessarily influence current perceptions. Many medieval Europeans believed Islam to be a false religion, tending to see Muhammad as a fraudulent prophet and his followers as the agents of impiety and disorder. For hundreds of years, the armies and navies of Muslim rulers posed a genuine threat to European states. This resulted in the proliferation of narratives that painted Islam in dark colours. Even when Muslim societies entered a period of decline and Europe a period of ascendency, fear of "Mohammedanism" remained latent. Through continual reinforcement of the notion that the Muslim Other was essentially a savage in need of civilization, it was possible to justify the colonial control of her land and person. The resilience of age-old notions about Islam is evident in the ease with which they can still be used by contemporary Northern propagandists.

Prior to the collapse of the USSR, the confrontations of Western powers with state and non-state Muslim actors seemed to prepare the way for "Islam" to become a post-Cold War Other. Over the last few decades, reportage of various Middle Eastern wars, "the OPEC crisis," the Iranian and Lebanese hostage situations, "the Rushdie Affair," the conflicts in Afghanistan, Algeria, Azerbaijan, Egypt, Indonesia, Iran, Iraq, Kashmir, Lebanon, Mindanao, and Sudan, as well as of the terrorist acts committed by Muslims often tends to attribute blame explicitly or implicitly to a monolithic Islam, regardless of these separate events' specific historical, economic, and political factors. Since the age-old cognitive models of the religion embedded over the centuries in European lore are of discord, the credibility of current media accounts about Muslims as being inherently disruptive tend not to be contested. Even though contemporary Northern discourses are secular, the memory of a medieval Christendom in military conflict with Muslim societies seems latent in present-day attitudes. Referring to the conflict in Bosnia-Herzegovina, Susan Sontag notes,

> Not to be underestimated...is the pervasiveness of anti-Muslim prejudice, a reflex reaction to a people the majority of whom are as secular, and as imbued with contemporary consumer-society culture, as their other Southern European neighbours. To bolster the fiction that this is, at its deepest source, a religious war, the label "Muslim" is invariably used to describe the victims, their army and their government—though no one would think of describing the [Serbian and Croat] invaders as the Orthodox and the Catholics. Do many secular "Western" intellectuals who might be expected to have raised their voices to defend Bosnia share these prejudices? Of course they do.[20]

The reluctant intervention of Western powers in Bosnia and in Kosovo, under the respective aegis of the UN and NATO, took place more due to concerns about the spread of the conflicts in central Europe than to rescue the Muslim-majority populations. They made little attempt, however, to assist the Chechens, apart from issuing pious protests against the massive abuses by the Russian military.

Whereas there remain other forces opposed to the hegemony of Northern elites, such as the governments of China, North Korea and Cuba, "narco-terrorists" in Colombia and South-East Asia, as well as popularly-based movements in the industrialized and non-industrialized societies like the environmentalist and the women's movements, Islam, with its world-wide body of adherents, is often constructed as presenting the most dangerous threat. From time to time it is linked variously to communism, fascism, Nazism, or anti-Semitism. These propagandic themes capitalize on traditional Northern images of Muslims as violent and as irrational barbarians intent on destroying civilization. A monolithic and static "Islam" is presented as the antithesis of the Western liberal values developed over the last 300 years. In the aftermath of the Cold War, "the Islamic peril" has become a convenient common enemy of the West and Eastern Europe since it can be presented as a fundamental threat to civilization. However, since Northern powers frequently seek allies in majority-Muslim states, the conflict with Islam cannot be portrayed as a clear-cut struggle such as that which was perceived to exist between NATO and the Warsaw Pact. Nevertheless, the image of the religion, when required, is used effectively to demonize certain enemies: the use of terms such as "Islamic," "Shia," "jihad" frequently serve in dominant Northern discourses to discredit Muslim groups. These tendencies are further exacerbated by the advent of the third Christian millennium and the rise in belief in prophecies about the Apocalypse: "Islam" has occasionally emerged as embodying the Antichrist.[21]

Several Muslim groups and individuals have attempted to respond in non-violent manners to the long-standing hegemonic status of the North that has existed since the colonial era and has come to be part of the "natural" scheme of things in dominant global discourses. However, this resistance is usually portrayed by Northern propagandists as being irrational and unwarranted, and as stemming from the supposedly regressive nature of Islam. The broad range of alternative discourses seeking to counter the present dominance of the North over Muslim cultures is often lumped together with violent opposition and is called "Muslim extremism."

While the American government uses violence of various types around the world and has supported insurgent forces such as the Contras in Nicaragua and mujahideen groups in Afghanistan, the U.S. State Department maintains an internationally influential list of "terrorist states" that has included Iraq, Iran, Libya, South Yemen, Sudan, and Syria. The mass media in the U.S. generally adhere to such discourses of Washington's foreign policies.[22] These tendencies have global implications due to the worldwide dissemination of the American media content. Given the exclusive communications links between metropolitan centres and specific developing countries, the perspectives of the Northern-based transnational mass media even influence the ways particular countries in the South view their own neighbours. Through this process of global consensus creation those that are declared terrorist states by Northern powers, particularly the United States, tend to become pariah or rogue elements in the eyes of the most other countries.

For example, the changes in Iraq's relationship with the United States since the late 1970s seems to have determined its portrayal in the transnational mass media. In 1982, the U.S. State Department dropped Iraq from its list of terrorist states when it was at war with Iran. Washington supported the government of Saddam Hussein during that conflict even though it continued to sponsor terrorist groups and use chemical weapons against its own Kurdish citizens. Whereas the transnational media were critical of Baghdad, they continued to portray Saddam Hussein as the protector of the Gulf states from revolutionary Iran. Once the Iran-Iraq War was over and Iraq threatened, with its invasion of Kuwait in 1990, to emerge as a regional power independent of American control, the United States descended on it with apocalyptic fury. Integration propagandists in the transnational mass media seemed suddenly to discover the long-standing brutality of the Iraqi regime. One of the most effective ways to discredit Hussein seemed to be to portray his actions within the dominant frames of "terrorism" and "Islam." The reports from the global news agencies were used in most countries around the world.[23]

Alternative Northern discourses on "the Islamic threat" expressed by Northern scholars such as John Esposito, Fred Halliday, James Piscatori, John Sigler, Jochen Hippler, and Andrea Lueg[24] have attempted to demonstrate that the portrayals of "the Islamic peril" to the North are usually overstated. They do point out, however, that the primary danger is for Muslim societies which have been destabilized by militant Islamism. Some journalists such as Robert Fisk, Elaine Sciolino, David Hirst, Paul Koring, Yousseff Ibrahim, Gwynne Dyer, and Thomas Friedman regularly attempt to present insightful reporting that steers away from hackneyed and formulaic reporting about Muslims. But these voices are drowned out by the constant din of the discourses that capitalize on the store of negative images to present "Islam" as a primary obstacle to global peace.

Northern journalists have available to them specific fields of meanings which they use in constructing discourses on the respective places of the North, of Muslims, of terrorists etc. The North-based transnational mass media, which have sophisticated hardware and organizational systems, are much more effective than Muslim sources in creating globally dominant interpretations. The transnational media infrastructure militates against information that runs counter to the mainly North-South flows, notwithstanding the rampant growth of global networking over the Internet. Even though individual Muslims have made inroads into mainstream media institutions in some Northern countries, they collectively lack access to dominant discourses. David Lloyd speaks of the adherence of the media of all countries to "a global narrative which allows for only one version of human history, [and] the gradual incorporation of all nations by a Western notion of development or modernity."[25] With the growing planetary concentration of media ownership and the reach of major Northern print and broadcast networks around the planet, this observation rings increasingly true. The dominant discourses about Islam and other topics are transmitted regularly to media outlets around the world and reproduced in newspapers and news broadcasts. Whereas oppositional and alternative discourses do regularly challenge global narratives, the latter ultimately triumph. Even the long-established media systems in smaller industrialized countries seem unable to produce reporting that is completely independent of the globally hegemonic discourses.

This book looks at the dependence of Canadian print media on the global narrative on Islam that is sustained by the transnational media. Newspapers in Canada tend to be heavily reliant on American, British, and French global wire services for foreign news.[26] Although Canadian media institutions do operate a few foreign news bureaus, these are small and understaffed. Apart from regularly using copy from the UK-based Reuters and Agence France Presse, Canadian dailies' foreign news content is often based on reports by correspondents of American sources like the Associated Press, *The New York Times*, *The Los Angeles Times*, Knight-Ridder, Cox News, and Scripps Howard. As a consequence, the coverage of foreign news in Canada is significantly influenced by the manners in which American journalists perceive it—this factor becomes crucial when considering regions of the world in which the U.S. government has strong foreign policy interests. Walter Soderlund notes about the press coverage of Salvadoran elections in 1982 and 1984, "While the elections received twice as much coverage in the American press as they did in the Canadian press, with the exception of some differences in leader evaluation and emphasis on issues,

Canadians received essentially the same media portrayal of the elections as did Americans."[27] A study by Jack Maybee of Canadian foreign coverage showed that *The Globe and Mail* (Toronto) and *The Toronto Star* were largely dependent on American news services, and missed opportunities on reporting on the Canadian angle of the Iranian revolution.[28]

The Canadian mass media share with the mass media of other Northern countries the myths of modern technological society, which provide the primary fields of meanings for the interpretation of events taking place in the world. Jacques Ellul, in his seminal work on *Propaganda*[29] indicates how these myths are used in an integrative way to create consensus in contemporary societies about critical matters; these can include the right of holding power by certain individuals or groups, the legitimacy of uses of violence by the state, and the illegitimacy of certain kinds of opposition to the nation-state. They also help engineer agreement about implicit hierarchies among nations, the relationships between them, and the place of non-governmental organizations in the world of nation-states. This consensus is at the basis of the global media narrative. A significant part of the Canadian mass media's coverage of Muslim societies involves an interpretation of Muslim responses to the North's, often American, cultural, ideological, economic, and military influence over those parts of the world. So completely absorbed are Canadian newspapers in global narratives that during the period of hostage-takings of Westerners in Beirut in the late 1980s and early 1990s, they paid more attention to American and British hostages than to Canadian ones held in Lebanon and elsewhere.

This book looks at the specific narrative forms these transnational discourses used in reconstructing the Muslim East as the nemesis of the West in the twilight of the second millennium. The relationship of the prominence given to news stories with their correspondence to dominant stereotypes; the uninformed use of Muslim terminology in mainstream journalistic discourses, especially headlines; and the adoption of formulaic frames like "Sunni versus Shi'a" or "Islam versus the West" to explain complex situations are all closely examined. The book analyses the Orientalist framing of contemporary terrorism carried out by Muslims; the ritualistic presentation of Lebanese hostage crises as struggles between good and evil; the dramatic casting of Jews, Muslims and Christians as heroes, villains and victims on the media stage of the Holy Land; the ideological effort of opinion leaders to depict the Gulf War as a clash of civilizations; and the strategic uses of the jihad model to narrate territorial wars in the Balkans and the Caucasus. The final chapter explores ways in which more informed and conscientious reporting in the twenty-first century can contribute to the mitigation of transnational conflict.

Notes

1. Samuel Huntington, *The Clash of Civilizations and the Remaking of World Order* (New York: Simon and Schuster, 1996) and Benjamin R. Barber, *Jihad vs. McWorld* (New York: Times Books/Random House, 1995). Also see Benjamin Netanyahu's construction of the

West's war against terrorism as a struggle "between the forces of civilization and the forces of barbarism." Benjamin Netanyahu, *Terrorism: How the West Can Win* (New York: Avon, 1987), p. ix.

2. Daniel Lerner, *The Passing of Traditional Society: Modernizing the Middle East* (Glencoe, Illinois: Free Press, 1958).

3. John L. Esposito, *The Islamic Threat: Myth or Reality?* (New York: Oxford University Press, 1992), p. 7. On the social-psychological need to have an enemy see Mehdi Semati, "Terrorists, Moslems, fundamentalists and other bad objects in the midst of 'us,' " *Journal of International Communication* 4:1 (1997), pp. 41-46.

4. Fred Halliday. *Islam and the Myth of Confrontation: Religion and Politics in the Middle East*. (London: I.B. Tauris, 1996), p. 183.

5. Stuart Hall, "Culture, Media and the 'Ideological Effect.'" In James Curran, Michael Gurevitch and Janet Woollacott, eds., *Mass Communication and Society*. Beverly Hills: Sage, 1979, pp. 343-344.

6. Institutional messages are propagandic since they are always slanted, however slightly, in favour of the vested interests that impart them. Hence, no information is objective. Whereas the overt, aggressive promotion of a cause is the popularly understood meaning of (agitation) propaganda, integration propaganda is a more subtle yet ubiquitous discursive form that continually leads the members of a society to conform to dominant discourses and structures of power. See Jacques Ellul, *Propaganda: The Formation of Men's Attitudes*, translated by Konrad Kellen and Jean Lerner (New York: Alfred A. Knopf, 1969).

7. The use of the terms "opposite" and "alternative" here is contrary to that of Raymond Williams in *Marxism and Literature* (Oxford: Oxford University Press, 1977), p. 113. The present study presents oppositional discourses as operating within the broad philosophical frameworks of the societies in which the dominant discourses exercise their hegemony, and alternative discourses as those that challenge the primary bases of dominant ones. See Karim H. Karim, "Reconstructing the Multicultural Community in Canada: Discursive Strategies of Inclusion and Exclusion," *International Journal of Politics, Culture and Society* 7:2 (1993), pp. 189-207.

8. See Louis W. Pauly, *Who Elected the Bankers? Surveillance and Control in the World Economy* (Ithaca, N.Y.: Cornell University Press, 1997) and Catherine Caufield, *Masters of Illusion: The World Bank and the Poverty of Nations* (New York: Henry Holt, 1997).

9. Aziz Al-Azmeh, *Islams and Modernities* (London: Verso, 1993), p. 1.

10. Akbar S. Ahmed, *Postmodernism and Islam: Predicament and Promise* (London: Routledge, 1992), pp. 36-37. For one of the more concise and articulate discussions of the religious, cultural, and historical manifestations of Muslim diversity, see Marshall G.S. Hodgson, *The Venture of Islam: Conscience and History in a World Civilization* Vol. 1 (Chicago: University of Chicago Press, 1974), pp. 71-99.

11. Mohammed Arkoun, "Islamic Cultures, Developing Societies, Modern Thought," in Hayat Salam, ed, *Expressions of Islam in Buildings* (Geneva: Aga Khan Trust for Culture), p. 50.

12. Mohammed Arkoun, "Islam, Urbanism and Human Existence Today," in The Aga Khan Award for Architecture, *Architecture as Symbol and Self-Identity* (Geneva: Aga Khan Awards), p. 51.

13. Ibid; also see his *Rethinking Islam: Common Questions, Uncommon Answers*, translated by Robert D. Lee (Boulder, Colo.: Westview Press), pp. 15-17 and Al-Azmeh, *Islams and Modernities*, pp. 60-61.

14. Edward W. Said, "The Phony Islamic Threat," *The New York Times Magazine*, November 21, 1993, p. 64.

15. Al-Azmeh, *Islams and Modernities*, pp. 60-88.

16. For two different perspectives on the inaccuracy of this term in Muslim contexts see Fazlur Rahman, *Islam and Modernity: Transformation of an Intellectual Tradition*, (Chicago: University of Chicago, 1982), p. 142 and Abdur-Rahman Momin, "On 'Islamic Fundamentalism': The Genealogy of a Stereotype," *Hamdard Islamicus* 10:4 (1987), pp. 35-46.

17. Edward W. Said, *Covering Islam: How the Media and the Experts Determine How We See the Rest of the World* (New York: Pantheon Books, 1981).

18. Ibid, p. ix.

19. Gordon W. Allport, *The Nature of Prejudice* (Garden City, New York: Doubleday Anchor Books, 1958), p. 175.

20. Susan Sontag, "'There' and 'Here': A Lament for Bosnia," *The Nation*, December 25, 1995, p. 819.

21. For example, Homero Aridjis, *The Lord of the Last Days: Visions of the Year 1000*, translated by Betty Fowler (London: Morrow, 1995).

22. See Abbas Malek (ed.), *News Media and Foreign Relations: A Multi-faceted Perspective* (Norwood, N.J.: Ablex Publishing, 1996); Lance Bennet, "The Media and the Foreign Policy Process," in D. Deese, ed., *The New Politics of American Foreign Policy* (New York: St. Martin's Press, 1994), pp. 168-88; and Nicholas Berry, *Foreign Policy and the Press: An Analysis of the New York Times' Coverage of U.S. Foreign Policy* (New York: Greenwood Press, 1990).

23. Hamid Mowlana, George Gerbner and Herbert I. Schiller (eds.), *Triumph of the Image: The Media's War in the Persian Gulf—A Global Perspective* (Boulder, Colo.: Westview, 1992).

24. Esposito, *op cit*; Halliday, *op cit*; James Piscatori (ed.), *Islamic Fundamentalisms and the Gulf Crisis* (Chicago: American Academy of Arts and Sciences, 1991); John Sigler, "Understanding the Resurgence of Islam: The Case of Political Islam," *Middle East Affairs Journal* 2:4 (1996), pp. 79-91; and Jochen Hippler and Andrea Lueg (eds.), *The Next Threat: Western Perceptions of Islam*, translated by Loula Friese (London: Pluto Press, 1995).

25. Quoted in Farrel Corcoran, "War Reporting: Collateral Damage in the European Theater," in Hamid Mowlana, George Gerbner and Herbert I. Schiller, eds., *Triumph of the Image: The Media's War in the Persian Gulf—A Global Perspective* (Boulder, Colo.: Westview, 1992), p. 117.

26. See Jack Maybee, "Reporting the Third World: The Canadian Angle," *Carleton Journalism Review* (Winter 1980), pp. 6-9; Gertrude J. Robinson, "Foreign News Values in Quebec, English Canadian and U.S. Press: A Comparison Study," *Canadian Journal of Communication* 9:3 (1983), pp. 1-32; Walter C. Soderlund, "Press Reporting on El Salvador and Nicaragua in Leading Canadian and American Newspapers," *Canadian Journal of Communication* 11:4 (1985), pp. 353-68; Stuart H. Surlin and Marlene Cuthbert, "Symbiotic News Coverage of the Grenada Crisis in Canada and the Caribbean," *Canadian Journal of Communication* 12:3-4 (1986), pp. 53-73; Walter C. Soderlund, "A Comparison of Press Coverage in Canada and the United States of the 1982 and 1984 Salvadoran Elections," *Canadian Journal of Political Science* 23:1 (March 1990), pp. 59-72; Walter C. Soderlund, Robert M. Krause and Richard G. Price "Canadian Daily Newspaper Editors' Evaluation of International Reporting," *Canadian Journal of Communication* 16 (1991), pp. 5-18; Walter C. Soderlund, Ronald H. Wagenberg and Ian C. Pemberton, "Cheerleader or Critic? Television News Coverage in Canada and the United States of the U.S. Invasion of Panama," *Canadian Journal of Political Science* 27:3 (September 1994), pp. 581-604.

27. Soderlund, "A Comparison of Press Coverage," p. 61.

28. Jack Maybee, "Reporting the Third World."

29. Op cit.

CHAPTER 1

VIOLENCE AND THE MEDIA

The Naming Of Violence

Media portrayals of "Islamic violence" are influenced by the dominant cultural meanings attached to both "Islam" and "violence." Societal consensus determines which actions are to be considered violent and which ones are not. This consensus is usually not a formal one, but is based on the myths to which the particular group subscribes. Joseph Gusfield[1] identifies three steps through which societal consensus on specific issues is engineered: naming the problem, giving it public status by assigning responsibility to deal with it, and legitimating a particular way of viewing the problem. Various discourses compete in the naming of violence, a phenomenon which is an integral, albeit enigmatic, feature of human history. Whereas force is often utilised to repress people, it is also a means to oppose and develop checks against excessive power. George Gerbner, who has carried out extensive studies of violence in television programming, states: "Violence is a legitimate and necessary cultural expression. It is a dramatic balancing of deadly conflicts against tragic costs."[2] Since there is an integral link between power and violence, those who hold power have a vested interest in ensuring that their preferred meanings remain dominant.

Symbolic violence has long been used in rituals to bind communities and stave off real, destructive violence.[3] It is sublimated in a variety of contemporary socio-cultural institutions that have adversarial structures, for example courts of justice where lawyers "fight" cases (harking back to the times when knights jousted to determine the justness of particular causes), parliamentary houses of assembly where members of rival political parties debate and hurl ritual insults at each other, and sports arenas in which opposing teams endeavour to "beat" each other. A primary feature of our myths, violence in symbolic forms emerges as a functional imperative that structures relationships within communities and underlies the manners in which societies are organized. Its public display and narration seem ubiquitous in all cultures since its use is often intimately related to the constructions of respective moral and socio-political orders. Physical and psychological violence is used by societies to penalize non-conformity to their particular rules and laws. Power is maintained to a significant extent, even in liberal democracies, on the demonstrated or potential capability for violence: hierarchies from the smallest to the global community are created and maintained through its symbolic or actual uses.

Actual physical violence is endowed with high symbolic value when it is depicted as supporting one or another view of political and social reality. Narratives that dramatize deadly struggles involving heroes, villains, and victims give meaning to the conflicts that exist in human society. Portrayals of particular uses of violence by specific kinds of people identify which social roles they are playing. Those who control the production and dissemination of these dramaturges have the means to influence public opinion regarding the types of people that are to be considered as the heroes, the villains, and the victims in society. Due to their very nature, incidents of terrorism allow very dramatic renderings. Since dominant discourses will have already established the proper and improper uses of violence, the integration propagandist does not have to expend much ideological labour in constructing scenarios of struggles between the "right" and the "wrong" sides and can almost perfunctorily endow specific actors in these incidents the roles of hero, villain, and victim. Philip Elliot tells us that in "the human interest accounts of incidents and their aftermath people are portrayed acting out their roles with the appropriate emotions as prescribed by the norms and traditions of their culture."[4] Mainstream journalists help sustain consensus on the moral order that supports the *status quo* by portraying state agents as heroes who apply force in the cause of national security, terrorists as villains who use it to destroy life and property, and citizens as victims whose security is maintained by state agents and threatened by terrorists. Such dramaturgical enactments are among the potent rites through which the legitimacy of the incumbent structures of power is continually validated: they provide opportunities for the public depiction of "correct" symbolic actions by the agents of the state, their opponents, and the citizenry.

Dominant discourses support the actions of existing hegemonic powers to preserve themselves from threats that they themselves name as violent and terroristic. The London-based *Independent*'s Middle East correspondent, Robert Fisk, whose reporting often provides alternative views on power and violence, notes that

> ...'terrorism' no longer means terrorism. It is not a definition; it is a political contrivance. 'Terrorists' are those who use violence against the side that is using the word. The only terrorists whom Israel acknowledges are those who oppose Israel. The only terrorists the United States acknowledges are those who oppose the United States or their allies. The only terrorists Palestinians acknowledge—for they too use the word—are those opposed to the Palestinians.[5]

Johan Galtung, a renowned scholar of peace studies, provides useful analytical concepts to study violence. He offers the notion of "structural violence," manifested in the denial of basic material needs (poverty), human rights (repression) and "higher needs" (alienation) as distinct from direct or "classical" violence[6], thus allowing for the placing of violent actions within a larger framework that takes into account historical and social situations from which they arise. Consequences of systemic institutional behaviour that does not involve direct, physical force but that, nevertheless, leads to alienation, deprival, disability or death, as under poor working conditions, is also not usually described as violent in dominant political discourses. However, direct, forceful reactions to such structural violence are invariably called violent. As no immediate violent causes can be uncovered for such (re)actions within dominant conceptualizations of violence, they are often described as being irrational.

Whereas violence is integral to the operative dynamics of society, it is also a social problem since it continually threatens to disrupt social order. In a utopic state, where absolute order is conceived to be the norm, violence would be an anomaly. However, in practice, the state and the socio-economic elite continually use various kinds of structural and direct violence to exercise and maintain power, especially against those who challenge the *status quo*. Max Weber asserted that,

> Today the relation between the state and violence is an especially intimate one. In the past, the most varied institutions—beginning with the sib—have known the use of physical force as quite normal. Today, however, we have to say that a state is a human community that (successfully) claims the *monopoly of the legitimate use of physical force* within a given territory…Specifically, at the present time, the right to use physical force is ascribed to other institutions or to individuals only to the extent to which the state permits it. The state is considered the sole source of the "right" to use violence.[7]

Those who carry out violence without authorization from the state are punished by the state's "bureaucracy of violence (police, army, jails)."[8] However, the modern state tends to downplay its own massive and systemic use of violence as it simultaneously emphasizes its opponents' violent acts.

A wide range of legitimate violence, from surveillance to execution, is available to the state and is administered by its bureaucratic structures. Governmental retribution for use of direct violence by members of society generally takes the form of the violence involved in incarceration, corporal punishment, or death. The state's harshest measures are reserved for actions against itself, such as treason and terrorism (whose definitions are provided by ruling elites). Naming of political opposition against the government is carried out according to the strength of the threats posed and the means used in the attempts to change the *status quo*. Whereas "activist" is used to denote those opponents who remain within what is considered legitimate opposition to the state, the term "terrorist" is often attached to someone who violently rejects the premises of the prevailing socio-political order. If the medium of reporting sympathises with the latter's cause it will call them "freedom fighters" or "resistance members"—a more neutral approach may use "guerillas." People who carry out state-sanctioned violence are "secret service operatives," "soldiers," "commandos," "tactical squads," "SWAT teams," "riots corps," "police," "prison guards," "executioners."

Historical applications of direct violence to establish the ruling elite are generally made invisible through processes of dehistoricization. The hegemonic structure is depicted as being part of a natural and rational social order in which violence is an anomaly. Thus, ignoring the blood-soaked American past and present, a U.S. judge could declare: "Violence in pursuit of any goal is an aberration in American society and simply cannot be tolerated."[9] Yet, when there arises a threat to the *status quo*, the state immediately marshals its own massive means of violence to stem it. In democratic regimes, where public opinion needs to be assured of the benevolence of the state, the latter has to strive harder than in autocratic ones to veil the force that it itself applies against its citizens or those of another country. State propagandists present it as being in the interests of maintaining order, security and justice and as being carried out within a rational and moral framework.[10] The applications of force to maintain the hegemonic structure are thus put outside the dominant discourses on violence, which instead revolve around criminality, irrationality, and deviance.

The term "violence" is generally reserved for the use of force by persons who are not state agents; and the political violence of those who seek to upset the *status quo* is characterized as terrorism. "More violent than the violent—such is terrorism," notes Jean Baudrillard.[11] Thomas Friedman, a former *New York Times* correspondent in the Middle East, writes about the Israeli military's failure to respond to the slaughter of Palestinian refugees and others in the Sabra and Shatila refugee camps in 1982:

> The Israeli soldiers did not see innocent civilians being massacred and they did not hear the screams of innocent children going to their graves. What they saw was a "terrorist infestation" being "mopped up" and "terrorist nurses" scurrying about and "terrorist teenagers" trying to defend them, and what they heard was "terrorist women" screaming.[12]

The demonization of all Palestinians was so complete in their minds that they could not seem to bring themselves to think of them as victims of violence even in such circumstances.

The Landau Commission appointed by the Israeli government found in 1987 that "abusive interrogation methods" were systematically used by Shin Bet, the Israeli security police, which had been lying to military courts in the West Bank and Gaza for seventeen years.[13] Nevertheless, the commission's report recommended that none of the Shin Bet agents should be prosecuted or even disciplined either for abusing detainees or for perjury. At the same time, it also endorsed "non-violent psychological pressure" in the interrogation of security detainees and, if this did not suffice, "a moderate measure of physical pressure."[14] Whereas structural violence by the state remains almost completely invisible in dominant political discourses, even direct violence by its agents—when publicly uncovered—is usually left unpunished or dismissed with a mere slap on the wrist. On the other hand, the violent resistance to governmental violence is highlighted as "terrorism."

The second in Gusfield's three steps of consensus-construction is to assign responsibility for dealing with the social problem. There is general acceptance that certain issues are to be handled by persons playing particular public roles or holding specific offices which can command public attention, trust, and influence. "Experts" from government, the military, academia, and the media emerge as the owners of dominant discourses on terrorism, making themselves readily available to the public through the mass media to define and describe the problem as well as to respond to alternative discourses on the issue. This does not mean that they are engaged in a conscious, coordinated conspiracy to produce a monolithic view, but that they subscribe to a general common purpose and to a common field of meanings. "Authorized knowers"[15] have a privileged say in the two other aspects of assigning responsibility for the problem of terrorism: who and what causes it and who and what will deal with it. They usually disassociate issues involving political violence from their structural causes and place them under rubrics such as "right-wing terrorism," "left-wing terrorism," "narco-terrorism," "nuclear terrorism," or "Islamic terrorism." Lack of security is often pinpointed as a key reason for the occurrence of terrorist incidents and the solutions are seen in technological and legislative improvements by the state to better detect, prevent, and punish terrorism. Persons who are not agents of the state and who use violence for political reasons are portrayed as criminals—they are to be dealt within the legal structures that normally process violent criminals. Public attention is thus kept focused on the *violence* rather than the *politics* of political violence.

The last step in consensus-engineering is legitimating a particular way of viewing the problem. Once the *status quo* has been determined as a just arrangement for all citizens, there can be no logical or legitimate reason for rebellion. If the modern state is considered to be the most rational model for organizing political community and represents the cultural and intellectual achievements of (Northern) civilization, then militant opposition to its power structures is irrational. When the structural and direct violence of the state is viewed as being non-existent, the violence against it can be presented as terroristic. Once the massive violence of the colonial era and its continuing effects have been glossed over, the contemporary world order comes to be perceived as a natural consequence of a benign history. Since international structures and the global activities of powerful Northern states are seen as beneficial for all humankind, the atrocities by certain Muslims against symbols of Northern hegemony can be attributed solely to the barbarism of "Islamic terrorism." Decontextualized dominant discourses help create moral consensus about the nature of political violence by influencing how public opinion perceives correct and incorrect modes of political behaviour in modern states and in international relations.

Adherence to global structures such as those of trade, which operate in favour of the North, are also supported by the dominant global discourses.

Punishment meted out by hegemonic powers for non-compliance spans the range from economic sanctions to outright bombing and invasion of territory. The violent world order also includes the political and military support of powerful states for what Noam Chomsky and Edward Herman term "National Security States."[16] These states oppress their populations to keep an uninterrupted supply of raw materials and cheap labour available to Northern multinational companies—this is the "real terror network" in the alternative discourse of Herman and Chomsky. They describe how the "Free Press" has in various periods overlooked U.S. involvement in supplying and training the armies of repressive regimes such as those in Guatemala, Brazil, Argentina, Chile, El Salvador, South Vietnam, South Korea, Burma, the Philippines, Indonesia, Turkey, Pakistan, Iran, and Israel, all of which carried out massive violence against subject populations in the last few decades. Dominant discourses on terrorism avert their eyes from what the authors call "wholesale violence" perpetrated by hegemonic states and their clients,[17] and focus instead on the "retail violence" of non-compliant states and groups. The mass media generally frame the latter's actions within the hegemonic discourses, demonizing them as practitioners of terrorism while largely disregarding the global terrorism of Northern powers conducted directly or through client states.

How The Media Explain Conflict

Whereas mainstream journalists do not always subscribe overtly to official views on terrorism, the field of meanings they choose to operate within inevitably leads them to produce only certain interpretations of political violence. Ellul maintains that integration propaganda in the technological state would not be possible without the elite-owned or controlled mass media, in which it appears constantly and consistently.[18] Unlike the overt tendencies of agitation propaganda, integration propaganda does not involve the aggressive presentation of specific views but a more subtle and ubiquitous mode which operates within dominant discourses. Although mainstream journalists in technological societies do challenge the day-to-day functioning of incumbent governments, they rarely bring into question the fundamental structures of thought or of power. Operating within a particular ideological system (be it free market, socialist, Islamist etc.), mass media workers consciously or unconsciously produce integration propaganda that serves the overall interests of elites.

Stuart Hall describes how, although it is ostensibly autonomous of the political and economic elites, professional journalism in the liberal state operationally and structurally tends to reproduce dominant discourses:

> The professional code...operates *within* the 'hegemony' of the dominant code. Indeed, it serves to reproduce the dominant definitions precisely by bracketing their hegemonic quality and operating instead with displaced professional codings which foreground such apparently neutral-technical questions as quality, 'professionalism' and so on. The hegemonic interpretations...are principally generated by political and military elites:

the particular choice of presentational occasions and formats, the selection
of personnel, the choice of images, the staging of debates are selected and
combined through the operation of the professional code...the
professionals are linked with the defining elites not only by the institutional
position of broadcasting itself as an 'ideological apparatus' but also by the
structure of *access* (that is, the systematic 'over-accessing' of selective elite
personnel and their 'definition of the situation' in television).[19]

Authorized knowers, drawn from elite ranks, are usually sought out for
interviews; indeed, the perspectives favoured by them are generally presented as
being rational and natural. The elites also ensure, through the various
mechanisms of censorship, licensing, access, and advertising, that the mass media
primarily disseminate continual and overriding streams of messages that promote
the social and economic values helping to maintain the *status quo*.

However, the media should not be viewed as monolithic vehicles for only one
type of discourse. Depending on the latitude allowed by owners, they do function as
sites of contestation between various views. Oppositional, alternative, and populist
perspectives may appear from time to time in media content, often in the back pages
of a newspaper or near the end of a news broadcast. Frequently, an alternative
narrative in the text of a write-up is subverted by the adjacent placing of the
dominant discourse in more prominent parts of the article format such as the
headline or an accompanying photograph. Occasionally, alternative views may even
appear in high-profile parts of a newspaper, such as the editorial, opinion columns,
and the front page. However, the dominant discourse's sheer ubiquity, omnipresence,
and manoeuvrability mitigates the impact of alternative perspectives.

The state usually appears in the mass media as the locus and the guardian
of social order. Its leaders and agents are generally depicted as representing the
populace. Within this framework, attempts to upset societal power structures are
generally characterized as attacks on the entire population. Whereas the mass
media's coverage may frequently challenge ruling elites, it usually adheres to
dominant political discourses during crisis situations, such as those involving
terrorism.[20] (On the other hand, alternative media—which report from
marginalized perspectives—tend to present materials that question specific
aspects of the *status quo*'s structures and operations; however, these media
usually do not have broad-based audiences and remain sidelined.) Denied access
to the mainstream media, marginalized groups "must assemble in the wrong
places at the wrong time to do the wrong thing."[21] in order to pass over the news
threshold. Some even carry out atrocities. Frantz Fanon points out that one way
in which militant groups attempt to appropriate the power of the state is by
partaking in the very violence over which the state has a monopoly.[22] They seek
to shake the credibility of hegemonic classes and initiate alternative discourses on
power with their public uses of violence. Lacking in military strength, they
specialize in limited but high-profile acts of sabotage, destruction, kidnapping,
and assassination. However, such attempts at influencing public opinion are

generally unsuccessful as dominant societal assumptions regarding the uses of violence are strongly influenced by the socio-political elites. Whereas the symbolic acts of militants may gain the temporary attention of audiences, they are systematically recoded by mainstream journalists who present them as deviant and irrational. The use of force by those who are not in power is presented by the mass media as a disruption of the social order and the targeting of the entire population, rather than as a revolt against the *status quo*.

The media utilize various narrative modes in attempting to get their views of reality across to their public. When producing news, journalists make the implicit assumption that audiences possess the same general ways of understanding information as themselves. Such consonance is vital in making their accounts seem rational and logical. In order for this to happen, both parties have to adhere to similar cognitive structures that frame the images of specific groups of people. The archetypal myth of the Other forms the basis for primary stereotypes (topoi) about her. Such longer-term cognitive macrostructures, which are held in collective cultural memories, give rise to the specific images that are generated according to changes in time and place. The topoi about the Other also inform the cognitive scripts, models, and frames that guide everyday interactions with her. Scripts "contain all we know in our culture about a specific stereotypical type of episode"[23]: they tell us how certain types of people (members of a professional group, adherents of a religion etc.) behave in particular situations.

Cognitive models operate as the referential bases of interpretation and are essential in making textual accounts involving specific actors seem coherent. Distinct from the abstract nature of the information about general behaviour held in scripts, models carry impressions about particular, identifiable individuals or groups acting in particular manners in certain kinds of circumstances.

> For instance, if we process media reports about the attack of the U.S. Air Force on Libya in April 1986, we build a mental model of that event with the help of the information from these reports. Part of that particular model, however, is also instantiated fragments of general information we already had about military operations, Libya, the Mediterranean, the Middle East, or terrorism—information that might have been derived from previous media reports. Later texts about this event may be used to update the model with new details, and that is precisely one of the central cognitive functions of news discourse.[24]

Integration propagandists therefore use dominant models to frame a series of occurrences; Gaye Tuchman has shown how such framing transforms "*occurrences* and *happenings* (strips of the everyday world) into defined *events*."[25] Muslims depicted in media narratives that present the core stereotype of "the violent man of Islam" as the manifestation of the Other frequently act according to the behaviour prescribed for them in dominant scripts. Cognitive models about Libyan, Iranian, Pakistani, or Malaysian Muslims in specific situations determine the kinds of accounts that will be given of their actions.

Journalists perform certain rituals in order to get across their messages. David Chaney lists three forms of ritualized media operations: "First there are rituals which are to be reported; secondly, there are ways of reporting which are themselves rituals; and thirdly, the medium itself may be a ritual or collective ceremony."[26] Since the functioning of human institutions is characterized by ritualized behaviour, journalists routinely report on the range of activities that include communal, professional, and political rituals. State ceremonies such as inaugurations, the opening and closing of national assemblies, speeches by the head of state, state banquets, state funerals etc. are vital for the continual legitimization of the incumbent structures of power and for the continual re-enactment of the imaginary community of the nation. In addition to reporting rituals, the ways in which incidents are covered by the media are also ritualized. These routine performances include the professional methods by which journalists do their work, such as the manners in which they collect information, compose news, and disseminate it. They also constitute the ways in which media workers present material within formats that pit one group against another.

Chaney considers the mass media themselves to constitute a ritual because they are part of the day-to-day existence of the community which they address. Mass consumption of the daily news narrated from a specific perspective is part of the ritual that helps holds the community together. The secular rituals of the mass media are akin to religious rituals in that they both frame their truth within the myths operative in their respective spheres. Just as priests re-enact rites based on religious belief, journalists couch their reporting in narratives that adhere to dominant societal discourses. And, like religious performances, journalistic rituals also need to be repeated regularly. Battles in which good triumphs over evil are related again and again.

Journalists also impart their views of the world through dramaturgical depictions, which can be deconstructed through dramatistic examination. "Dramatism is a method of analysis and a corresponding critique of terminology designed to show that the most direct route to the study of human relations and human motives is via a methodological inquiry into cycles or clusters of terms and their functions."[27] Dramatistic analysis involves study of actors, actions, scenes, purposes, and agencies described in a text. However, in looking at the dramaturgical aspects of media texts, the present inquiry is limited to scrutinizing the presentation of actors and their actions. It studies how dramaturgical portrayal constructs scenarios in which those who wield "good violence" fight with the perpetrators of "bad violence" so as to re-establish order in the universe. Since dominant discourses will have already defined the proper and improper uses of violence, the integration propagandist does not have to expend much ideological labour in constructing scenarios of struggles between the "right" and the "wrong" sides in these violent conflicts and can almost perfunctorily endow specific types of actors the roles of hero, villain and victim. Mainstream journalists help sustain consensus on the moral order that supports the *status quo* by dramaturgically portraying state agents as heroes, terrorists as villains, and citizens as victims.

This dramaturgy, however, does allow some room for transmutation of characterizations: a hero can become a victim (martyr) when harmed by the villain-terrorists, and victims can become heroes when they kill or capture the latter or when they bravely withstand their violence. But villain-terrorists cannot become heroes or what Herman and Chomsky term "worthy victims."[28] Citizens, who play the role of actual or potential victims in this scenario, do not generally carry out violence, but are either threatened by the violence of the terrorist or are saved by that of the state agent. In these ways the mass media symbolically portray good and bad, right and wrong, and winners and losers in society. Through such dramaturgical engineering of reality, mainstream journalists construct an elaborate societal hierarchy, placing various kinds of people (men, women, children, the elderly, persons with disabilities, ethnic and religious minorities, foreigners) in specific inter-relationships of dominance and subservience. George Gerbner notes that "The pattern of violence and victimization projects a mean world in which everyone is at risk (though some more than others). Its calculus of danger and ratio of winners and losers sets up a structure of power that puts every social group in its 'place'."[29] Structural violence of the state or of socio-economic institutions is usually invisible in these constructions.

Dramaturgical enactments of the "war against terrorism" are among the potent rites through which the legitimacy of the incumbent structures of power is continually validated: they provide opportunities for the public depiction of "correct" symbolic actions by the agents of the state, their opponents, and the citizenry. The moral counterweight of terrorists and other nefarious enemies of the state helps affirm (through combat between the forces of good and evil) the goodness of the *status quo*. Regular media depiction of the drama of the "war against terrorism" therefore becomes a vital ritual for the integration propagandist to assert the continuing viability of the existing socio-economic order. In this, violence operates as a rite of symbolic cleansing that rids society of evil:

> If sociodramas of blood, violence, and war are mounted as rites of purification, then torture, killing, and wounding become not only "necessary," but "noble." These sociodramas are not only merely symbolic screens, or metaphors in which we clothe the reality of politics, economics and sex. They *are* social reality *because* they are forms of social integration.[30]

For this reason it is important for integration propagandists to give disproportionate levels of prominence, space and time to violent challenges to the state even though the actual damage caused by them is insignificant when compared to other forms of violence and destruction that exist in society.[31] When media consumers, influenced by such portrayals, become convinced of their victimhood at the hands of villainous terrorists and of their need for protection from heroic state agents they are more willing to acquiesce to the right of state agents to carry out violence. They also become amenable to the suspension of their own rights in cases of state-declared emergencies.

Constructing The (Violent) World Order

A high degree of consensus on the right of the state to use violence legitimately is also present at the transnational level. Indeed it is part of what has emerged as the "global culture." Rather than disappear under pressures of globalization, national entities remain the effective loci for the vertical power structures of domestic elites. And within the "community of nations," the elite states retain power by developing consensus on the validity of their dominant status in international structures; or, alternatively, they use coercive means. Economic dominance of the North, particularly that of Western countries, is a remnant of the essentially violent colonial period during which the bases of presently-existing global trading structures were forcibly established. The massive historical violence that helped shape the political map of the world is rarely questioned in contemporary narratives of dominant international discourses. Individuals and states which challenge the current configurations of power in the international system with violence are termed "international terrorists" and "terrorist states."

Whereas retail terrorism is sometimes carried out for mercenary, religious, or pathological reasons, its root causes in the South frequently lie in the rejection of the configurations of imperialist power prevalent even in the aftermath of colonialism. European colonialism created a world of specifically demarcated countries where there had previously been vaguely-defined and shifting borders between administrative areas. People who had interacted with each other for millennia were split apart in order to be labelled the subjects of national governments dominated by narrow ranges of interest. Tribes, extended families, religious communities, and other integral social, economic, and cultural units in Africa, Asia and the Americas were dissected by map-drawers sitting in European capitals. Commercial, linguistic, and communications links of specific Southern countries extended like umbilical cords to their "mother nations" in Europe, while ties with their immediate neighbours grew weak. Even following the "birth" of independent nations, the economic and communications global infrastructures developed over decades of colonial rule have largely maintained the influence of Northern nations over former colonies to this day. Avuncular, non-colonizing states in Europe, North America, and Australasia have also benefitted from the current international order that is the legacy of colonialism. Indeed, in the aftermath of World War II and particularly in the post-Cold War era, Uncle Sam has emerged as the global patriarch.

Boundaries drawn by European cartographers are largely respected as sacrosanct and immutable divisions of peoples in the South despite the arbitrary natures of these borders. One of the most resilient legacies of the colonial era is the continuing pre-eminence of the concept of the modern nation-state in which power and violence are concentrated at a historically unprecedented level. Born out of the specific experience of Europe, it continues to remain the framework within which political communities around the world arrange their respective internal and inter-national relationships. Alternative concepts of global structures, such as those based on traditional Muslim conceptions of the relations between various peoples of the world,[32] are dismissed as being irrelevant in the modern age.

The dominant construction of the "war against terrorism" as a conflict between the forces of civilization and barbarism has deep cultural roots in the manners that European cultures have historically characterized the world. The Eurocentric world view, according to Stephen Rosow, has traditionally divided humanity into categories which have significantly influenced global discourses:

> Internationalization is a process of movement from national to international society, a movement of incorporating those outside the boundaries of the system into it...Three characterizations, three types of narratives of...others have prevailed in the European tradition: the barbarian, the heretic, and the primitive. It is important that each of these narratives developed so as to enable relations between Europeans and others and constituted those relations as different from relations within the European system. In particular cases, such as orientalism and U.S. foreign policy,...all three intertwine, drawing on each other and blending into one another.[33]

These historic stereotypes have been integrated into contemporary global discourses which view the North as the domain of rationality, order and democracy, and the South (particularly Muslim societies) as that of irrationality, instability and tyranny.[34] The latter is also seen as a primary source of "international terrorism," presenting a major challenge to the world order created in the image of Europe. Although Muslim (and other Southern) countries have been incorporated into the international system of states, they cannot, according to Eurocentric discourses, be considered equals to countries of the North. Whereas the modern liberal state in the North is viewed as being only nominally Christian, its Muslim antagonist is generally seen as still holding on to the beliefs perceived as being integral to barbarism. Therefore, in the dramaturgy of these dominant discourse, the Eurocentric civilization is pitted against the barbaric world, which throws up the challenges of "Islamic terrorism," "narco-terrorism," "nuclear terrorism" etc. that the former has to contain forcefully. In this way the hegemonic status of certain states on the global stage merges with older world views to create a *dramatis personae* of heroes and villains who engage in a violent struggle that defines the global moral order.

Power on the international scale is arranged even more overtly than the domestic on the capability for violence. Following the essentially violent colonial era, the "community of nations" has become institutionalized in the United Nations Organization and other international and regional associations. A well-recognized hierarchy of states exists in the structure of the United Nations (formed in the wake of World War II), that is based on military prowess: as

Permanent Members of the Security Council, the five victors of the Second World War were accorded a status superior to all other UN member states.[35] In this lay the creation of a planetary moral order which assigns the security of the world to the five elite states. The United States and the Soviet Union (and later, just the U.S.) became universally acknowledged in dominant global discourses as having superpower status due to their respective military strengths. During the Cold War, the two superpowers became the protagonists on the global stage—deciding the fate of the planet in their armaments negotiations at which all other states constituted little more than an attentive audience.

Global trade and financial structures, which have their origins in the colonial era, are weighted in favour of the North. The pressure on poorer Southern governments to conform to the dictates of Northern-based conglomerates has increased considerably in recent years with phenomenal amounts in loans outstanding to Northern banks. Where it has been unable to acquire the consensus of local elites, the American superpower, acting alone or as the head of UN or NATO forces, has exerted its military might—in Grenada, Panama, Iraq, Somalia, Haiti, Afghanistan, Sudan, and Yugoslavia (but not always successfully). Despite various challenges to the Northern-dominated global economic system, it remains intact. The primary players in the contemporary reorganization of global trade structures continue to be the U.S., the powerful states in the European Union (France, Germany, and the UK), and Japan, as evidenced in international trade negotiations; while the interests of the South are generally relegated to the sidelines.

Hamid Mowlana sees three major trends emerging in the relationship of the mass media and geopolitics since World War I. These are the increasing alignment of the transnational media with the superpower-dominated global order, shifting the mobilization of public opinion from the national to the planetary level as "a prerequisite for the conduct of modern international warfare," and the decline of the roles of government and the media as watchdogs over each other.[36] When elite powers are involved in confrontations with Southern entities, the transnational media agencies—based in the North—largely align themselves with the hegemonic position. This has led to the growth of a global media narrative in which civilized nation states led by the U.S. are besieged by "Terrorism International."

Despite periodic revelations about the involvement of the United States government in supporting structural and direct violence in various parts of the world, the mass media generally adhere to discourses that present it as a benevolent superpower. For example, an "end-of-decade" review of terrorism in December 1989 by a staff writer for *The Ottawa Citizen*, while mentioning France's "state terror" against the Greenpeace ship, the Rainbow Warrior, and the activities of "para-military death squads" in El Salvador, mainly dwelt on the struggles of elite states (especially the United States) against the political violence of non-governmental groups. The write-up did not consider the support of dominant powers for the wholesale terrorism perpetrated by various National

Security States against their own nationals. And while the author warned that "narco-terrorism promises to be the one to watch in the early part of the nineties," he failed to explain the global infrastructural causes behind the economic incentives for many developing countries to produce cash crops that are much in demand in the North. An accompanying article in the same issue of the daily lamented that while "Peace Breaks Out [between the two superpowers]...Third World tensions threaten to boil over." Although the writer did state that "Global spending on weapons had passed $1-trillion-a-year mark" she made no mention of the promoters of this international trade, who were in large part the two superpowers themselves and the other three permanent members of the United Nation's Security Council; they had together accounted for 74 percent in global arms sales between 1982 and 1986.[37] Similarly, at the end of 1999 and the beginning of 2000, there were a spate of articles warning of an explosion of terrorism at the eve of the new millennium and the continuing threats in the new century, especially from Muslim groups.[38] An opinion piece by John F. Burns masquerading as a news feature in the January 2, 2000 issue of *The New York Times* predicted that Algeria, described as being near the other end of the Muslim "crescent" from Iran, would be the source of future turbulence. The role of the North in generating violence in much of the world through its structural dominance over the global economic system, the sale of armaments to Southern countries, and covert operations does not form part of dominant global discourses.

Dramaturges in which the Permanent Members of the Security Council act as guardians of the planet seem to be integral to these narratives. Even though there is frequent criticism of their respective policies, the five hegemonic states have come to be portrayed in global media narratives as having the implicit right to own and deploy nuclear armaments and other weapons of mass destruction. An example of this global discourse was a story in *The Ottawa Citizen* by the UK-based Reuters news agency, that reported on November 5, 1988 the alarm raised by a London newspaper about the spread of nuclear arms to countries which are "outside the scrutiny of the International Atomic Energy Agency" (IAEA), a United Nations body. The function of IAEA's "safeguards inspection program" was described as "aimed at stopping the spread of nuclear arms from the five long-standing nuclear weapons states—the United States, the Soviet Union, China, Britain and France." No other reason was given by the news agency based in one of these five countries explaining why they were allowed, above all others, to own nuclear weapons. The operative journalistic model did not require the report to go beyond stating than that they were "long-standing nuclear weapons states." Since these hegemonic relationships have become normalized globally, the report from the British wire service seemed coherent enough to print without explanation by the Canadian newspaper. The "natural" order of power relationships in the world is supported by transnational communications media based in militarily hegemonic countries as well as by their subservient customers in the North and the South. Global consensus on the current configurations of the international system is thus maintained through the mass media as well as through the international agencies of coercion (the Security Council, IAEA), which themselves depend for their continued validation on this consensus.

The self-contained and self-sustaining ambit of power does not allow global discourses on violence to focus on the fundamental issue of the *existence* of weapons of mass destruction. Instead, the possession of such arms by the five elite states becomes integral to the preservation of the global moral order. The dramaturgy of armaments negotiations between Washington and Moscow are presented in the mass media as occurring within a rational setting in which the actors operate in accordance with the norms of international diplomatic discourse. However, the conflict of the hegemonic states with ("barbaric") Southern ones who challenge the international *status quo* is presented as a struggle between the upholders of global order and those promoting chaos. In a feature article on the proliferation of cruise and ballistic missiles, the London-based *Economist*, which has a world-wide circulation, stated in its January 4, 1997 edition that "The greatest potential menace are the five 'rogue' regimes, some of which have helped each other's missile programmes: Iran, Iraq, Libya, Syria and North Korea." This pentad of "rogue states" has become the evil counterpart of the five benevolent Permanent Members of the Security Council in the planetary dramaturgy of journalistic discourses.[39]

A frequent media ritual consists of reporting favourably on "sting operations" in which terrorist suspects are arrested by law enforcement agencies, thereby symbolically asserting the legitimacy and efficiency of state agents' violence and de-emphasizing any impropriety on their part. As the information veers away from the dominant script, it is either not reported or is given less prominence. In September 1987, *The Ottawa Citizen*, using various American news sources, printed several stories on the capture of a suspected Lebanese hijacker, Fawaz Yunis, by the U.S. Federal Bureau of Investigation. The FBI had lured him into a trap with the pretence of conducting a drug deal. On September 18, the paper published an article on page A6 from *The Chicago Tribune* stating: "Justice Department officials said Fawaz Yunis, 28, a Beirut resident, was arrested in international waters Sunday after he voluntarily boarded the vessel." The journalist seemed to be operating within the dominant model of the confrontation between American law enforcers and "Islamic terrorists."

On the following day, the *Citizen* carried a piece on page A18 from United Press International, which gave the first hint (appearing at the very end of the article) that the manner in which Yunis was captured was not viewed by everyone as legitimate: "In Beirut, Nabih Berri, chief of the Shiite Amal militia and Lebanon's Justice Minister, accused the United States of 'piracy against international law' and 'aggression on Lebanon's dignity.'" The headline of another write-up a week later, also from UPI, stated with a note of alarm: "Hijack suspect's broken wrists may threaten FBI case." What had initially appeared as a heroic victory in the war against terrorism had soured because it seemed that the alleged terrorist's captors may have carried out the kind of practice that only the opponents of law and order are supposed to indulge in. Interestingly, this story appeared far from the front sections, on page D16. Once the facts began to differ from the preferred script the developments were no longer considered worth highlighting and the story was relegated to being a filler in a section containing classified advertisements. However, upon the conviction of Fawaz by an American court one and a half years later it returned to the front section of the *Citizen*, where a short article on page A5 concluded: "The verdict was viewed as an affirmation of a 1984 law asserting U.S. jurisdiction over the taking of American hostages abroad." This mode of reporting also reaffirmed the consistency of the dominant script that was followed faithfully in the newspaper's coverage of the running story. The legitimacy of the superpower's actions in apprehending suspected criminals anywhere on the planet was underlined in the reportage of the transnational incident by the Canadian newspaper, which had relied completely on American news sources for the story.

Integration propagandists appear to do their job so well that significant proportions of the publics in Northern states seem to favour strong measures against terrorists that include increasing state powers to place suspects under surveillance and to hunt down and kill those who have escaped to other countries.[40] In late 1984 and early 1985, the Reagan administration in the United States attempted to organize a world-wide economic boycott of Libya to penalize its sponsorship of terrorist groups opposed to the former's interests. Following wide support of this campaign in the materials of the U.S. news services used by Canadian mass media, a poll found 57 percent of Canadian respondents in favour of these measures. Ironically, at the same time that the U.S. government was leading the international campaign against Libya, senior White House officials were surreptitiously supplying arms to Iran (which the U.S. State Department had also listed as a "terrorist state") and to the Nicaraguan Contras, thus contravening legislation passed by the U.S. Congress.[41]

The demonization of Libya and its leader Muammar Qadhafi by the U.S. mass media had served to deflect attention from the more serious terrorism that the Reagan administration was supporting elsewhere in the world. It had been evident for some time that Qadhafi's government had supported terrorist activities externally (apart from engaging domestically, like other states, in structural and direct violence). However,

> "The striking feature of Libyan atrocities," two commentators observe in reviewing the Amnesty International study of state terror, "is that they are the only ones whose numbers are sufficiently limited that the individual cases can be enumerated," in striking contrast to Argentina, Indonesia, and the Central American states where the emperor [the U.S. government] molests the world.

> In short, Libya is indeed a terrorist state. But in the world of international terrorism, it is hardly even a bit player.[42]

In Noam Chomsky's alternative discourse, Libya's retail terrorism paled in comparison to the wholesale terrorism supported by the U.S. However, through the continual bombardment of messages in global media narratives, consensus was built up among the public of various states that this particular country was one of the worst exponents of terrorism.

The transnational media clearly play an important role in the construction of agreement about violence and terrorism. Whereas one cannot generalize about the ideological machinations of all mainstream journalists, the operational nature of mass media institutions leads to the continual production of hegemonic messages which veil the structural and direct violence of dominant states while highlighting the violent activities of "terrorists" and "terrorist states." Operating within and contributing to these discourses, the mass media consciously or unconsciously use presentational formats, imagery, placements of information, and selections of sources to further particular viewpoints. In naming only certain kinds of political violence as terrorism, in assigning causal and remedial responsibilities for this public problem, and in legitimating a depoliticized way of viewing it, the mass media are vital participants in engineering consensus about this issue. The sensationalistic coverage of retail terrorism harnesses popular notions about the legitimacy and illegitimacy of certain kinds of violence. Journalistic narratives sketch heroes, villains and victims, according to their fit with the roles scripted by dominant fields of meanings. Domestic and transnational hierarchies are culturally constructed in the reporting of conflicts—"terrorists" and "terrorist states" are portrayed as global outlaws intent on creating worldwide mayhem, while powerful Northern states are generally presented as supplying, deploying and using weapons in the interests of peace, order and security, even if large numbers of the innocent are injured and killed by them. Akbar Ahmed suggests that mainstream journalists in the North carry out discursive violence when they support or underplay the repression carried out by hegemonic powers. Writing about the relationship of transnational television networks with Muslim societies, he refers to CNN and BBC as "storm troopers."[43]

NOTES

1. Joseph R. Gusfield, *The Culture of Public Problems: Drinking-Driving and the Symbolic Order* (Chicago: University of Chicago, 1981).

2. George Gerbner, "Violence and Terror in and by the Media," in Marc Raboy and Bernard Dagenais, eds., *Media, Crisis and Democracy* (London: Sage, 1992), p. 97.

3. René Girard, *Violence and the Sacred*, translated by Patrick Gregory (Baltimore: John Hopkins University, 1979).

4. Philip Elliot, "Press Performance as Political Ritual," in Harry Christian, ed., *The Sociology of Journalism and the Press* (London: Constable, 1979), p. 161.

5. Robert Fisk, *Pity the Nation: Lebanon at War* (Oxford: Oxford University Press, 1990), p. 441.

6. Johan Galtung, "The Specific Contribution of Peace Research to the Study of Violence," in

UNESCO, *Violence and Its Causes* (Paris: UNESCO, 1981); also see Jamil Salmi, *Violence and Democratic Society: New Approaches to Human Rights* (London: Zed Books,1993).

7. Max Weber, *From Max Weber: Essays in Sociology*, translated by H.H. Gerth and C. Wright Mills (New York: Oxford University Press, 1946), p. 78.

8. David I. Kertzer, *Ritual, Politics, and Power* (New Haven, Conn.: Yale University, 1988), p. 132.

9. United Press International, "3 Montrealers jailed in U.S. bomb case," *The Ottawa Citizen*, June 23, 1988, p. A23.

10. During the Gulf War fought between the United Nations Coalition and Iraq, president George Bush proclaimed that the American military actions were "moral." George Bush, "State of the Union," *Vital Speeches of the Day* 57:9 (Feb. 1991), p. 261.

11. Jean Baudrillard, *Fatal Strategies*, translated by Philip Beitchman and W.G.J. Niesluchowski, edited by Jim Fleming (New York: Semiotext[e], 1990), p. 34.

12. Thomas L. Friedman, *From Beirut to Jerusalem* (New York: Anchor Books, 1990), p. 163.

13. Aryeh Neier, "Watching Rights," *The Nation*, June 24, 1991, p. 841.

14. Ibid.; also see B'Tselem, *The Interrogation of Palestinians During the Intifada: Ill-Treatment, Moderate Physical Pressure or Torture* (Jerusalem: Israeli Information Centre for Human Rights in the Occupied Territories, 1991).

15. James Winter, *Common Cents: Media Portrayal of the Gulf War and Other Events* (Montreal: Black Rose Books, 1992), p. 40.

16. Noam Chomsky, "International Terrorism: Image and Reality," in Alexander George, ed., *Western State Terrorism* (New York: Routledge, 1991), pp. 12-38 and Edward S. Herman, *The Real Terror Network: Terrorism in Fact and Propaganda* (Montreal: Black Rose Books, 1985).

17. In 1995, Washington approved a funding package of $18 million to support covert action by the CIA to overthrow the government of Iran. David Corn, "Newt's Blown Cover," *The Nation*, February 26, 1996, pp. 3-4. The shipment of another $20 million dollars in surplus military equipment to Sudanese opposition groups was given the go-ahead in 1996. David B. Ottaway, The Washington Post, "U.S. to Aid Opposition to Sudan," *The Guardian Weekly*, November 17, 1996, p. 19. The U.S. government also appears to have supported the Taliban's war and takeover of the government in Afghanistan by proxy through Pakistan. Nael Mokhayber, Al-Watan al-Arabi, "America's Link to the Taliban," *World Press Review*, January 1997, pp. 22-23 and John-Thor Dahlburg, The Los Angeles Times, " 'U.S. suspected of supporting rise of the Taliban," *The Ottawa Citizen*, October 5, 1996, p. A8. The U.S. continues to pour massive amounts of money into the coffers of a repressive Colombian government, ostensibly in the effort to fight the "war against drugs." Also see William Blum, *Killing Hope: U.S. Military and CIA Intervention Since World War II* (Montreal: Black Rose Books, 1998).

18. Jacques Ellul, *Propaganda: The Formation of Men's Attitudes*, translated by Konrad Kellen and Jean Lerner (New York: Alfred A. Knopf, 1969).

19. Stuart Hall "Encoding/decoding," in Stuart Hall et al, eds., *Culture, Media and Language* (Birmingham: Centre for Contemporary Cultural Studies, 1980), pp. 136-137.

20. For an extensive analysis of the role of the mass media acting as integration propagandists in the coverage of terrorism see Edward S. Herman, *The Real Terror Network*, pp. 139-199. Whereas governments and the mass media *are* often at odds about the coverage of terrorists this usually involves disagreements over matters of style rather than ideology; the former fear that the mere portrayal of and interviews with terrorists serve a legitimating function while the mass media are determined not to deprive themselves of covering some of the most dramatic events in current affairs. The two generally remain united on their view of terrorism as an illegitimate means of political struggle and work to present it as such to the public. For example, see the views of some prominent Northern

journalists in "Conference Report: Terrorism and the Media," *Political Communication and Persuasion* 3:2 (1985), pp. 185-90.

21. Gaye Tuchman, "Myth and the Consciousness Industry: A New Look at the Effects of the Mass Media," in Elihu Katz and Tamás Szecskö, eds., *Mass Media and Social Change* (Beverly Hills: Sage, 1981), pp. 89-90.

22. Frantz Fanon, *The Wretched of the Earth*, translated by Constance Farrington (New York: Grove, 1963).

23. Tuen A. van Dijk, *News Analysis: Case Studies of International and National News in the Press* (Hillsdale, New Jersey: Lawrence Erlbaum, 1988), p. 13.

24. Ibid, p. 22.

25. Gaye Tuchman, *Making News: A Study in the Construction of Reality* (New York: Free Press, 1978), p. 7; also see Erving Goffman, *Frame Analysis: An Essay on the Organization of Experience* (Cambridge, Mass.: Harvard University Press, 1974).

26. David Chaney, "The Symbolic Form of Ritual in Mass Communication," in Peter Golding, Graham Murdock and Philip Schlesinger, eds., *Communicating Politics: Mass Communications and the Political Process* (New York: Holmes and Meier, 1986), p. 117.

27. Kenneth Burke, "Dramatism," in D. Sills, ed., *The International Encyclopedia of the Social Sciences*, Vol. 7 (New York: Macmillan, 1968), p. 445.

28. Edward S. Herman and Noam Chomsky, *Manufacturing Consent: The Political Economy of the Mass Media* (New York: Pantheon, 1988), pp. 58-60.

29. Gerbner, George, "Violence and Terror in and by Media," paper circulated at the Media and Crisis conference, Laval University, Quebec, October 1990, p. 18. The second sentence in this quotation appears in the paper prepared by George Gerbner for the international conference on "Media and Crisis" at Laval University in Quebec city in October 1990, but not in the published version published with the same title in Marc Raboy and Bernard Dagenais, eds., *Media, Crisis and Democracy* (London: Sage, 1992), pp. 94-107.

30. Hugh Dalziel Duncan, *Symbols in Society* (Oxford: Oxford University Press, 1968), p. 237.

31. Gerbner, 1992, pp. 100-106.

32. Cf. Imran Nazar Hosein, "Islam and United Nations Organization," *Muslim Education Quarterly* 6:3 (1989), pp. 22-27; Waheed uz-Zaman, "Doctrinal Position of Islam Concerning Inter-State and International Relations," *Hamdard Islamicus* 9:1 (1986), pp. 81-91; and Sharif al-Mujahid, "Muslim Nationalism: Iqbal's Synthesis of Pan-Islamism and Nationalism," *American Journal of Islamic Social Sciences* 2:1 (1985), pp. 29-40.

33. Stephen J. Rosow, "The Forms of Internationalization: Representation of Western Culture on a Global Scale," *Alternatives* 15 (1990), p. 294.

34. Eastern Europe, which left the fold of the capitalist, Christian West, was cast in the mode of a heretic, is now being welcomed back upon its reconversion.

35. China is the only Southern country that is a Permanent Member of the UN Security Council; neither India (with its population of over one billion), "the Muslim world" (which constitutes some twenty percent of the world's population), nor any other countries from Asia, Africa, or Latin America have this status. (Even Germany and Japan, the losers of World War II, have not been successful in gaining this particular position despite their presently elevated economic status.)

36. Hamid Mowlana, "Roots of War: The Long Road of Intervention," in Hamid Mowlana, George Gerbner and Herbert I. Schiller, eds., *Triumph of the Image: The Media's War in the Persian Gulf - A Global Perspective* (Boulder, Colo.: Westview, 1992), p. 31.

37. Keith Krause, "The International Trade in Arms," *Canadian Institute for International Peace and Security Background Paper* 28 (March 1989), p. 2.

38. Massimo Calabresi, "The Terror Countdown," *Time*, December 27, 1999, p. 33; Joanna McGeary, "New Year's Evil?" *Time*, December 31, 1999, pp. 155-157; John F. Burns and Craig Pyes, "Radical Islamic Network May Have Come to U.S.," *The New York Times*, December 31, 1999, p. A16; Daniel Klaidman and Evan Thomas, "Americans on Alert," *Newsweek*, January 1, 2000, pp. 10-13; Daniel Benjamin and Steven Simon, "The New Face of Terrorism," *The New York Times*, January 4, 2000, p. A19; Evan Thomas and Michael Hirsh, "The Future of Terror," *Newsweek*, January 10, 2000, pp. 35-37; and Bruce Wallace, "The Terror Hunt," *Maclean's*, January 24, 2000, pp. 22-26.

39. U.S. officials sometimes speak openly about using nuclear arms against these states. President Clinton warned North Korea in July 1993 that it faced nuclear holocaust if it used a nuclear weapon. Newsday, "Ditch A-bomb plan, U.S. tells North Korea," *The Toronto Star*, July 11, 1993, p. A3. A U.S. nuclear policy directive explicitly allows for a nuclear strike against a "rogue state" threatening the use of chemical or biological weapons. In April 1996, the Assistant Secretary of Defence Kenneth Bacon said that the American government was considering a number of options for destroying a Libyan chemical weapons plant, including the use of nuclear weapons. Michael T. Klare, "Nuking Libya," July 8, 1996, pp. 5-6. General George Lee Butler, former commander of the U.S. Strategic Command, told the Washington press club in February 1998 that planning for the Gulf War included the possible use of nuclear arms. Editorial, "Bombast on Baghdad," *The Nation*, March 2, 1998, p. 3.

40. Connie DeBoer, "The Polls: Terrorism and Hijacking," *Public Opinion Quarterly* 43 (Fall 1979), pp. 410-418.

41. Jonathan Marshall, Peter Dale Scott, and Jane Hunter, *The Iran Contra Connection: Secret Teams and Covert Operations in the Reagan Era* (Montreal: Black Rose Books, 1987).

42. Noam Chomsky, *Pirates and Emporers: International Terrorism in the Real World* (Montreal: Black Rose Books, 1987), pp. 116-17.

43. Akbar S. Ahmed, *Postmodernism and Islam: Predicament and Promise* (London: Routledge, 1992), p. 259.

CHAPTER 2

JIHAD

Religion and Violence

Dominant media discourses usually translate the Arabic word "jihad" as "holy war"; it is frequently viewed as the ultimate expression of the Muslim's violent tendencies and as being synonymous with "Islamic terrorism." Seen from the perspective of a Christian disdain of worldly matters, it seems to be a perversion of religion even though violence in the name of God is not a concept that is completely alien to Christian thought and practice. Whereas religious war does not occupy the level of prominence in Christianity that it does in Muslim doctrine, the Crusades and colonial conquests carried out in the name of Christ have been fairly bloody. Nevertheless, the Western Christian Self tends to view itself as essentially restrained and non-violent in juxtaposition to the image of the Muslim Other driven to killing by fanatical frenzy.

In its dominant meanings, holy war is thought of as a means to weaken or destroy another religion and to acquire converts. Medieval Arabs are often portrayed in Northern discourses as attacking neighbouring lands carrying a sword in one hand and the Koran in another. Such views hold that conquered peoples were forced to embrace Islam upon pain of death even though "conversion by force, while not unknown in Muslim countries, was, in fact, rare."[1] Rudolph Peters, who has extensively studied medieval and modern discourses on jihad, remarks:

> The image of the dreadful Turk, clad in a long robe and brandishing his scimitar, ready to slaughter any infidel that might come his way and would refuse to be converted to the religion of Mahomet, has been a stereotype in Western literature for a long time. Nowadays this image has been replaced by that of the Arab "terrorist" in battledress, armed with a Kalashnikov gun and prepared to murder in cold blood innocent Jewish and Christian women and children. The assumption underlying these stereotypes is that Moslems, often loosely called Arabs, are innately bloodthirsty and inimical towards persons of a different persuasion, and that owing to their religion,

which allegedly preaches intolerance, fanaticism and continuous warfare against unbelievers.[2]

The image of the jihad-inspired Muslim ready to pounce upon Christians was used by European powers to justify massive structural and direct violence against Muslim interests during the colonial era. This tendency has survived into the present, helping to legitimize highly destructive actions such as the intensive bombing by Western powers of Iraqi cities during the Gulf War, the Serbian slaughter of Bosnian Muslims, and the Russian assault on Chechens.

Northern critics have found in the practice of jihad evidence that Islam promotes fanatical violence. Such approaches disregard the complexity of the concept as well as the debates that Muslims have engaged on it over the last fourteen centuries. In the discourses of modernist Muslims, jihad is presented as an essentially defensive mode of war—it is carried out only when the existence of the faith is in danger. They emphasize those parts of the Koran and the traditions (hadith) of the prophet Muhammad which counsel peacemaking with adversaries. Militant Islamists, however, tend to promote jihad as the means to establish the "Islamic state." They take an aggressive stance towards the current national and international orders, which they seek to challenge with force. Their readings of Islamic scriptures confirms for them the legitimacy of direct violence against their enemies. Others, such as Mohammed Arkoun, attempt to deconstruct the epistemological bases underlying such discourses: he argues against rigid interpretations of the Koran to support one view or another, and instead proposes the exploration of the "unthinkable, which can only be reached by going beyond the frontiers of the closed dogmatic system."[3]

The conduct and the avoidance of violence appear to have a fundamental place in the activities of human society. In his acclaimed study on Violence and the Sacred, René Girard presents evidence from ancient myths, Greek tragedy, biblical narratives, rituals of animist religions, and contemporary judicial systems to demonstrate the central place of violence in human existence. Various societies have held it to be an irrepressible force that has to be placated or diverted so that it does not destroy them. One way to deal with the problem has been the institution of sacrifice, including that of humans. It is important, however, that the victim be "pure" so that her death is not avenged—thus breaking the cycle of violence. These victims, who are chosen for their absence of or weak links with members of society, are manifestations of the Other: prisoners of war, slaves, and even uninitiated youth, who in some cultures are considered marginal. As an extension of these beliefs, war is waged against the outsider or infidel in order to channel violence away from the in-group.

Girard compares such legitimization of violence by religion with that by modern judicial systems. Indeed, the state, which has a monopoly over legitimate violence, is very effective in curbing the cycle of vengeance. Since the modern judiciary is supposed to be objective and independent, it can sanction punitive violence without fear of reprisal from members of society. Girard's functionalist perspective finds similarities in how religious and technological culture have dealt with the social problem of violence: "To understand religious thought requires an empirical approach. The goal of religious thinking is exactly the same as that of technological research—namely, practical action."[4] Paradoxically, the practical action (the ritual or technique) which religious and technological societies have adopted for the avoidance of violence, is violence itself. Utopia, where there will be no violence, can be achieved through continual progress involving the repetition of ritual or the refinement of technique. Thus, holy or just wars are fought to end all wars by eradicating the Other.

Kenneth Vaux, a scholar of ethics, traces the evolution of the modern concept of just war to Jewish and Christian notions of holy war. Whereas its roots are to be found in ancient Greece and Rome, medieval Christian philosophers contributed significantly to the development of the idea. During the Gulf War, President George Bush acknowledged this as he sought to justify American military action against Iraq. Speaking at a prayer breakfast of the National Religious Broadcasters Convention, during the second week of the hostilities, he said,

> The war in the Gulf is not a Christian war, a Jewish war, or a Moslem war—it is a just war. And it is a war with which good will prevail. (Applause.) We're told that the principles of a just war originated with classical Greek and Roman philosophers like Plato and Cicero. And later they were expounded by such Christian theologians as Ambrose, Augustine, Thomas Aquinas.[5]

Whereas the Western integration propagandists did not present their governments' involvement in the Gulf War in religious frames, they did highlight its religious characteristics (good will prevail) and Christian pedigree. It was also significant that Bush presented the moral justification for the war at the National Religious Broadcasters Convention. His personal religious conviction appears to have influenced his rationalization for engaging the U.S. in the conflict. The "born again"[6] American president raised the matter with his own Episcopal congregation and engaged in worship and prayer with his closest advisers and with evangelist Billy Graham prior to the war. The search for religious sanction for war appears to have been intense in both Washington and Baghdad (where Saddam Hussein couched it in terms of jihad).

The ultimate aim of the Gulf War in Bush's rhetoric was the global peace that would be ushered through a New World Order. This echoed centuries of justifications for holy war which promised eternal peace. Holy war in the Old Testament was carried out to establish *shalom* (peace). One cannot peer into the hearts of those who made the decisions to carry out the Gulf War to ascertain their innermost convictions about the righteousness of their actions, but we do know that their words did appeal to the moral and ethical, if not the religious traditions of their respective societies. A utopic peace would be ushered in for the whole region, which would justify the large scale killing and destruction preceding it.

Human societies have had to contend with the contradiction between the human propensity for violence and the religious/ethical taboo against shedding blood ("thou shalt not kill"). The resolution of this paradox has been the formulation of the concept of holy war/just war, which becomes a legitimate form of war. Killing is justified, indeed made obligatory, in the name of a higher authority—God or the State. The French Foreign Legion's Code of Honour commands its members that "A mission once given to you becomes sacred to you, you will accomplish it to the end and at all cost." Killing others is rewarded and putting one's own life in danger while conducting war is recognized with high honours; death is honoured with the status of martyrdom (both religious and secular).

> The mythologies and rituals of holy war in early Israel, Islam, and the Christian Crusades served exactly the same purpose and had the same "truth value" and ethical import as rational theory in seventeenth-century Europe and modern jurisprudential theory about the law of war. Each asked: why shall we go to war and how shall war be fought?[7]

The early Jewish (Davidic) code of war, outlining the purposes and manners in which fighting should be carried out, forms the basis of the Christian, Muslim, and modern international codes of war. Christian views on war, conflicting with the New Testament's advice of "turning the other cheek," evolved with Augustine's attempt to reconcile Christian pacifism with the contingency of defending Christendom against its enemies. Aquinas developed the principles of just war, thus providing the theological justification for the more aggressive Crusades.

Interestingly, among the first modern theorists of just war were the Spanish Jesuits Francisco de Vitoria and Francisco Suarez who wrote during the era of Spanish colonial expansion. The concept of just war was used by emerging monarchies during the 15th century, aiding the birth of "national consciousness."[8] A vital contribution was also made in this area by the Calvinist Hugo Grotius, whose work, in laying out a doctrine of ownership and expropriation of land and resources, formed the foundation of contemporary international law. While maintaining, in adherence to Old Testament tradition, that the goal of any warfare is the achievement of peace, he was instrumental in rationalizing the forceful acquisition by European powers of the non-European/non-Christian Other's territories. True peace could only be established under European Christian rule. According to Grotius, the conduct of war must be governed by a discerning conscience—a notion that was echoed by George Bush in the State of the Union address made during the Gulf War.

> Our cause is just. Our cause is moral. Our cause is right.

> Let future generations understand the burden and the blessings of freedom. Let them say, we stood where duty required us to stand.

> Let them know together, we affirmed America, and the world, as a community of conscience.[9]

Thus, whereas just war ethics have been secularized enough to become part of the technological society's dominant discourses, they carry very strong traces of Christian thought. In fact, the regulation of relations and conflicts among European states until 1856 was carried out according to a set of rules referred to as Christian international law, which is the basis for contemporary international law. Although the latter has been extended around the globe, Northern interests have resisted the addition of elements from non-Christian religious traditions.

The Origins of Jihad

The term jihad means "effort," "exertion," or "struggle." Whereas other Arabic words such as *harb* (war) and *qital* (fighting) specifically denote bloodshed, jihad does not necessarily involve physical conflict; the former are usually used to describe non-religious (e.g., tribal and nationalist) wars. The fourteenth-century Arab social historian Ibn Khaldun described three other kinds of war apart from jihad: that between neighbouring groups, that caused by hostility, and dynastic war.[10] Although dominant Muslim discourses have traditionally favoured the meaning of religious struggle through fighting, this interpretation has coexisted with others. A primary non-martial connotation of jihad is the ongoing spiritual struggle against one's own evil desires. The basis for this view is a tradition of the prophet Muhammad, who is said to have remarked upon coming home to Medina from a battle: "We have returned from the lesser jihad to the greater jihad."[11]

The degree of self-control that is expected of a Muslim in conducting a jihad is related by Jalal al-din Rumi, a prominent 13th century sufi master, in narrating the heroic exploits of Ali, the Prophet's cousin and son-in-law. (The historical role of Ali is especially significant because he was the last of the Rightly-Guided Caliphs and is held to be the founder of Shi'ism.) During the course of a battle, just as Ali was about to strike a lethal blow with his sword his opponent spat at him. At this point Ali checked himself, stopped fighting, and turned away. When asked to explain his action, he replied:

In the hour of battle, O knight,

When thou didst spit in my face, my fleshy self was aroused and my (good) disposition was corrupted.

Half (of my fighting) came to be for God's sake, and half (for) idle passion: in God's affair partnership is not allowable.[12]

Jihad fi sabil Allah ("struggle in the way of God") is viewed here as a very complex endeavour that demands the level of self-control that can discern, even in the heat of battle, the difference between acting out of one's own emotions and selfless service to God. Such self-assessment of changing circumstances enables the individual to elude the trap of rigid and dogmatic prescriptions.

This form of jihad is also referred to as "jihad of the heart." The "jihad of the tongue," involving the verbal encouragement of good deeds, and that of the pen are ways to engage in spiritual endeavour through education. "Jihad of the hand" means the physical administration of disciplinary measures by those in authority to prevent sinful behaviour. And "jihad of the sword" is fighting unbelievers for the sake of religion.[13] The latter has become the most commonly-understood meaning of jihad when it is used without qualification. However, a prominent Islamist leader declared,

> Islam wishes to press into service all forces which can bring about a revolution and a composite term for the use of all these forces is "Jihad." To change the outlook of the people and initiate a mental revolution among them through speech or writing is a form of "Jihad." To alter the old tyrannical social system and establish a new just order of life by the power of sword is also "Jihad" and to expend goods and exert physically for this cause is "Jihad" too.[14]

As with many other religious issues, various Muslim authorities hold differing opinions on the nature and characteristics of jihad.

The origins of the concept are to be found in the Koran and the traditions (*hadith*) of the Prophet. However, there is seemingly contradictory guidance in the various Koranic verses and various *hadiths*, which have led to the adoption of differing positions by Muslim schools of law. Divine advice in the form of *Koranic* verses on relations with non-believers differed in the various periods of Muhammad's prophethood. Dominant Muslim discourses view the guidance about the response to those who attacked Muslims as becoming increasingly aggressive in the course of the Prophet's mission. In the early phase he was told merely to deliver his message without engaging in discussion: "proclaim that which thou art commanded, and withdraw from the idolaters" (XV: 94).[15] Later on, even though Muhammad was taunted and his followers were attacked physically, he was instructed only to "Call unto the way of thy Lord with wisdom and fair exhortation, and reason with them in the better way" (XVI: 125). Despite this peaceful approach the persecution of Muslims increased, causing them to migrate from Mecca to Medina in 622. However, they continued to be harassed by the Meccan raiding parties. Subsequently, sanction to fight was given to those who had been wronged, but only as a defence against attacks by the unbelievers. "Fight in the way of Allah against those who fight against you, but begin not hostilities" (II: 190) and (XXII: 39).

Finally, as Meccan attacks intensified, the unconditional command to fight all unbelievers was received in what are known as the two "verses of the sword" (IX: 5 and IX: 29): "Then, when the sacred months have passed, slay the idolaters wherever ye find them, and take them (captive), and besiege them, and prepare for them each [an] ambush. But if they repent and establish worship and pay the poor-due, then leave their way free. Lo! Allah is Forgiving, Merciful" (IX: 5). With this revelation, war against polytheist tribes in the Arabian peninsula became a legitimate activity for Muslims striving to bring the inhabitants of Arabia into the fold. Violence was seen as a means to pacify the land and usher in utopia. The Koranic quest for *salam* (peace) through jihad seems to reflect the Old Testament's search for *shalom* through holy war. Jews and Christians were given the option, without converting to Islam, of becoming protected peoples (ahl al-dhimma), under Muslim suzerainty. With the increasing leeway in the Koran to engage polytheists in battle, the dominant legal-theological discourses after Muhammad's death eventually treated this as the prescribed course of action (although there were prominent dissenters from this view, such as the fifteenth century scholar, al-Suyuti). According to the linear application of the rule of *naskh* (abrogation), a later Koranic verse repealed a previous one on a particular issue. In reducing jihad to ritual and to legalism, dominant Muslim discourses deprived it of the powerful dialectic within the self, as in the action of Ali described by Jalal al-din Rumi. The continual inner jihad of an individual to strive for truth was superseded by jihad as a legal/religious requirement.

Jihad was deemed to be a communal responsibility which would be organized and conducted under the leadership of the Muslim state. However, it became individual duty in the cases when an enemy attacked Muslim territory—in such an event it was incumbent upon all Muslims to fight back with or without the declaration of a formal campaign. Based on pertinent references in the Koran and the *hadith*, legal scholars developed specific rules regarding the waging of jihad, which in many ways resemble the Davidic code of war inspired by the Old Testament. Particular categories of people (women, minors, those with mental or physical disabilities etc.) were made exempt from the communal duty; before launching an attack, the enemy had to be given the opportunity to accept Muslim rule; the kinds of permissible weapons were listed; the classes of persons who could not be harmed and the specific circumstances under which non-combatants could be attacked were identified; while the seizure of enemy property was allowed, burning or other forms of destruction of vegetation was not; Muslim combatants were not permitted to flee from the battlefield; assistance from non-Muslims was acceptable under certain circumstances; whereas trading could be carried out with enemy powers, particular kinds of goods could not be exported to them; the leader (*imam*) was to make decisions regarding the fate of prisoners of war; quarter could be granted to particular persons in a hostile territory and safe-conduct to individuals at the borders of Muslim lands; treaties of peaceful coexistence could be conducted with enemy powers; finally, jihad was to be terminated upon the conversion of unbelievers to Islam or when they submitted themselves to Muslim government without converting.[16] Whereas this was the general tenor of regulations regarding jihad, there did not exist complete agreement on these points among the various schools of law.

Dominant Muslim discourses divided the world into two parts: the Territory of Islam (*dar al-Islam*) and the Territory of War (*dar al-harb*). A third category existed according to the Shafi'i school—the Territory of Treaty (*dar al-sulh* or *dar al-'ahd*), which referred to lands occupied by rulers who had made treaties with the Muslim state. The Territory of Islam could be transformed into the Territory of War under three conditions, according to the founder of the Hanafi school:

- Application of the laws of unbelievers;
- Adjacency to the Territory of War;

- Absence of the original security of life and property for the Muslims and the protected non-Muslims (dhimmis).[17]

In this, medieval Muslim world views had developed the characteristics which defined the loci of the collective Self and Other. In so far as the known world was divided into the territories of Islam and War, it was analogous to the dichotomization of humanity by Hugo Grotius between Europe and the non-Christian/non-civilized Other and that which existed during the Cold War between the communist and capitalist blocs. As in these cases, the relationship between the two spheres was essentially confrontationary: ideology, whether religious or political, exhorted followers to commit themselves to fighting the Other.

Putting one's life in danger "in the way of God" has been an important religious duty in dominant Muslim discourses, with believers expected to respond enthusiastically to the call to arms. Jihad has been presented as an obligation for every believing male who does not belong to one of the exempt categories. Paradise would be denied to those who fail to perform this or any other important religious duty prescribed by the shariah. Death during jihad, on the other hand, guaranteed salvation. Ayatollah Khomeini sought to revive the notion of martyrdom through jihad among the Twelver Shia. The effect that his teachings had was apparent in the 1980s, especially among certain individuals in the Iranian military and militant Shia groups in Lebanon.

Jihad In History

After the death of Muhammad in 632, Muslim armies emerged from Arabia and within a few centuries conquered a broad swath of territory from the Iberian peninsula in the west to India in the east. The well-trained and equipped legions of the Iranian (Sassanid) and Byzantine empires, which were exhausted through continual warring against each other, were defeated by a few thousand poorly-armed and mostly nomadic Arabs. Vanquished peoples were accorded the status of the protected ahl al-dhimma, who did not serve in the Muslim army and paid poll taxes distinct from the religious dues that were obligatory for Muslims. In many cases the local Monophysite, Coptic, and Nestorian Christian as well as Jewish populations, which had been oppressed by the Greek Orthodox Byzantines and Zoroastrian Sassanids, were eager to expel the latter powers and were in favour of gaining protected status from the Muslim state.[18]

Inspired by the mission of carrying the Koranic message to all humanity, Muslim armies were poised to reach far into Europe. Their advance was, however, stopped by Charles Martel at Poitiers (in what is presently France) in 732—a century after Muhammad's death. The Muslim empire became sedentary as it absorbed the ways of conquered peoples, and jihad gave way to treaties with neighbouring powers. Nomadic Turkic tribes arriving from their home in Mongolia from the tenth century onwards, converted to Islam, and became the new warrior class. Not only did they stop the Mongols, who followed them west, from completely devastating the central lands of the Muslim realm, but also carried the jihad westwards into the Balkans after conquering Constantinople in

1453. Some Muslim rulers found it in their interests to identify their wars, even against other Muslims, as jihad. This served to give religious legitimacy to the military campaigns which brought them worldly profit.

No one made more consistent use of the technique than Timur-i Lenk [Tamarlane], the Turkish Muslim Lord of Samarkand in Central Asia, who devastated the Islamic East under the banner of "holy war."

At the end of the fourteenth century, he visited the Muslims of Delhi with a terrible "jihad," and sacked and destroyed it on the pretence that the country was still full of infidels (who, however, were paying tribute).[19]

The pious purposes of "striving in the way of God" appear to have been abandoned for material gains. A plurality of sultans fought with each other, and the caliph—who technically had the sole authority to proclaim the jihad—remained powerless. (Iraq as well as Saudi Arabia—which was on the side of the United Nations Coalition—both declared jihad against each other during the Gulf War.)

Following European incursions into Africa and Asia, jihad was adopted as an important ideological and tactical means of opposition to colonialism. Several nineteenth-century Muslim movements in India, Sudan, Egypt and Palestine fought against the British, in Libya against the Italians, in Somalia against both the British and Italians, in Algeria against the French, in Indonesia against the Dutch, and in Central Asia against the Russians. Jihad was both a means to mobilize people for resistance and to legitimize military action. According to a *fatwa* (legal opinion) issued by a prominent Indian theologian in 1803, India had reverted to being a Territory of War because it was under non-Muslim rule. The Tariqa-i Muhammadi movement which carried out a jihad against the British administration had a large following of peasants and craftspeople who had suffered from the economic and social consequences of the colonial order. Despite military defeat and the death of its founding leaders, the movement survived underground.

It was against this background that the famous "Sepoy Mutiny" of Indian soldiers in the British army took place in 1857. Whereas the followers of Tariqa-i Muhammadi played a role in inciting the civilian Muslim population, in many places Hindus and Muslims fought together against the colonial masters. But the British saw the uprising as an attempt of Muslim landed and military aristocracy to restore the rule of the Mughal sultan, and singled them out for particular repression in its aftermath. In an attempt to show that Muslims posed no threat to the colonial regime, many legal opinions, edicts and statements by modernist Muslim elements were issued to the effect that India was not a Territory of War and that military action against the British would be illegitimate under the *shariah*. This echoed an earlier verdict of the Egyptian religious authorities at Al-Azhar, Sunnism's premier seat of learning, which had declared that attempts at resisting Napoleon's army were "against God's will."[20] Another reason for not carrying out the jihad against European colonial rulers, provided by religious scholars in India and Algeria, was the weak probability of success. Indian modernists, led by Sayyid Ahmad Khan, asserted that jihad was essentially limited to defence against the religious persecution that specifically impeded the performance of what dominant Muslim discourses consider to be the five pillars of Islam: the profession of faith, prayer, religious dues, fasting and pilgrimage. In thus removing jihad from the political sphere and limiting it to the defence of the fundamentals of the faith, Sayyid Ahmad Khan made a separation of Church and State—which was hitherto alien to dominant Muslim discourses.

By the end of the nineteenth century the notion that jihad was defensive had become current in many other Muslim societies, including those in the Middle East. However, unlike their Indian counterparts, modernists there considered it legitimate to carry out the jihad against colonial powers who did not necessarily prevent the practice of Islam. Nevertheless, the Koran's guidance received in the last period of Muhammad's life, which seemed to sanction war against polytheists unconditionally, was reinterpreted through contextual exegesis by Sheikh Mahmud Shaltut, an Egyptian religious authority. He argued that the verses of the sword had been meant to counter people who refused to respect pledges. In this way he mitigated what was dominantly considered the unrestricted command to fight all unbelievers. This reflected the acceptance by modernists of the principle of peaceful relations between the Muslim state and the rest of the world. The Territory of War was transformed into what Sayyid Ahmad Khan termed "Dar-ul-aman, or 'land of security', in which the Moslem may lawfully reside as moostamin, or seeker of aman [security]."[21]

As dominant Northern discourses have taken hold in Muslim societies, the discourses of modernist Muslims have increasingly been couched within the concept of the nation-state. With the secularization of the Muslim polity, national conflicts have become coextensive with jihad—which itself has been secularized in some cases. During the Arab-Israeli war in 1973, the Rector of Cairo's Al-Azhar University, appealing to the nationalist sentiments of Muslim and Christian Egyptians, declared:

> Jihad is an obligation for all, without distinction between Moslems and Christians. It is the first duty of all who live under the sky of Egypt, the fatherland of all...Being killed (istishhad) [literally, "martyred"] for the sake of the fatherland gives access to Paradise.[22]

A former Tunisian president, Habib Bourguiba, addressing the subject of national development, stated: "Escaping from [economic] backwardness is jihad-obligation, ruled by the same prescription as jihad by the means of sword."[23] Religious and national duty appear to have merged in these discourses, which promise utopia upon performance of the ritual/technique of jihad. Whereas medieval Muslim jurists reduced jihad from an inner spiritual dialectic to legalism, it is currently being harnessed to modernist world views by those Muslims acting as integration propagandists of dominant global discourses. Militant Islamists, on the other hand, have been working to reinstate the medieval status of the concept.

Contemporary Debates On Jihad

There has emerged from militant sources a defence of jihad that is unapologetic and unbending. This discourse sees the concept as the means to save Muslim societies from self-destruction. Militant Islamist groups are vehemently critical of the interpretations provided by modernists and are deeply suspicious of Northern interests. Abul A'la Maududi, one of the key Islamist ideologues in South Asia, was speaking out as early as the 1930s against European colonists for characterizing Muslims as being endemically violent when they themselves had acquired much of the world through military conquest. His ideas were influential in other Muslim societies including Egypt, where the Muslim Brethren organization has since the early decades of this century been preaching the return to a society ruled by the *shariah*. Its members were involved in a jihad in Palestine against Jewish forces before and after the formation of Israel. Over the years, it has been periodically banned and reinstated by the Egyptian government, and its leaders and members have been jailed and some executed. Among the Muslim Brethren's most outspoken leaders was Sayyid Qutb, who was tried and executed in 1966.

According to Qutb, the North was in decline and was devoid of the values necessary for the future of human civilization. Borrowing from Koranic narratives, he characterized the contemporary situation as that existing during the time of Moses and the Pharaoh—whose story has popular resonance in Egyptian society. Through this he indicated that the current government, based on a Northern model, had to be overthrown by "a vanguard of dedicated fighters, using every means, including *jihad*, which should not be undertaken until the fighters had achieved inner purity, but should then be pursued, if necessary, not for defence only, but to destroy all worship of false gods and remove all the obstacles which prevented men from accepting Islam."[24] Qutb's proposal that the contemporary Egyptian state be violently displaced due to its "unIslamic" nature was a novel idea among Islamists, who had hitherto not preached jihad against domestic Muslim rulers. Qutb also lambasted the latter for promoting *jahiliyya* (literally, a state of ignorance)—the Koranic term applied to the societal chaos of pre-Islamic Arabia—which made armed revolt against them legitimate. These ideas were to have a profound effect on the next generation of Muslim militants.

In the wake of the Six-Day War (1967), in which Arab countries led by Egypt were soundly defeated by Israel, the Islamist movement grew rapidly. The sheer scale of the military debacle was interpreted by many as punishment from God upon the Arab secular state for supposedly abandoning religious faith in God. There was a deliberate turning away from Northern influences back to religion by large numbers of Egyptian Muslims (as well as Christians). While many Muslims returned to traditional forms of piety, some found the activist messages of the various Islamist groups more appealing. It is interesting to note that a number of the leaders and ideologues of Egyptian Islamist groups operating in the 1970s had received training in the applied sciences but no formal education in Islamic theology.[25] Whereas the Islamist movement was strong in universities based on Northern models, its presence in traditional institutions of learning such as Al-Azhar was rare. The sudden replacement of the religious world view by a secular, empiricist discourse appears to have played a part in driving certain individuals to Islamism.

Some of the Egyptian groups which these people joined were dedicated to overthrowing the government through jihad. They carried out wide-ranging activities against the state from political agitation to attacks on government representatives. One of these groups, the Tanzim al-Jihad, succeeded in assassinating President Anwar Sadat in October 1981. A key document that sheds light on the views of such groups is a pamphlet published in December 1981 by Tanzim al-Jihad's ideologue, Muhammad Abd al-Salam Faraj. *Al-Farida al-Gha'iba* ("The Neglected Duty") referred to jihad as a religious obligation which Muslims had disregarded.

> Jihad...for God's cause, in spite of its extreme importance and its great significance for the future of this religion, has been neglected by the *ulama* [leading Muslim scholars] of this age. They have feigned ignorance of it, but they know that it is the only way to the return and the establishment of the glory of Islam anew.[26]

Muslims had to carry out religious war in order to re-establish the earthly utopia of the Islamic state.

The document made selective use of source material from the Koran, Muhammad's traditions, legal treatises, and historical sources, refuting out of hand any contrary opinions. Faraj attacked the current government of Egypt. He based his case on the opinions of Ibn Taymiyya, a 13th-14th century scholar renowned for his puritanical tendencies and for inspiring revivalist movements. The "ungodly rulers" of Muslim lands whom Ibn Taymiyya had assailed in his day were the Mongols; Faraj compared them to the current regime in Cairo. Since the local leaders were viewed as pivotal in implementing Northern imperialism in Egypt they had to be dealt with as an initial step: "We must concentrate on our own Islamic situation: we have to establish the Rule of God's Religion in our own country first, and to make the Word of God supreme."[27] The contemporary Egyptian leaders were even more culpable than either Northerners or the Mongol rulers of the past because they were seen as being in apostasy from Islam—a heinous offence according to the *shariah*.

Founding a political party to oppose the government within parliament would entail cooperating with the dominant order and ensuring its continuation. This was considered pointless by Faraj because the ultimate purpose of his program was the destruction of the existing state. He believed that his group's purposes could only be achieved through a radically different discourse that promoted violent revolution and the overturning of the established system. Faraj preached jihad against the Muslims whom he considered to have strayed from the straight and narrow. The document quoted from Ibn Taymiyya to support this position: "Any group of people that rebels against any prescript of the clear and reliably transmitted prescripts of Islam has to be fought, according to the leading scholars of Islam, even if members of this group pronounce the Islamic Confession of Faith."[28] Ibn Taymiyya himself had attacked the rationalist methodology of many of his contemporaries and that of the Muslim philosophers and theologians who had preceded him. Taking a leaf from the medieval scholar's book, Faraj assailed the religious leadership of Al-Azhar stating that it had paid obeisance to imperialism since the time of Napoleon. Deriding the *ulama*, he declared that jihad in the form of fighting was superior to that carried out in the quest for knowledge.

However, Faraj seemed to contradict himself when, arguing for active involvement of Muslims to rectify Egypt's political situation, he quoted this tradition of Muhammad: "The best form of *jihad* is a word of truth (spoken to) a tyrannical Ruler."[29] Despite this, he considered the "jihad of the sword" to be more important than the "jihad of the tongue." The "jihad of the heart" was rejected outright. Faraj considered the tradition in which Muhammad is said to have described the struggle against the self as "the greater jihad" and religious war as "the lesser jihad" to be fabricated. Any dilution of the militant interpretation of jihad—which provides the religious legitimacy for their violent programs—is shunned by groups like Tanzim al-Jihad. Having decided that only extreme measures can effect the societal changes they deem necessary, they are focused on the coercive and are almost completely devoid of the consensual.

But while militant Islamists appear to reject the dominant technological discourses, the concept of the national polity is not entirely absent in their world view. *The Neglected Duty* preached rebellion against the Egyptian state, not a general uprising against all secular governments with Muslim populations and even less a worldwide revolution against the international order (not yet at least). By limiting its approach to the retransformation of a particular state into an "Islamic" one the Tanzim al-Jihad was subscribing to the modernist idea of the nation-state. Faraj wanted Egypt to be ruled by the *shariah*, which would enable it to "have a brilliant future both economically and agriculturally."[29] However, his arguments failed to provide a real alternative to dominant technological discourses. The precise manners in which a contemporary "Islamic state" would be run was also left unsaid. As Aziz Al-Azmeh notes, this is not unusual for such groups:

> Islamist political discourse is loath to specify the political system that the Islamic state would create and invigilate. It normally rests content with emphasizing the uniqueness of this society, it being one where God is the sole legislator. Beyond the legal order which re-enacts the primitivist utopia, nothing remains but a savage vitalism: the social order will "emerge vitally" from doctrine.[30]

Muhammad Abd al-Salam Faraj's pamphlet has been the focus of much scholarly discussion. The official response from the religious establishment at Al-Azhar, which Faraj had attacked, came in the form of a *fatwa* (legal opinion) issued in 1982 by Egypt's *mufti* (leading *shariah* scholar), Sheikh Jadd al-Haqq. He tackled

Faraj's arguments point by point, attempting to refute them by quoting scripture and legal sources. The sheikh disagreed with the sole interpretation of jihad as fighting: he referred to the end of one Koranic "verse of the sword" to indicate the essentially peaceful premise upon which it was made conditional: "But if they repent and establish worship and pay the poor-due, then leave their way free. Lo! Allah is Forgiving, Merciful" (IX: 5). In this respect, jihad could not be legally waged against the rulers of Egypt who were practising Muslims. Furthermore, Jadd al-Haqq pointed out, the verse was addressed to the pagan Arabs in Muhammad's time who did not have a treaty with the Muslim state. He also challenged Ibn Taymiyya's strict rules of belief and apostasy by citing the Koran (IV: 94) and Muhammad's traditions, according to which the only sin which can render a Muslim an apostate is the denial of *tawhid*—the unity of God.

Additionally, the *mufti* discounted the validity of comparing the "savage destructive Mongols on the one hand, and the rulers and the inhabitants of Egypt on the other.[31] Jadd al-Haqq stated that whereas Islamic scripture commanded Muslims to resist the enemies of Islam, it did not order them to attack other Muslims or non-Muslim citizens, who had equal rights in the contemporary state. "The character of *jihad*, so we must understand, has now changed radically, because the defence of country and religion is nowadays the duty of the regular army, and this army carries out the collective duty of *jihad* on behalf of all citizens."[32] The *mufti* used this modernist interpretation of the concept to turn the tables on Faraj. He declared that since the system of conscription into the army was the present-day equivalent of pledging loyalty to the prophet Muhammad, the Tanzim al-Jihad were actually fighting against God and His prophet.

Jadd al-Haqq upheld the validity of the notion of jihad against the self. And in response to Faraj's specific charges against the *ulama* he insisted that the quest for knowledge was indeed integral to jihad. The sheikh charged that the Tanzim al-Jihad was promoting disregard for both the religious as well as the secular sciences and that their document was a call for illiteracy and primitivism in the name of Islam. Responding to Faraj's reference to the Egyptian *ulama*'s collaboration with Napoleon, the *mufti* claimed that the religious establishment had played a leadership role in resisting colonialism. Whereas the sheikh did not deny the violent aspects of jihad, he attempted to emphasize the specific conditions under which they could be manifested. Like other modernist explanations of the concept, his is supported by contextual analysis of scripture indicating how particular courses of action were recommended only under specific circumstances. And also like other modernists, he attempted to find antecedents of various features of the contemporary state in early Muslim history. Whereas Faraj also adhered to the concept of the nation, he rejected the secular manifestations of the modern state; the *mufti*, on the other hand, appeared to merge the religious and the secular.

We find a more profound analysis in Mohammed Arkoun's commentary on *The Neglected Duty*. He carries out an epistemological study of the document by scrutinizing its underlying cognitive system. Arkoun contends that the political consensus achieved among Islamist movements since the 1970s

> ...tends to obscure the theological issues and historiographical debates that were considered crucial by classical thinkers. There has therefore been an epistemic shift within the cognitive system characteristic of Islamic thought: the principle of returning to the basic texts is maintained, or applied even more rigidly than before, but the semantic and discursive handling of the texts is made wholly subordinate to an ideological objective, ruling out all the 'scientific' procedures (syntax, semantics, rhetoric, history, theology or even philosophy) which previously every doctor of Law (*Imam mujtahid*) was required to master.[33]

Although Faraj had laced his work with quotations from scripture and revered legal authorities, his ignorance of the traditional methods was apparent in the presentation of arguments. There was little concern for the philological or the contextual—two important indices in traditional Muslim exegesis—in what was essentially an exhortative and polemical tract. Thus, according to Arkoun, Faraj presented Muslim scripture as a static body of texts that was not open to analysis and discussion: jihad became fixed in the particular interpretation which the latter imposed on it, veiling the wide variety of opinions (historical and contemporary) about its nature and characteristics.

Arkoun identifies seven tendencies manifested in *The Neglected Duty* which constitute the epistemic framework of Islamist discourses that present the Koran as a "closed official corpus":

- "Everything occurs within the closed dogmatic system made up of the Koranic corpus and the semantic, legal and theological extensions selected, consecrated and transmitted by 'orthodox' tradition";
- "Attention is fixed on the divine Commandment and the duty of every believer to obey it";
- "The legal prevails over the theological" in that the overriding regard for the guidance about practical behaviour regarding jihad in the two "verses of the sword" overshadows 114 other Koranic verses which counsel living in peace as a general mode of behaviour for Muslims;
- The crucial question of abrogation of earlier Koranic verses by later ones is presented as having been settled once and for all by selected authorities whom Faraj cites, thus obscuring the debate on the principle and procedures of Koranic exegesis among classical theologians;
- "Polytheists, infidels and the faithful are no longer considered as competing social groups" in varying historical contexts but are accorded static theological and legal status;
- The historical and sociological contingencies of responding to the devastating violence of the Meccans that motivated the divine commands in the verses of the sword are fixed as being valid for all time; and

- In the Islamist discourse, scholars like Ibn Taymiyya and the founders of the schools of law participate fully and authentically in the phenomenon of Koranic revelation—seemingly on par with the Prophet himself: "their information is incontestable and their interpretations infallible; each represents a benchmark of dogma ensuring the 'logical' and 'coherent' functioning of the shared Islamic discourse."[34]

It is within this closed dogmatic system that personhood is constructed by Islamist discourses, and as a corollary, the militants' justification to carry out jihad against individuals who are deemed non-persons. Unbelievers, apostates, and others living in the Territory of War—characterized as such by the consecrated traditional authorities—thus become legitimate targets.

The official discourses of the religious establishment, which contrives modernist explications of scripture for the secular state, and the oppositional discourses of the militants, who favour rigid anti-modernist interpretations, both operate within the closed dogmatic system. Arkoun's alternative discourse does not see scripture as a fixed corpus but as a source of "permanent tension between God...and man...This is not a static dualist opposition, but a continuous dialectic tension."[35] He proposes the study of Islamic concepts such as jihad by stepping outside dogmatic discourses.

Therefore, whereas jihad has been dominantly viewed as denoting fighting, this perception has been challenged continually within Muslim societies. The intolerant attitude which interprets scriptural guidance as giving permission for unconditional war against unbelievers has been promoted, among others, by those who have wanted to profit materially from wars as well as those driven by socio-economic and political circumstances to fight their oppressors. Northern journalists, who usually translate jihad as "Islamic holy war," are generally unaware of the debates in Muslim discourses on the nature of jihad, the technical points of exegesis such as abrogation of Koranic verses, the validity of specific prophetic traditions, the consecration of particular theological authorities, or even the similarities between jihad and Northern conceptions of holy war/just war. Their work, adhering to the dominant Northern discourses on Islam, serve to make an *essential* link between jihad and terrorism.

NOTES

1. Ira Lapidus, *A History of Islamic Societies* (Cambridge: Cambridge University Press, 1988), p. 244.

2. Rudolph Peters, *Islam and Colonialism: The Doctrine of Jihad in Modern History* (The Hague: Mouton Publishers, 1979), pp. 4-5.

3. Mohammed Arkoun, "The Topicality of the Problem of the Person in Islamic Thought," *International Social Science Journal* 117 (Aug. 1988), pp. 407-422.

4. René Girard, *Violence and the Sacred*, translated by Patrick Gregory (Baltimore: John Hopkins University, 1979), p. 32.

5. Kenneth L. Vaux, *Ethics and the Gulf War: Religion, Rhetoric, and Righteousness* (Boulder, Colo.: Westview, 1992), p. 92.

6. "In 1988 Bush had declared that he had been 'born again' and had accepted Christ as his personal saviour." Ibid, p. 91.

7. Ibid, p. 42.

8. Esther Cohen and Sophia Menaché, "Holy Wars and Sainted Warriors: Christian War Propaganda in the Middle Ages," *Journal of Communication* 36:2 (1986), pp. 52-62.

9. Vaux, *Ethics and the Gulf War*, p. 261.

10. Ibn Khaldun, *The Muqaddimah: An Introduction to History* Vol. 2, translated by Franz Rosenthal (Princeton: Princeton University Press, 1967), p. 74.

11. John Alden Williams, ed., *Themes of Islamic Civilization* (Berkeley: University of California Press, 1971), p. 281.

12. Jalaluddin Rumi, *The Mathnawi of Jalaluddin Rumi* Vol. 1, translated by Reynold A. Nicholson (London: Luzac, 1977), p. 215.

13. Peters, *Islam and Colonialism*, p. 10; also see R.C.Martin, "Religious Violence in Islam: Towards an Understanding of the Discourse on *Jihad* in Modern Egypt," in Paul Wilkinson and Alasdair M. Stewart, eds., *Contemporary Research on Terrorism* (Aberdeen: Aberdeen University Press, 1987), pp. 55-71.

14. S. Abul A'la Maududi, *Jihad in Islam* (Lahore, Pakistan: Islamic Publications, 1976), p. 7.

15. All Koranic references are to Muhammad Marmaduke Pickthall, *The Glorious Qur'an* (Mecca: Muslim World League-Rabita, 1977).

16. Peters, *Islam and Colonialism*, pp. 15-37.

17. Ibid, p.12.

18. Lapidus, *A History of Islamic Societies*, pp. 37-53.

19. Williams, *Themes of Islamic Civilization*, p. 285.

20. Johannes G. Jansen, *The Neglected Duty: The Creed of Sadat's Assassins and Islamic Resurgence in the Middle East* (New York: MacMillan Press, 1986), p. 15.

21. Peters, *Islam and Colonialism*, p. 52.

22. Ibid, p. 134.

23. Ibid, p. 119.

24. Albert Hourani, *A History of the Arab Peoples* (Cambridge, Mass.: Harvard, 1991), p. 446.

25. Saad Eddin Ibrahim, "Anatomy of Egypt's Militant Islamic Groups: Methodological Note and Preliminary Findings," *International Journal of Middle Eastern Studies* 12:4 (1980), p. 436.

26. Jansen, *The Neglected Duty*, pp. 160-161.

27. Ibid, p. 193.

28. Ibid, p. 192.

29. Jansen, p. 184.

30. Aziz Al-Azmeh, *Islams and Modernities* (London: Verso, 1993), p. 28.

31. Jansen, p. 56.

32. Ibid, p. 60.

33. Arkoun, "The Topicality of the Problem of the Person," p. 417.

34. Ibid, pp. 417-418.

35. Mohammed Arkoun, "The Notion of Revelation: From *Ahl al-Kitab* to the Societies of the Book," in Axel Havemann and Baber Johansen, eds., *Gegenwart als Geschichte: Islamwissenschaftliche Studien* (Leiden: E.J. Brill, 1988), p. 69.

CHAPTER 3

ORIENTALIST IMAGINARIES

The Origins Of Orientalism

Current Northern images of the Muslim as post-Cold War Other have roots in age-old ideas about Islam. Certain basic notions about the characteristics of Muslims, having survived hundreds of years, feed the dominant discourses of contemporary media—just as the primary stereotypes that Muslims have about Northerners inform their current constructions of Europe and North America.[1] However, Muslim societies have not institutionalized their imaginaries about Northern societies to the extent that the latter have done of Islam, especially over the last two centuries. Edward Said has contributed significantly to the understanding of this process. In *Orientalism* he analyses the works of painters, belle lettrists, historians, linguists, archaeologists, travellers, colonial bureaucrats, and statesmen to demonstrate the links between knowledge and power in the context of the relationship between Western and Muslim societies. Said describes Orientalism as "the corporate institution for dealing with the Orient—dealing with it by making statements about it, authorizing views of it, describing it, by teaching it, settling it, ruling over it: in short, Orientalism as a Western style for dominating, restructuring, and having authority over the Orient."[2] (Although the "Orient" in certain uses refers to East Asia or the "Far East," in Said's parlance it refers primarily to Muslim lands in Africa and Asia.) It should be noted, however, that despite the numerous examples of Orientalist writing which clearly exhibit ideological tendencies, it would be a serious mistake to dismiss all Orientalist scholarship. Many Orientalists have taken great pains to provide well-considered research that has added much to the understanding of Muslim societies.

There have been a number of efforts to locate the origins of Orientalist imaginaries in European history. Maxime Rodinson asserts that whereas Christian polemical attacks on Islam had begun with the earliest contacts of the two religions' adherents, it was not until Europe embarked on enlarging its ambit that its typifications of Muslims began to take a clear shape: "The image of Islam arose, not so much as some have said from the Crusades, as from the slowly

welded ideological unity of the Latin Christian world which led both to a clearer
view of the enemy's features and also to a channelling of effort towards the
Crusades."[3] Indeed, the Muslim Other became more sharply defined just as there
was emerging, near the end of the Middle Ages, the idea of a Christian Europe as
Self. Later, during the European colonization of Asian and African territories,
Orientalists provided "scientific" justifications for subjecting foreign peoples. The
need to develop negative images of the enemy exists because "a people strongly
committed to the ideal of peace but simultaneously faced with the reality of war,
must believe that the fault for any such disruption of their ideal lies with others."[4]

   Shiraz Dossa seeks to take the origins of Orientalism even further back to
ancient Greece. He does not find the division of the human universe into the
West and the Orient in Homer; but by the time of the historian Herodotus the
Greeks generally felt that as a community and as a culture they were indisputably
superior to the Orientals. One especially finds the image of "Orientals as
barbarians '*par excellence*'"[5] in the writings of the tragic dramatists like Aeschylus.
The medium of drama allowed for the polarization of good and bad personified
by Greek and Oriental characters. The task of developing a theory that attempted
to explain an essential difference between the Hellenes and the Oriental Other
was taken up by the political philosophers. In *The Republic*, Plato asserted that
the "love of knowledge" is "ascribed chiefly to our own part of the world" while
"the love of money" is attributed to "Phoenicia and Egypt."[6]

> For Plato, the tendency to slavishness was intrinsic to the character of the
> Oriental and this was the reason Orientals could never produce a just polity.
> Unjust by nature, they were incapable of understanding justice, being just, or
> treating their fellow-barbarians with justice.[7]

Since she was slavish by nature, the Oriental barbarian was only fit for
enslavement by Greeks.

   Aristotle's premises of who was fit to rule were also based on the
essentialist notions of who was free and who was a slave. He wrote in *The Politics*
that all non-Greeks were slaves, and since the Greeks must rule over barbarians
the "barbarian and slave are by nature identical."[8] According to this philosopher,
it was only the Greek (men) who were capable of establishing a *polis* governed by
rational and just means; all others were characterized by their tyrannical rule.
Whereas the ancient Greeks seemed to have been concerned with defining
themselves in opposition to *all* other "barbarians," the notion of a Europe and an
Orient in binary opposition does not appear to have emerged until later. The
evolution of the contemporary concept of "the West" underwent several stages
that included the schism of the Christian Church between its eastern and western
branches, the emergence of Islam in the East, and later, the establishment of
communism in Eastern Europe. The East was conceptualized as the Other by
Western Europeans in each of these cases; it was defined as being different and
the place from which threats to the West seemed to emerge. Neither the West nor
the Orient exist as absolute categories but are conceptualized in relation to each

other. They are not clearly demarcated or static geographical regions of the world, but are continually redefined by history and ideology.

Edward Said traces the emergence of Orientalist attitudes towards Muslim societies to the time when Europe began to see itself in the Middle Ages as one great Christian community. From the works of Dante Alighieri, Peter the Venerable, Guibert of Nogent, Roger Bacon, William of Tripoli, Burchard of Mount Syon, and Martin Luther, as well as in the *Poema del Cid* and the *Chanson de Roland*, there developed the image of the Muslim as Other. The latter became a standard figure in medieval Europe's dramaturgy of good and evil. An imaginative geography emerged, consisting of a series of tropes whose relationship to the actual Orient was like that of stylized costumes to characters in a play. At the level of myth, the Muslims portrayed in this literature were not meant to be truly representative figures but personifications of the Other. However, "Islam" was a geopolitical problem as well:

> It lay uneasily close to Christianity, geographically and culturally. It drew on Judeo-Hellenic traditions, it borrowed creatively from Christianity, it could boast of unrivalled military and political successes. Nor was this all. The Islamic lands sit adjacent to and even on top of the Biblical lands; moreover, the heart of the Islamic domain has always been the region closest to Europe, what has been called the Near Orient or Near East. Arabic and Hebrew are Semitic languages, and together they dispose and redispose of material that is urgently important to Christianity.[9]

At the eve of the project of global colonization, the Muslim realm stood as a rival that occupied parts of Europe and barred overland access to the fabled riches of India and China. Although large parts of India and eastern Asia were vanquished by the mid-18th century, the Middle East remained largely unconquered upon Napoleon's arrival in Egypt in 1798. In the meantime, European travellers such as Anquetil-Duperron and William Jones had begun the systematic study of Orientals, including Muslims. With this began to grow the body of Orientalist literature that described the Orient through the eyes of the European colonialist.

One part of the world came to study another in such an intensive manner as had not happened before. European social scientists, archaeologists, historians, biblical scholars, travellers, and colonial administrators streamed out to the East digging, searching, measuring, recording, inventing. The medieval lore about the Orient was reframed into the rationalism engendered by the Enlightenment. Biblical world views were reshaped by an empirically more accurate picture within secular structures of thought. Muhammad was now not to be viewed as "a diabolical miscreant" but as a historical figure, and the primary division between the Christian and non-Christian communities was replaced by that which factored in "race, color, origin, temperament, character, and types."[10] Nevertheless, most of this work was based on fundamental preconceptions of what the Orient stood for. Each generation of Orientalist writers was influenced by previous ones, absorbing the biases and prejudices that went back centuries. This created a textual attitude which lent greater credence to written material about the subject matter than to actual experiences. What is more, certain strongly-held and oft-repeated beliefs about the Orient functioned as self-fulfilling prophecies. Aided by the silence of the defeated Oriental, the received Orientalist wisdom gained the status of self-evident truth. In search of resources, markets, and colonies, Europeans actually created in the Orient what Orientalist texts had constructed only in an imaginary sense. The subdued Oriental, overwhelmed by Occidental technology and the violent destruction of her own social, economic, and scientific infrastructures, generally played out the role of the passive, intellectually backward native that Orientalism had scripted for her. Whenever she rebelled, she was characterized as a deviant and then brutally crushed. This tragic scenario was repeated over and over again in the annals of European colonialism.[11]

Orientalism became very much part of the colonial and foreign policy-making apparatus of Northern powers as the expertise of Orientalists was harnessed for adventures abroad. The involvements of Britain, France, Germany, Russia, the Netherlands, Italy, Portugal, and Spain in the Middle East, Africa, Central Asia, South Asia and South-East Asia were reflected by the growing number of institutes and university departments devoted to the study of these regions and their inhabitants. Their graduates also filled administrative posts in the mother countries and in the colonies, bringing with them the love of Orientalism. Explorers, travellers, poets, and writers all drew from the store of images—adding as they went. "Transmitted from one generation to another, it was part of the culture, as much a language about a part of reality as geometry or physics. Orientalism was able to survive revolutions, world wars, and the literal dismemberment of empires."[12] It thus continues to flourish in the era of neo-colonialism in which Northern powers no longer administer colonies but nevertheless influence the destinies of Southern countries through global economic and communications structures.

What is remarkable is not that there should be a study of one culture by another but its one-sidedness. Even today there is not an "Occidentalism" in the Orient that could serve as a reciprocal counterpart to Orientalism. The rationalization for this is attempted by Gustave von Grunebaum, a leading European Orientalist who, like his fellows such as Hamilton Gibb and Bernard Lewis, crossed the Atlantic to America in the mid 20th century:

> It is essential to realize that Muslim civilization is a cultural entity that does not share our primary assumptions. It is not vitally interested in the structured study of other cultures, either as an end in itself or as a means towards clearer understanding of its own character and history. If this observation were to be valid merely for contemporary Islam, one might be inclined to connect it with the profoundly disturbed state of Islam, which does not permit it to look beyond itself unless forced to do so. But as it is valid for the past as well, one may perhaps seek to connect it with the basic anti-humanism of this civilization, that is, the determined refusal to accept

man to any extent whatever as the arbiter or the measure of things, and the tendency to be satisfied with the truth as the description of mental structures, or in other worlds, with psychological truths.[13]

It is ironic that such reductionism and generalization should come from a historian who had studied the truly remarkable achievements of Muslims. Von Grunebaum's arguments seem to indicate that whereas Orientalists can interpret the East within the legitimacy of their academic discipline, Easterners, lacking intellectual inclination or tradition, have to be satisfied with analyses of the Occident carried out by Occidentals themselves. This is true not only in academia but in the domain that has a more ubiquitous presence in the contemporary world—the mass media, which "raid the orientalist cupboard for alimentation, picking up old prejudices and scatological bits of information."[14] The dominance of the North-based transnational news agencies and the communications structures, whose foundations were built under colonialism, help in producing the largely one-sided views of the world.

In *Covering Islam*[15] Said scrutinizes the Northern mass media's constructions of Muslim societies. He attempts to demonstrate how events such as the oil crisis in the mid-1970s and the overthrow of the staunch American ally in the Middle East, the Shah of Iran, by Islamist militants were viewed by journalists within Orientalist perspectives that have roots in medieval Europe. The foreign correspondents who report on Muslim countries are generally ill-equipped to provide adequate understanding of current events in those countries. (Said does, however, make a distinction here between American correspondents, who are usually moved around from one "hot spot" to another and their European counterparts, some of whom tend to remain in the region for relatively long periods and are familiar with local languages.) "Islam" becomes a timeless entity in much of the reporting, which is replete with stereotypical generalizations and clichés. Phrases such as "the Islamic mind-set," "the crescent of crisis," and "the Shi'ite penchant for martyrdom" have posed as standard explanations for events that most journalists do not bother to explore in a meaningful way.

Illustration 3: Media clichés about Islamic resurgence

Said sees the Western, particularly the American, media taking a consensual approach towards those Muslim societies which are ideologically aligned with their respective governments' foreign policies. He does not view this process as being conscious and deliberate but as operating within a dominant field of meanings:

> The simplest and, I think, the most accurate way of characterizing it is to say that it sets limits and maintains pressures. It does not dictate content, and it does not mechanically reflect a certain class or economic groups' interests. We must think of it as drawing invisible lines beyond which a reporter or commentator does not feel it necessary to go...When the American hostages were seized and held in Teheran [1979-81], the consensus immediately came into play, decreeing more or less that only what took place concerning the hostages was important about Iran; the rest of the country, its political processes, its daily life, its personalities, its geography and history, were eminently ignorable: Iran and the Iranian people were defined in terms of whether they were for or against the United States.[16]

Just as academic Orientalism's textual attitude produced sets of self-evident truths about the Orient, the Northern mass media's dominant discourses on Islam continue to be marked by many unsubstantiated impressions that recur with predictable regularity in the daily output.

Whereas Said's work has had a great impact on the study of power relationships between cultural groups, it has been criticized for overestimating the hegemony of Orientalist discourses. *Orientalism* tends to condemn almost all Northern discourses on the Orient without attempting to provide suggestions for an alternative approach. Robert Young says about Said: "By assuming that any 'method' must be univocal and totalizing, his own anti-method simply takes up the opposite pole of the antagonistic dialectic he has created. As we might expect, this means that he then inevitably acts out and repeats at a textual level the dualistic structures from which he is unable to free himself."[17] In this, Young sees *Orientalism* as merely adopting what I have described above as an oppositional discourse, which is often applied by sources that consciously or unconsciously perpetuate some of the basic structures and assumptions of the systems which they oppose.

The approach in the present study, which views dominant discourses as being in continual struggle with oppositional and alternative discourses, seeks to overcome the problems associated with overemphasizing the hegemony of dominant discourses. Whereas Orientalism is viewed in this book as a vehicle for dominant Northern discourses on Islam, it would be a gross exaggeration to suggest that it is a monolithic instrument of hegemonic constructions. Even though it does generally adhere to a fundamental dichotomy between the Occident and the Orient, there have been within it strands of oppositional discourse and alternative ideas about the relationship between Christian and Muslim societies. For example, the phenomenological approaches of Louis

Massignon, Henri Corbin, and Fritjof Schuon, who extensively studied Muslim spiritual traditions, went against those tendencies of Orientalist discourses that are more supportive of an imperialistic viewpoint. (It is noteworthy that Said himself lauds Massignon for attempting a non-hegemonic approach to Islam).

Fred Halliday[18] faults Said for not carrying out an analysis of the ideas and ideologies of the Middle East itself. In defence of Said, it should be pointed out that neither *Orientalism* nor *Covering Islam* were studies of the Middle East but of *external* perceptions of the Middle East, as is this book. In any case Halliday's own book, *Islam and the Myth of Confrontation*, does an excellent job of elucidating the political and ideological aspects of the contemporary religious revival in Muslim societies. Nor does Said deny, as Halliday suggests, that Muslim peoples have stereotypes of others; he seeks to demonstrate that Orientalist stereotypes have had a much more devastating effect due to the power relationship between the colonizers and the colonized. I do concur with Halliday's criticism regarding the imprecise use of the terms "Orient" and "Orientalism" by Said; however, since this enquiry borrows substantially from the work of Said, it replicates by necessity his particular use of the terms to refer, respectively, to the Muslim East and to its study.

Generative Stereotypes

One central theme emerges from Edward Said's writings: that "Islam" is often manipulated to mean what the particular source wants it to mean. "Islam," "Islamic," "Muslim," "Muslim fundamentalist," "Islamic radical," "Islamic terrorist" etc., are generally used in undefined manners by Northern observers, particularly journalists, who tend to portray the one billion Muslims of the world as a monolith. Even though there are significant amounts of media coverage about matters "Islamic," no coherent picture of "Islam" ever seems to appear. Endless streams of episodic "facts" are reported about events in Muslim countries, but little attempt is made to impart an understanding of the larger picture of Muslims' relationships among themselves and others. This ambiguity combined with the media consumer's tendency to forget the details of previous reportage leaves the integration propagandist free to manipulate the meaning of "Islam" according to her current needs.

Certain "essential thematic clusters" in the media coverage of the Middle East can be identified, according to Said:

> One: The pervasive presence of generally Middle Eastern, more particularly Arab and/or Islamic, terrorism, Arab or Islamic terrorist states and groups, as well as a "terrorist network" comprising Arab and Islamic groups and states...Terrorism here is most often characterized as congenital, not as having any foundation in grievances, prior violence, or continuing conflicts.

> Two: The rise of Islamic and Muslim fundamentalism, usually but not always Shi'i, associated with such names as Khomeini, Qadhafi, Hizballah, as well as, to coin a phrase, "the return of Islam."

Three. The Middle East as a place whose violent and incomprehensible events are routinely referred back to a distant past full of "ancient" tribal, religious, or ethnic hatreds.

Four. The Middle East as a contested site in which "our" side is represented by the civilized and democratic West, the United States, and Israel. Sometimes Turkey is included here, most often not.

Five. The Middle East as a locale for the re-emergence of a virulent quasi-European (i.e. Nazi) type of anti-Semitism.

Six. The Middle East as the *fons en origo*, the hatching ground, of the gratuitous evils of the PLO.[19]

Whereas some of these themes may be receiving less emphasis since Said outlined them at a conference in 1986, they generally reflect the ways in which Northern journalists frame their coverage of Muslim societies. Robert Ivie's work helps in understanding how some basic stereotypes (topoi) can be reproduced with variations over a long period of time to fulfil the same underlying purpose. Whereas Ivie looked at the remarkable consistency of American characterizations of the different military enemies that the U.S. faced over two centuries, his method can be applied here to the images that peoples of European origins have had of Muslims over the last millennium. According to Ivie, "The topoi, metaphorically speaking, are a 'reservoir' of ideas or core images from which specific rhetoric statements can be generated."[20] Such core images enable dominant groups to sustain the ideological legitimization of hierarchical societal structures that put every individual in his or her place.

Specific topoi that characterize dominant Northern representations of Islam can be identified. According to Jack Shaheen, television tends to perpetuate four primary stereotypes about Arabs: "they are all fabulously wealthy; they are barbaric and uncultured; they are sex maniacs with a penchant for white slavery; and they revel in acts of terrorism."[21] Such core images have been the bases for dominant Northern perceptions of Arabs/Muslims since the Middle Ages when they were viewed as being "war-mongers," "luxury lovers" and "sex-maniacs."[22] Although these topoi may vary from time to time in emphasis and in relation to the particular Muslim groups to which they have been applied, they remain the most resilient of Northern images about Muslims. Variations of the four primary stereotypes of Muslims having fabulous but undeserved wealth (they have not *earned* it), being barbaric and regressive, indulging in sexual excess, and the most persistent image of "the violent Muslim" have not only been reproduced in newspapers and television, but generally appear as the representations of the Muslim Other in popular culture, art, music, literature, school textbooks, public discourse, and in computerized formats.[23] Some Muslims may indeed exhibit such characteristics, but it would be grossly inaccurate to suggest that they are shared by significant proportions of Islam's adherents.

These generic notions about Islam, which emerged as the basic frames in the European Christian polemic against the "Saracens," often discursively interlink with each other in contemporary Northern narratives about Muslims. The image of Arab Muslims converting by "the sword of Islam" those whom they conquered is a popular image in the North.[24] Out of the scores of Muslim caliphs and sultans, the few despots who persecuted non-Muslims as well as Muslim sectarians are often presented as being typical. Violence has come to be linked with the very nature of Islam as a religion and of Muslims as its adherents. This image intermingles with that of Arabs as lovers of luxury with the implication that their wealth is an indication of avarice and is usually obtained through illicit means. Linked to the desire for worldly pleasures are the notions of sloth and greed as well as of lust for sexual and political power.[25] Technological and cultural differences between Muslim and Northern societies are often viewed as evidence of barbarism and intellectual backwardness. Personifications of these topoi are to be found in figures such as the cruel, barbaric, and lascivious but fabulously wealthy sheikh, who is a common figure in Northern representations of Muslims.

Inherent in these imaginaries is the idea of exoticism: "the exotic East" evokes simultaneous but contradictory feelings of attraction and revulsion, of fascination and terror; it invites prurient indulgence, but is to be kept at a distance. Shakespeare's *Othello* seems to imply that a violent end awaits European women who choose to consort with such men as the "Black Moor": the two topoi of lust and greed come together here in the notion of sexual jealousy, which ultimately explodes in violent rage. The immense popularity in Europe and North America of the "Arabian Nights" (out of all the literature produced in Arabic), the depictions of exotic Muslims in alternatively violent or languorous poses by artists such as Eugène Delacroix and Jean-Léon Gérôme, the early Hollywood production of "The Sheik" (1921) followed by the numerous films of this genre, and the portrayal of "oil sheiks" by editorial cartoonists all illustrate, despite their internal contradictions, the seeming inseparability of the images of "sensuality, promise, terror, sublimity, idyllic pleasure, intense energy"[26] in Northern ideas about the Muslim Other.

Central to the ideological construction in the Middle Ages of the "Islam" that had to be defeated was the single-minded assault on the character of the prophet Muhammad. At the basis of the European image of the Islamic prophet were contrasts with the ascetic picture of Christ: not only was Muhammad married, he was also a ruler and led armies into battles. In the eyes of many medieval Christians this seemed not only to deny his holiness but also to confirm his sinfulness as well as the fraudulent nature of his prophethood. To them Muhammad seemed to be the antithesis of what Christ was supposed to stand for; indeed, for some he became the Antichrist.[27] One of the more ironic illustrations of this trend was the use by Dante Alighieri of Islamic eschatology, derived from the Arabo-Spanish narratives of the Muhammad's *Miraj* (heavenly ascent), in developing the structure of his *Divine Comedy*. Despite this literary debt to the Islamic prophet, Dante placed him in the nether extremities of the Inferno.

Even as contact with the relatively advanced medieval Muslim civilization was enabling Europe to emerge out of its Dark Ages, the vituperation against the founder of Islam seemed to increase. Norman Daniel, whose work stands as one of the most detailed studies of this subject, isolates "three marks of Muhammad's life" in European Christian polemical writing. These were "the violence and force with which he imposed his religion; the salacity and laxness with which he bribed followers whom he did not compel; and finally his evident humanity, which it was constantly believed to be necessary to prove, although no Muslim denied it, or even wished to deny."[28] We have in these impressions of the Islamic prophet the topoi with which Islam is characterized in dominant Northern discourses: violence, a "bad" sexuality, and a lack of ethics in worldly dealings.

The greatest threat from Islam in the view of Christian Europe seemed to lie not in the differences but rather in the actual similarities of Muhammad's message to the monotheistic biblical tradition. Whereas the Koran repudiated the concept of the godliness of Jesus, it revered him as a major figure in the series of prophets in which Muhammad was considered the final and most important. The Church had reason in seeing Islam as an ideological rival, since Muslims believed their religion to be the culmination of the tradition of Abraham, Moses, and Jesus. Some Christian observers tended to view "Mohammadanism" as one of the many heresies that abounded in the Middle Ages. Its prophet was initially presented as, among other things, a Roman Catholic cardinal who, "thwarted in his ambition to become Pope, revolted, fled to Arabia and there founded a church of his own."[29] Whereas the Enlightenment produced some less polemical discussions of the life of Muhammad by writers such as Thomas Carlyle, others like Voltaire continued to attack the prophet for being violent, salacious, and irrational. Even as late as the twentieth century a biography, which was "strongly recommended" by Islamicists, could carry this summation:

> In spite of everything that can be said in defence of Mohammed's religious integrity and his loyalty to his call, his endurance, his liberality, and his generosity, we are not doing the Prophet of Islam an injustice when we conclude that his moral personality does not stand upon the same level with his other endowments; and indeed, not even upon the same level with his religious endowments.[30]

What is found lacking in the morality of the prophet of Islam is also present in the characterizations of his followers: violence, lust, avarice, and barbarism have become the archetypal sins of "Mohammedans" in their dealings with Northerners.

These features continue today to be integral to dominant Northern discourses on Islam; for example, a description of Muslim notions of revolution advanced by Bernard Lewis (a major figure in the Anglo-American Orientalist establishment for over half a century), who associated the Arabic term *thawra* (revolution) with the image of a camel rising and with feelings of excitement.[31] Edward Said criticized this description as implying that Arabs and Muslims were not capable of serious political action and were ruled by their emotions and their sexuality.[32] He argued that the systemic linking of Muslims' violence to motives that are less than noble serves to delegitimize it—their political activities can readily be interpreted as motivated by characteristic lust/greed for power than by a sense of social justice. Even if Said is faulted for overinterpreting Lewis, one would expect the latter to know that in popular Northern culture dromedarian analogies are the common currency of racist insults against Arabs.[33] Although Lewis dismissed Said's reading in a rebuttal,[34] it is interesting to note that he did not re-use the metaphor of excitement for the description of *thawra* in a later work on *The Political Language of Islam*.[35]

Reeva Simon has traced portrayals of Middle Eastern characters in British and American crime fiction, indicating how—whereas the images of Arabs or Turks may change depending on the current political circumstances—the topos of the violent Muslim remains irrepressible.

> This perennial Western fear, that of a resurgent Islam, is part of the Western historical memory. The sword-wielding Muslim thundering across the Straits of Gibraltar or laying siege to Vienna, the Old Man of the Mountain's Assassins high on drugs launched to kill political leaders, white slavers, and Barbary pirates have been reincarnated as plane hijackers, embassy bombers, and nefarious creators of long gas lines. In the fiction of the "paranoid" and "vicious" categories, the conspiracy, the hero, and the villain are basic elements for thriller/spy novel success. One of the most popular conspiracies, the Islamic threat, has been a plot motif threaded throughout crime fiction since John Buchan's *Greenmantle* (1916).[36]

This tendency seems to be intensifying with the darker drawings of Muslim characters by contemporary novelists; for example, in the millennialist *The Lord of the Last Days: Visions of the Year 1000* by Homero Aridjis, Christians battle with Muslims, who appear in the guise of the Antichrist. The basic social myth of the Other, which allows the endowment of a range of negative characteristics upon the perceived rival, is superimposed onto the Muslim enemy whose evil status has been validated by the vast repertoire of the negative images she has acquired in Northern discourses over the last 14 centuries. Consequently, the Muslim's depiction as a villain carries a high level of plausibility in cultural entertainment that portrays the struggles of the good against the bad.

Not only does the representation of the violent Muslim serve a propagandic purpose, it is also highly profitable. Apart from painters and writers of fiction, the utility of presenting Muslims in negative ways has been exploited extensively by producers of films, television dramas, advertising, comics, and toys. Commercial and ideological purposes dovetail neatly in products that exploit the basic stereotypes of Arabs and Muslims.

> Viciously anti-Arab prejudices are moulded to serve contemporary imperial politics: like the Coleco children's toy Rambo and his enemy "Nomad" with swarthy features, unmistakable head-dress, and Arabic writing on his cloak. The packaging tells us: "The desert is the country of the treacherous

soldier Nomad. He is as unreliable as the sand, as cold as the nights and as dangerous as the deadly scorpions that live there. His family is a gang of assassins and wandering thieves. They are men without honour, who use their knowledge of the desert to attack innocent villages."[37]

Children are thus socialized into identifying the Other in the form of an Arab or Muslim. Ritual fights can be staged in play between the "good guy," who is the representation of the Northern technological civilization, with the "bad guy," who comes from a backward desert land. Television cartoons also frequently have villainous characters with cultural traits generally considered to be those of Arabs or Muslims.

There is substantial evidence to indicate the negative effect that these ubiquitous representations are having on Northern publics' attitudes. One poll of American perceptions about Arabs elicited the responses, "anti-American," "anti-Christian," "cunning," "unfriendly," and "warlike,"[38] and another received around 40 percent agreement on the statement: "Muslims belong to a religion that condones or supports terrorism."[39] Two surveys that inquired about Canadians' comfort levels in their relations with various groups in the country, placed Muslims near the bottom of the lists.[40] A study measuring the social distance of Australians to various groups placed Muslims the furthest.[41] When Mordecai Briemberg, a teacher in a Canadian senior high school, carried out a word association exercise in a history class, responses to "Muslim" were "Cult. Black. Ayatollah. Palestinian. Barbarians. Terrorists."[42] 80 percent in a British survey identified Islam as "the next major threat after communism."[43] Similar apprehensions about Muslims were also indicated by a French poll.[44]

The "Islamic terrorist" has come to be a major figure in the typology of characters who perform in Northern dramaturges about Muslim societies. It does not appear to require much ideological labour to create such a role given the repertoire of Northern images arising from the topos of "the violent man of Islam." The widely-reported activities of the relatively few Muslims who practice terrorism also serve to strengthen this core image. For the Northern propagandist, the generative framework of the violent Muslim becomes the matrix upon which to base the portrayal of the careers of people as distinct in character and in time as the prophet Muhammad, Saladin (Salah ad-Din), Rashid al-Din Sinan, Hassan-i Sabbah, Tamerlane (Taimur Lang), Jamal al-Din Afghani, Gamal Abdel Nasser, Muammar Qadhafi, Yasser Arafat, Abu Nidal, Ruhollah Khomeini, Saddam Hussein, and Osama bin Laden

Verbal and Visual Signifiers

The figure of Saddam Hussein as an "Islamic" despot calling Muslims to jihad made him a focal point of the propaganda deriving from the dominant discourses on violence and on Islam. An editorial in the January 22, 1991 issue of *The Ottawa Sun* stated:

While *we* may be fighting a war in the Persian Gulf, Saddam Hussein and his followers are fighting a *jihad*. The difference is enormous.

Jihad is an Arabic word meaning "holy war," and, indeed, it explains why Saddam's strategies may be unpredictable, even incomprehensible, and will be right until this conflict reaches its inevitable end:

The defeat of Saddam Hussein.

The concept of *jihad* has become the wild card in the Gulf War. It makes it impossible to understand fully the goals, aims and objectives of Saddam Hussein.

Ordinary rules play no role in a *jihad*—only God's law as interpreted by those who believe in *jihad*.

Jihad's supposed inexplicability allows those going to war with Iraq to name the problem, legitimate a particular way of viewing it, and assign responsibility to particular military powers to deal with the problem. The writers of the editorial seemed oblivious to the divergent views of Muslims regarding jihad. Subscribing to the same discourses on Islam and on violence, audiences were willing to overlook the fact that it was Northern arms suppliers themselves that had spurred Saddam Hussein's ambition for regional hegemony.[45]

That some "good Muslims" on the side of the UN Coalition had also declared a jihad seemed to be irrelevant to those propagandists who used Saddam Hussein's supposed "Islamicness" to demonize him. Dominant Western discourses on Islam systematically tend to make distinctions between those Muslims who are allied to the West and those who are not. Whereas the term *mujahideen* refers to people who carry out a jihad, it developed a generally positive connotation in the transnational mass media in the 1980s. Anti-Soviet and anti-Iranian Muslim groups using violence in their struggles were referred to as "mujahideen." For example, the Afghani guerrillas who fought the communist government in Kabul and Soviet troops in the country as well as an Iranian Muslim guerrilla organization fighting against the *ulama*-led government in Tehran were called "mujahideen"; but the term "jihad" was frequently emphasized in referring to Muslim groups in Egypt, Lebanon, and Kashmir fighting their respective national governments.

Benjamin R. Barber presents "jihad" and "McWorld" as the "two axial principles of our age," both of which are viewed as global threats to democracy.[46] "McWorld" (derived from the worldwide reach of the fast food restaurant chain McDonald's) refers to the increasing integration of the planet. "Jihad" in its interpretation as "Islamic holy war" becomes here the epitome of disorder and a trend towards the retribalization of the world. Rebellions against the nation-state and globalization are automatically interpreted as manifesting opposition to modernity; and what better way to portray such regressive tendencies than through jihad. Similarly, words like Shi'ite, ayatollah, and *fatwa*, derived from the Muslim discourses, become "labels of primary potency"[47] that are universalized to reflect all cultural tendencies perceived to be in a global war against progress. "Muslim" and "Islamic," which would refer to the entire religion, its institutions and adherents, are used mainly in conflictual contexts in headlines such as *Time* magazine's "Islam: The Militant Revival," *The Globe and Mail*'s "Islamic rioters demand freedom for arrested activists" and "Risking the wrath of Islam" and *The Ottawa Citizen's* "Muslims hear Hamas sermon at riot scene." This serves to demonize the entire faith as fanatical and present the militancy of particular sections of the Muslim community as a parody of the religion's entire body of adherents. Islamists, usually described in the transnational media as "fundamentalists," have come be a reduction of Islam.[48] *The Montreal Gazette* has routinely spoken of an "Islamic death threat," an "Islamic suicide mission," and an "Islamic powder keg." Northern journalists are usually loathe to use the adjectives "Christian" or "Judaic" in similar ways.

There have developed, particularly over the last few decades, a distinct, although not finite, set of visual signifiers in the transnational media's imaginaries of "Islamic fundamentalism." These include the *hijab* worn by Muslim women and girls, the cloak and turban worn by Muslim *ulama*, the Arab head-dress and cloak, the figure and the face of Ayatollah Khomeini, people prostrating in Islamic prayer, a mass of people performing the *hajj* (pilgrimage) at Mecca, children at a Koranic school, domes of mosques, minarets, a crescent with a five-pointed star, Arabic or Arabic-looking writing, Arabesque designs, scimitars, camels, and desert dunes. Illustrations in the print media and television stories on the growth of "Muslim fundamentalism" usually display such images that communicate a vast amount of information without verbalizing it. Photographs of individual visual signifiers of "Islamic" militancy similarly carry larger messages that have the potential to activate cognitive models of latent information. Thus a stern, bearded "middle-Eastern-looking" man wearing a black cloak and turban and carrying a rosary can trigger an entire series of images of a fanatical religious movement, of airplane hijackings, of Western hostages held helpless in dungeons, of truck bombs killing innocent people, of cruel punishments sanctioned by "Islamic law," of the suppression of women, and of people flagellating themselves in public—in sum, of intellectual and moral regression.

News pictures of funerals of Palestinian or Lebanese dead killed by Israelis have usually depicted masses of people, rather than close-ups of faces—which are often portrayed in pictures of people grieving for Israeli victims of war or of terrorism.

In newsreels or newsphotos, the Arab is always shown in large numbers. No individuality, no personal characteristics or experiences. Most of the pictures represent mass rage and misery, or irrational (hence hopelessly eccentric) gestures. Lurking behind all of these images is the menace of *jihad*. Consequence: a fear that the Muslims (or Arabs) will take over the world.[49]

Frequently, images of large numbers of Muslims in communal prayer become illustrations for a "fundamentalist" threat. On the other hand, it was possible in positive, non-threatening renderings of "good Muslims" to include visuals of the anti-Soviet *mujahideen* praying because the guerillas operated in small units scattered in the Afghan countryside.

Usually, the captions of news photographs reinforce their ideological messages. However, in order to work the illustration has to manifest established and widely-accepted cognitive themes. What Stuart Hall has indicated about the function of media portrayals of the Irish terrorist's image is applicable to that of "the violent Muslim":

> ...we can 'read' the meaning of the closely-cropped, densely compacted composition: the surly, saturnine face: the hard line of the mouth, eyes,...beard...the black suit: the bitter expression. These formal compositional and expressive meanings reinforce and amplify the ideological message. The ambiguities of the photo are here not resolved by a caption. But once the ideological theme has been signalled, the photo takes on a signifying power of its own—it adds or situates the ideological theme, and grounds it at another level. This, it says, is the face...[responsible for] another 'senseless' explosion in downtown Belfast [read: Beirut/Tel Aviv/Paris/London/New York]...This is its subject, its author. It is *also* a universal mythic sign—the face of all the 'hard men' in history, the portrait of Everyman as a 'dangerous wanted criminal'.[50]

The timeless face of "the violent Muslim" is based on this universal sign of the hard man as the mythical Other. Images of the faces of well-known Muslim "hard men" have often been used to inspire fear in American audiences by non-petroleum corporate interests. In order to make a point about alternative energy sources for Americans a New York utility company in the summer of 1980 ran a striking television commercial: "clips of various immediately recognizable OPEC personalities—Yamani, Qaddafi, lesser-known robed figures—alternated with stills as well as clips of other people associated with oil and Islam: Khomeini, Arafat, Hafez al-Assad. None of these figures were mentioned by name, but we were told that 'these men' control America's sources of oil."[51]

In 1989, the U.S. Council for Energy Awareness, a lobby organization for the American nuclear energy industry, ran print advertisements depicting a drawing of Khomeini holding a small Uncle Sam-like figure bound with string to the little finger of his left hand. The caption read: "IMPORTED OIL STRENGTHENS OUR TIES TO THE MIDDLE EAST." A 1991 version of the advertisement by the Council adopted a format similar to the 1980 TV commercial. It had four photos of unidentified men; they were Ayatollah Khomeini, Muammar Qadhafi, Saddam Hussein, and Ayatollah Beheshti. The caption was, "If you're uneasy about nuclear electricity, consider the alternatives." Representations of well-known figures in the mass media normally trigger patterns of thoughts and issues relating to them. So entrenched in dominant American culture are the negative perception of these "hard men of Islam" that the advertiser can be confident that their mere portrayal will elicit the desired response among readers. Violence and avarice—topoi that have been integral to Northern imaginaries of Islam—work here with contemporary images of the OPEC oil crisis, "Islamic terrorism," and the military conflicts with Iraq, Iran, and Libya to generate readings that arouse fear, anger, and even a desire for vengence.

NOTES

1. M. R. Ghanoonparvar, *In a Persian Mirror: Images of the West and Westerners in Iranian Fiction* (Austin: University of Texas, 1993); Akbar S. Ahmed, *Postmodernism and Islam: Predicament and Promise* (London: Routledge, 1992); Fatima Mernissi, *Islam and Democracy: Fear of the Modern World*, translated by Mary Jo Lakeland (New York: Addison Wesley, 1992); and Peter M. Clark and Hamid Mowlana, "Iran's Perception of Western Europe: A Study in National and Foreign Policy Articulation," *International Interactions* 4:2 (1978), pp. 99-123.

2. Edward W. Said, *Orientalism* (New York: Pantheon Books, 1978), p. 3.

3. Maxime Rodinson, "The Western Image and Western Studies of Islam," in Joseph Schacht and C.E. Bosworth, eds., *The Legacy of Islam* (Oxford: Oxford University Press, 1979), pp. 10-11.

4. Robert L. Ivie, "Images of Savagery in American Justifications for War," *Communications Monographs* 47 (Nov. 1980), p. 280.

5. Shiraz Dossa, "Political Philosophy and Orientalism: The Classical Origins of a Discourse," *Alternatives* 12 (1987), pp. 343-57.

6. Plato, *The Republic*, translated by Francis MacDonald Conford (Oxford: Oxford University Press, 1945), p. 132.

7. Dossa, "Political Philosophy and Orientalism," p. 347.

8. Aristotle, *The Politics*, translated by T.A. Sinclair (Harmondsworth, England: Penguin, 1962), pp. 26-27.

9. Said, *Orientalism*, p. 74.

10. Ibid, p. 120.

11. See V.G. Kiernan, *The Lords of Human Kind: European Attitudes to the Outside World in the Imperial Age* (London: Pelican, 1972) and Peter Worsely, *The Three Worlds: Culture and World Development* (Chicago: University of Chicago, 1981).

12. Said, p. 222.

13. Quoted by Said; ibid.

14. Ahmed, *Postmodernism and Islam*, p. 186.

15. Edward W. Said, *Covering Islam: How the Media and the Experts Determine How We See the Rest of the World* (New York: Pantheon Books, 1981).

16. Ibid, p. 50.

17. Robert Young, *White Mythologies: Writing History and the West* (London: Routledge, 1990), p. 136.

18. Fred Halliday, *Islam and the Myth of Confrontation: Religion and Politics in the Middle East* (London: I.B. Tauris, 1996), pp. 213-14.

19. "The MESA Debate: The Scholars, the Media, and the Middle East," *Journal of Palestinian Studies* 16:2 (1987), pp. 88-89.

20. Ivie, "Images of Savagery," p. 281.

21. Jack Shaheen, *The TV Arab* (Bowling Green, Ohio: Bowling Green State University Popular Press, 1984), p. 4.

22. Hanna E. Kassis, "Christian Misconceptions of Islam," in Mordecai Briemberg, ed., *It*

10000[""]

Was, It Was Not: Essays and Art on the War Against Iraq (Vancouver: New Star Books, 1992), p. 261.

23. For an extensive list of sources see Karim H. Karim, *Images of Arabs and Muslims: A Research Review* (Ottawa: Multiculturalism and Citizenship Canada, 1991).

24. For example, this phrase served as the title of a documentary produced by the UK-based Granada television in the late 1980s and of the June 15, 1992 cover story of *Time* magazine.

25. Karim H. Karim, "The Historical Resilience of Primary Stereotypes: Core Images of the Muslim Other," in Stephen Harold Riggins, ed., *The Language and Politics of Exclusion: Others in Discourse* (Thousand Oaks, California: Sage, 1997), pp. 171-76.

26. Said, *Orientalism*, p. 118.

27. Norman Daniel, *Islam and the West: The Making of an Image* (Edinburgh: Edinburgh University Press, 1960), p. 280.

28. Ibid, p. 107.

29. Albert Hourani, *Western Attitudes Towards Islam* (Southampton: University of Southampton 1974), p. 11.

30. Tor Andrae, *Mohammed: The Man and His Faith* (New York: Harper and Row, 1960), p. 191. This book was published in German in 1932 and later translated into English, Spanish and Italian. The back cover of the 1960 Harper and Row edition cites from, among others, a review by Arthur Jeffrey, a leading Islamicist: "As an introductory book on Mohammed, it is by far the best there is. Each year I recommend it strongly, and wish every student had his own copy to read and reread." It was a text for an Islamic studies course that I took at Columbia University in the mid-1970s.

31. Bernard Lewis, "Islamic Concepts of Revolution," in P.J. Vatikiotis, ed., *Revolution in the Middle East, and Other Case Studies* (London: George Allen and Unwin, 1972), pp. 31-40.

32. Said, *Orientalism*, pp. 314-16.

33. A common North American racial slur against Arabs is "camel jockey."

34. Bernard Lewis, "The Question of Orientalism," *New York Review of Books*, June 24, 1982, pp. 51.

35. Bernard Lewis, *The Political Language of Islam* (Chicago: University of Chicago, 1988).

36. Reeva S. Simon, *The Middle East in Crime Fiction: Mysteries, Spy Novels, and Thrillers From 1916 to the 1980s* (New York: Lilian Barber Press, 1989), pp. 52-53.

37. Paraphrased and translated from a conference paper given by Antonius Rachad in Mordecai Briemberg, "Sand in the Snow: Canadian High-brow Orientalism," in Mordecai Briemberg, ed., *It Was, It Was Not: Essays and Art on the War Against Iraq* (Vancouver: New Star Books, 1992), pp. 248-49.

38. Shaheen, *The TV Arab*, p. 7.

39. This survey, carried out for the National Conference of Christians and Jews, inquired into the attitudes of various American minority groups about each other. Agreement for the statement was 48 percent among Latino Americans, 41 percent among non-Muslim white Americans, 39 percent among black Americans, and 30 percent among Asian Americans. Ela Dutt, "Survey Unveils Groups' Biases," *India Abroad*, Mar. 11, 1994, p. 5.

40. Angus Reid Group, *Multiculturalism and Canadians: Attitude Study 1991* (Ottawa: Multiculturalism and Citizenship Canada, 1992), p. 51 and Decima Inc., *A Report to Canadian Council of Christians and Jews: Canadians' Attitudes Toward Race and Ethnic Relations in Canada* (Toronto: Decima Inc., 1993) pp. 39-40.

41. Ian McAllister and Rhonda Moore, "Ethnic Prejudice in Australian Society: Patterns, Intensity, and Explanations," Campbell, University of New South Wales, unpublished paper, pp. 7-13.

42. Briemberg, "Sand in the Snow," p. 251.

43. Ahmed, *Postmodernism and Islam*, p. 37.

44. Daniel Pipes, The Muslims Are Coming! The Muslims Are Coming! *National Review*, Nov. 19 1990, p. 29.

45. Mark Pythian, *Arming Iraq: How the U.S. and Britain Secretly Built Saddam's War Machine* (Boston: Northeastern University Press, 1997) and Alan Friedman, *Spider's Web: The Secret History of How the White House Illegally Armed Iraq* (New York: Bantam Books, 1993). One of the exceptions to the tendency in mainstream media to disregard the American government's previous relationship with Saddam Hussein was a December 19, 1998 article by Paul Koring, *The Globe and Mail*'s Washington correspondent, titled "Hussein's metamorphosis: He went from friend, to tolerated thug, to Washington's arch-nemesis." The publication of this alternative narrative was all the more remarkable since it took place as the U.S. and UK governments were preparing to bomb Iraqi targets.

46. Benjamin R. Barber, *Jihad vs. McWorld* (New York: Times Books/Random House, 1995).

47. Gordon W. Allport, *The Nature of Prejudice* (Garden City, New York: Doubleday Anchor Books. 1958), p. 175.

48. "The word 'fundamentalism' has come to mean ugly, intolerant and violent religious fanaticism in the Western media; it is also a code, sometimes subliminal, sometimes explicit, for Islam. If a Muslim admits to being a Muslim he is in danger of being labelled a fundamentalist; such is the power of the media." Ahmed, *Postmodernism and Islam*, p. 15.

49. Said, *Orientalism*, p. 287.

50. Stuart Hall, "The Determination of News Photographs," in Stanley Cohen and Jock Young, eds., *The Manufacture of News: Social Problems, Deviance and Mass Media* (London: Constable, 1973), p. 189.

51. Said, *Covering Islam*, p. 3.

CHAPTER 4

ASSASSINS, KIDNAPPERS, HOSTAGES

Inventing a Genealogy for "Islamic Terrorism"

The narratives of Northern journalists who report on Muslim societies draw upon the academic descriptions of Muslims. In the late 1970s and the 1980s leading Orientalists such as Bernard Lewis, Elie Kedourie, and Panyotidis Vatikiotis played a significant role in developing the dominant discourses on "Islamic terrorism," which has been key to the construction of Islam as a post-Cold War Other. The three of them presented their views in 1979 at a pivotal conference on terrorism organized in Jerusalem by the Jonathan Institute; it was attended by fifty government representatives, scholars, and journalists from several countries. Among those who made presentations were leading Israeli and American politicians such as Yitzhak Rabin, Moshe Arens, Yehuda Z. Blum, George P. Schultz, Daniel Patrick Moynihan, and Edwin Meese III. The conference was organized by the head of the Jonathan Foundation, Benjamin Netanyahu, who at that time held a diplomatic post in the Israeli government and then was prime minister from 1996 to 1999. He declared to the conference's participants that "the two main antagonists of democracy in the postwar world, communist totalitarianism and Islamic radicalism, have between them inspired virtually all of contemporary terrorism."[1]

Dominant global discourses have generally viewed Israel as an island of Western values in a sea of Arab and Muslim barbarism. This perception, which has strengthened significantly as a result of the Arab opposition to Israel, has been constructed in part through cultural presentations of Muslims as inherently violent people who have repressed non-Muslim minorities. However, most historians agree that Jewish and Christian minorities in Muslim lands, apart from some isolated outbursts of repression against them, had a significant level of communal autonomy to the extent of administering their own systems of communal and family law.[2] But much ideological effort has been expended in rewriting the history of the relationship between Muslims and Jews to show that the Arab-Israeli conflict has ancient roots. Bernard Lewis has been at the forefront of this reinterpretation that serves to portray Arab/Muslim countries as opposed essentially to Jews and Judaism instead of to the political ideology of Zionism.[3] This belief contributes to discourses on "Islamic terrorism" by linking Islam with the phenomenon of anti-Semitism and the history of anti-Semitic violence. In this rewriting of the history that partially transfers the locus of anti-Semitism from Europe to Muslim societies, the West and Israel become unified in the war against "Islamic terrorism."

At the 1979 conference, Lewis attempted to explain through a convoluted argument why "it is appropriate to use 'Islam' as a term of definition and classification in discussing present-day terrorism" even though "terrorism of the modern kind, directed against bystanders, non-combatants, and the innocent is not Islamic."[4] The use of the term "Islamic terrorism" was correct, according to him, because of "the essentially political character which the Islamic religion has had from its very foundation and retains to the present day" and "the reassertion of this association of Islam and politics at the present time...Thus it is inevitable that when the Islamic world confronts the problem of terrorism, that problem too, assumes a religious, indeed in a sense an Islamic, aspect."[5] (Lewis did not attempt to make any comparisons with the relationship between Judaism and politics in biblical or modern times nor did he bother to dwell on the contemporary terrorism of right-wing Jewish groups in Israel and the United States, to suggest that it would be equally appropriate to refer to a "Judaic terrorism.")[6]

Lewis went on to identify two main types of "Violent conflict as perceived in Islamic law and tradition, and as expressed in Islamic history." The first type is "between the world of Islam and the outside world of believers" which is

> ...to be conducted with due warning and declarations to the enemy on the eve of hostilities, and with the observance of the laws of war—not the ones we know at the present time, but the ones laid down by Islamic law. And these leave no place for what might be called terrorism, even by the wider definitions that have been proffered.[7]

The second type, according to him, is internal armed conflict among Muslims "where violence is called upon to defend God's state or, alternatively, to remove those who have somehow violated and usurped it" and which tends to manifest itself as terrorism. Giving the example of "the Assassins," a 11th-13th century Shia (Ismaili) group, he implied that whereas the first kind of violence was legitimate in the Muslim order, in so far as it adhered to the *shariah*, the second was not. He was attempting to demonstrate, on the one hand, that the terrorism of "the Assassins" was not within the norms of the legal-theological Muslim discourses, and was insisting, on the other, that there is such a thing as *"Islamic* terrorism." This is indicative of how Muslim history becomes extremely pliable in the hands of some Orientalists, who manipulate it to fit even contrary explanations for the same phenomenon. Although Lewis's presentation was ostensibly on the legitimacy of the term "Islamic terrorism" he did not touch on this in his conclusion; instead he stated that although "the Assassins" continued to operate for centuries, they "ended in total failure…having accomplished none of their purposes." After attempting to establish "the Assassins" as the progenitors of "Islamic terrorism," he sought ideological closure by seeking to demonstrate that it was futile and usually came to a dismal end.

The legend of "the Assassins," first popularized in Europe by the Crusaders and by Marco Polo, has become a standard tale in Northern discourses about "Islamic terrorism." This story, much embellished in the course of time, is about Nizari Ismailis who had managed to acquire a number of forts in northern Iran and in Syria/Lebanon during the eleventh century. Under attack from the vastly superior military powers such as the Seljuk sultanate and the Crusaders, they sometimes used the method of assassinating the military and administrative leaders of their enemies rather than engage them on the battlefield. Orientalist writings imputed that the Nizari Ismaili *fida'is* who took part in what seemed like suicidal missions were convinced into risking their lives by being drugged with hashish and then led to a paradisiacal garden populated with enchanting damsels; eternal residence in this garden was promised to them upon their death. (The etymological origin of the word "assassin" in European languages is consequently attributed to "hashish.") Dominant discourses regularly continue to reinscribe this lurid account even though it has been found to be lacking in historical evidence.[8]

The following paragraph, from an article titled "Terrorism: modern word for ancient violent acts," appeared in a September 23, 1989 *Ottawa Citizen* column by Harry Bruce on the origins and history of words.

Next year is the 900th anniversary of the founding of the Mohammedan order of Assassins, which flourished during the Crusades. Let's not celebrate with fireworks and folk dancing. The Assassins' sheikh, Hassan ben Sabbah (The Old Man of the Mountain) used to send them out to murder Christian leaders. A jolly bunch, they got themselves zonked on hashish before strapping on their scimitars.

The writer did not provide any context for the reasons why "the Assassins" sought to kill Christian leaders—the dominant script of Muslims as endemically violent and barbaric served as implicit explanation. Not only did he include the apocryphal detail about the use of hashish, but also confused Hasan-i Sabbah, an Ismaili leader in northern Iran, for Rashid al-din Sinan who was in command in Syria/Lebanon. Sinan had made peace with the Crusader ruler of Jerusalem (Amalric I) but was opposed by the Hospitaller and Templar military orders—details which would upset the neat, polarized scenario constructed by popular Northern accounts.[9]

The story of "the Assassins" appears in a variety of media apart from newspapers. For example, the August 22, 1997 issue of *Bioworld Today*, an American popular science periodical, stated the following in the lead paragraph of an article titled "Marijuana Compounds in Human Brian Hint at Drugs to Ease Cancer Chemotherapy,"

A millennium or so ago, Christian warriors who sallied forth in the Crusades to liberate the Holy Land from its Islamic occupiers were often set upon and murdered by Moslem fighters who cultivated the cult of hashish. By smoking or chewing this [plant]…these sons of the prophet acquired a high that spurred them psychologically to kill a Crusader on sight. They called themselves "hashishins," after the Arabic word for the plant, which in Western language came out as "assassins."

It appears remarkable the extent to which "scientific objectivity" appears to vanish when writing about Muslims. A novel by Daniel Easterman titled *The Last Assassin*[10] is among the publications which have revived the story to construct a global threat coming from the present-day successors of the medieval "Assassins." The tale has also found its way into the content of new communications technologies. Loren Miller states in a script for an adventure game listed as "GRASS/Assassins" in an on-line site that

…the Assassins are a perfect "evil" enemy for players. they [sic] could be the main enemy for a medieval campaign in the Levant, and would be a very dangerous one as they had the finest spy system in the world. (http://hops.wharton.upenn.edu/~loren/Links/grass/assassins.ss)

Despite the historical findings that have debunked the more fantastic aspects of the Assassins story, it appears that this group of Muslims will continue for some time to provide the characters of "the perfect 'evil' enemy" in Northern popular culture.

Elie Kedourie delineated further the genealogy of contemporary terrorism in the annals of the Muslim past at the Jonathan Institute's conference. He gave examples of what he considered to be terrorist groups in the 1400 years of Muslim history, attempting to demonstrate that Shi'ism was inherently terroristic. This echoed another article by Kedourie titled "Political Terror in the Muslim World," published in 1987 in the London-based *Encounter* magazine, in which he remarked: "the fact that political terrorism originating in the Muslim and the Arab world is constantly in the headlines must not obscure the perhaps more significant fact that this terrorism has an old history." Since, the contemporary actions of Muslims can always be related to what are viewed as their ancient tribal, religious, or ethnic hatreds, it seems logical for Kedourie to attempt to demonstrate the "Islamic" pedigree of contemporary Muslim terrorists. He did this by relating that the "first political assassination to take place in Islam" was that of Ali, the cousin of the prophet Muhammad, in 661; that Hasan-i Sabbah in 11th and 12th-century Iran "may be considered as a foremost exponent of the theory and practice of terrorism"; that Jamal al-din Afghani, a 19th-century Muslim reformer "certainly believed in assassination"; that during the 1940s and 50s the Muslim Brethren in Egypt, the Fedayan-i Islam in Iran and a communist group in Algeria engaged in terrorism; that the successive presidents of Egypt, Gamal Abdel Nasser and Anwar Sadat, had either contemplated or carried out assassination as young army officers; that "the Palestine Liberation Organisation is the best-known body in the Muslim world to derive its doctrine and practice from a European model" of terrorism; that members of a Muslim group attempted to kill president Assad of Syria and another one succeeded in assassinating Sadat in 1981; and that "Khomeini's Iran…exemplifies the idea of a 'terrorist state.'" While it may be considered logical and coherent for Kedourie to weave various persons drawn from the history of Muslims into a fabric of "Islamic terrorism," a similar tracing of assassinations from Julius Caesar to John F. Kennedy to demonstrate violent tendencies in the ways that the North treats its leaders would be considered laughable.

The strong image of Muslims as innately prone to violence and the dominant notion that transnational violence is only carried out by Southern states either against themselves or against Northern interests allow for the cultural constructions of "Islamic terrorism." The coalescence of these two discourses makes the terrorism carried out by Muslims the terrorism of the worst kind, because it is seen as being supported by a historical tradition of mindless violence and as opposing modern civilization with a barbaric irrationality. Kedourie's article opened with: "There is a prevalent (and justifiable) impression that an appreciable part of terrorist activities today originate, and frequently take place, in the world of Islam, and particularly in its Arab portion." Such attempts to equate the terrorist with the Muslim completely ignore the atrocities carried out by the terrorist groups of various religious and ethnic backgrounds around the world. They also disregard the much more deadly structural violence and wholesale terrorism conducted at the level of the state. Kedourie's narrative also implies that the religion of Islam supports, indeed encourages, the use of gratuitous violence.

At the Jerusalem conference, Kedourie cited what he termed as the "in-built Messianism" of Shi'ism (there were no comparisons with the "in-built messianism" of Judaism or Christianity): "This Messianism has usually encouraged political passivity, but it can also fuel political activism of an extreme kind, and lead to terrorist acts, as with the Assassins." In addition to Muslim precedents, Kedourie also credited (unspecified) European political theory for the rise of contemporary "Islamic terrorism."

> Modern European political thought and attitudes have a prominent strand of messianic activism and violence—of what can be called ideological thuggery. This feature of European political thought became part of the world-wide market of ideas and eventually passed, with much else into the world of Islam. One of the earliest figures associated with terrorism, in theory and in practice, was the well-known Jamal al-Din al-Afghani (1838-97), whose activities ranged over a large part of the Muslim world. Afghani was a Shiite, and his thought is a strange amalgam of Western and Eastern notions.[11]

He then went on to lump together secular revolutionary movements in the

Middle East like the Algerian Front de Libération Nationale and the Palestinian Liberation Organization with others who identify themselves with Islam such as the Muslim Brethren, the Takfir wa'l-Hijra, and the Tanzim al-Jihad. All become part of the undifferentiated phenomenon of "Islamic terrorism" which was presented as the spawn of nefarious Islamic and European (fascist, communist, Nazi?) ideas.

It was left to Benjamin Netanyahu to extend Kedourie's explanations in bringing together what some Orientalists have for decades held to be the twin evils of Islam and communism.[12]

> Though Islamic radicalism is opposed to communist secularism, their common antagonism to the West has often united them. Worlds apart in other matters, they join in utterly rejecting the central democratic tenet, that the governing authority is derived from popular consent and not from a religious or ideological decree. Both Islamic fundamentalists and communist totalitarians view the expansion, even the existence, of democratic ideas as inherently threatening to their own authority. This is how it is possible, indeed common, to find radical groups professing to be at the same time both Islamic and Marxist. The West will not be able to stem the tide of international terrorism without first facing squarely this alliance in terror.[13]

Structural violence was non-existent in this scenario. The powerful states' use of massive direct and indirect violence was also invisible. Netanyahu translated Muslim opposition to the cultural, ideological, and military hegemony of the North as opposition to democracy. Nothing was said about the viability of "the central democratic tenet" in Israel as it repressed millions of people in the territories it had occupied militarily, nor did Netanyahu specify which "radical groups" professed "to be at the same time both Islamic and Marxist." Yet the appeal of this singularly successful propagandist seemed to derive from the manner in which he was able to play on the worst fears of Western audiences with vague and unsubstantiated statements.[14] The marriage of the twin demons of Islam (which has been disparaged by Northern polemicists for centuries) and Marxism (the secular incarnation of evil), helped to outline in simple fashion a villain that could be clearly identified, feared, hated, and attacked. As Jacques Ellul has noted, "Each individual harbours a large number of stereotypes and established tendencies; from this arsenal the propagandist must select those easiest to mobilize, those which will give the greatest strength to the action he wants to precipitate."[15]

"Muslim Terrorism" In the Media

Following the collapse of the Soviet Union, Northern integration propagandists construct the most typical terrorists as those that have an adherence to Islam. An article by a former CIA employee, excerpted by *The Globe and Mail* on October 16, 1996 from *The Baltimore Sun*, declared: "The profile of today's international bomb-planting terrorist is that of an Arab male between the ages of 17 and 24, raised in the strict Muslim faith in a small rural town (somewhere like the remote Bekaa Valley of Lebanon), and harbouring a deep hatred of the United States and a fanatical willingness to martyr himself in the name of Allah." It is not surprising then that Muslims often seem to become immediate suspects in terrorist incidents around the world, even when evidence against them is non-existent. For example, the blame for the bombing of Jewish community centre in Buenos Aires in July 1994 and of U.S. federal buildings in Oklahoma City in April 1995 was laid initially on Muslims. As it turned out, members of a neo-Nazi organization in Argentina and "home-grown" anti-federalist Americans were eventually found to be the more likely suspects in the respective incidents—none were Muslims. There was similar speculation about the involvement of Muslims in the unexplained crash of a TWA airliner (Flight 800) in July 1996 off Long Island.[16] Persons of Arab backgrounds who happened to be in those cities at those respective times were apprehended and interrogated at length, primarily due to their ethnic and religious backgrounds. (Following the Oklahoma City incident, one man of Jordanian origins was even flown back from London to the U.S. for questioning by the FBI.) Whereas Muslims have been involved in a number of terrorist atrocities, the single-minded focus on them as the primary perpetrators of such acts actually permits the real culprits to get a head start in eluding the authorities. The suspicion of Muslim involvement in terrorist incidents around the world seems to resemble the Cold War paranoia about "reds" lurking under every bed.

Operating within the dominant discourses outlined by Orientalists and the state, journalists often use references to the Muslim past, including those to "the Assassins," to demonstrate the endemically violent nature of contemporary Muslim terrorists. In its April 21, 1986 issue, *Time* magazine had a cover story titled "Targeting Gaddafi," which attempted to make the case for the imminent bombing of Libya by American forces. A two-page article by Richard Stengel presented a profile with the headline, "Gaddafi: Obsessed by a Ruthless, Messianic Vision." It sought to link his known support for terrorism and with an "Islamic" fanaticism:

> ...his messianic vision, like the turbans in which he wraps himself, does not camouflage his vicious methods and his ruthless fanaticism. He believes his own erratic ends are justified by any means, however bloody. He has become the modern-day incarnation of the society of Assassins, which flourished from the 11th to the 13th century in the Middle East, only his victims are random and spread over the entire map. The primary tool of his effort to achieve Islamic unity and the elimination of Israel is terrorism. Qadhafi regards himself not only as the last great hope of pan-Islam but as the scourge of the West, which he fervently believes has humiliated the Arab world for centuries. It is a humiliation he intends to avenge.

The writer, conflating the Libyan leader's pan-Arabism with pan-Islamism, had clearly intended to create the image of an arch "Islamic" terrorist who had to be stopped. In the apparent effort to provide justification for the impending American action against Libya, the concluding line of the write-up stated: "Whatever his motive, whether it is the quest for pan-Islam or only a greater audience for himself, he will not rest until he has struck back or been struck down." The implication was that only once the Libyan leader had "been struck down" would there be peace. In fact, it seems that it was Washington's own overwhelming desire to seek revenge for a terrorist act—which it later turned out that Libya had not carried out[17]—that was being projected onto Qadhafi. The writer could capitalize on the cognitive model that already existed in the mind of the reader regarding "Islamic terrorism," Libya, Qadhafi, and American military operations. This propagandic technique was to be used again on a larger scale for the much more massive bombing of Iraq by Western powers in 1991.

The picture of "Islam" as the deadly enemy of the West and the source of terrorism regularly appears in American, British, and Canadian press articles with headlines like "Islamic Terror Group: Hint of U.S. Presence," in *The New York Times*, "Islam versus the West" in *Newsweek*, "The sword of Islam" and "The dark side of Islam" in *Time*, "The roots of Muslim rage" and "Jihad vs. McWorld" in *The Atlantic*, "Mozambique fears the growth of Islam" in *The Guardian Weekly*, "Islam's Holy Warriors" and "The Radical Origins of Islamic Terror in Lebanon" in *Maclean's*, "Islamic suicide mission organizer threatens more violence," "Islamic Terrorism an Extension of Arab Culture," and "Islamic powder keg" in *The Montreal Gazette*, and "Islamic extremists could retaliate, security analyst says" in *The Ottawa Citizen*. Such titles act as signals for the reader to activate the dominant cognitive models about "Islamic terrorism," within which the accompanying articles are rendered coherent.

The image of terrorism has been so completely enmeshed with Islam in the dominant Northern discourses that even Christian Middle Easterners involved in violent confrontations are presented as being Muslim. Although a significant proportion of the members of the PLO have been Christian, including George Habbash, the head of the Popular Front for the Liberation for the Liberation of Palestine (one of the most active terrorist organizations in the 1970s), the dominant image of the PLO was that its members were solely Muslim. When religious militancy began to emerge among Muslim Palestinians it challenged the secular and nationalist aspirations of the PLO. Yet, Northern journalists operating within the dominant script saw this differently. For example, the headline of a February 27, 1984 article printed in *The Montreal Gazette* from the Knight-Ridder news organization stated, "Infusion of Islamic Zeal Threatens to Revitalize PLO."

The transnational mass media implicitly lay the blame on Islam for the actions of those Muslims who carry out terrorist acts by reconfiguring the meanings of the same words (Islam, Islamic, Muslim) that hundreds of millions of other Muslims use to describe their peaceful world view and respect for humanity. When Islamists in Algeria ruthlessly killed fellow Muslims and other people in their self-righteous attempt to gain power they were called "Islam's cruel warriors" by the globally-influential *Economist* in August 13, 1994; the suspects in the bombing of the Jewish community building in Buenos Aires were described as "Islamic extremists" by *The Globe and Mail* on July 20, 1994 and as perpetrators of "Muslim terrorism" by the *Newsweek* on August 8, 1994.

Such descriptions contrast with the manners in which the violent actions of Christians are covered in the mass media narratives. Analysis of Reuters copy published in *The Ottawa Citizen* in May and June 1988 indicates an apparent reluctance to label as "Christian terrorists" those individuals and groups who carried out hostage-takings and who primarily identified themselves as Christian. This included the coverage of an Italian sect called the "Apostles of Christ," which was involved in kidnapping and armed bank robberies, and a Colombian group called "Christians for Peace and National Salvation," which held 42 hostages. Reuters copy in *The Toronto Star* in April 1995 referred to the Lord's Resistance Army, a Christian group in Uganda which had killed 82 civilians, as "religious fundamentalists" without indicating to which religion they belonged. A similar tendency was demonstrated in press narratives about the mass murders and suicides in October 1994 in Quebec and Switzerland and again in March 1997 in Quebec of members of the Order of the Solar Temple, a messianic group using the symbolism of the Templar Knights of the time of the Crusades. The initial massacre began with the ritual killing of a baby whom the leaders of the group portrayed as the Antichrist. And even though white supremacist organizations in North America use Christian scripture and symbols to promote their cause, they are rarely identified in religious terms.

The simultaneous reporting of two events in the March 15, 1993 issues of *Time*, *Newsweek*, and *Maclean's* demonstrate the differential treatment given to the illegal activities of Muslim and Christian groups by all three weeklies. The stories were, respectively, the probable involvement of Sheikh Omar Abdel-Rahman in the bombing of the World Trade Centre in New York and the deadly clash of the Branch Davidians with U.S. federal agents in Waco, Texas. The articles about the former incident were punctuated with references such as "Muslim cleric," "Islamic holy war," "Sunni worshippers," "Muslim fundamentalist," "Islamic fundamentalist movements" in *Time*, "Islamic link," "Muslim sect," "Sunni sect," "Islamic community," "the Islamic movement," "Islamic populism," "Muslim fundamentalism," and "Islamic fundamentalist" in *Newsweek*, "Muslim fundamentalist," "extremist Muslim terrorist groups," "Muslim militants" in *Maclean's*. However, the three North American news magazines seemed reluctant to use the adjective "Christian" to describe the Branch Davidians, even though they did all report that David Koresh, the leader of what was repeatedly referred to as a "cult," had claimed to be Christ and quoted from Christian scriptures. Whether conscious or unconscious, there does appear to be a tendency in dominant discourses to avoid describing as "Christian" the violent groups drawn from the Christian tradition. On the other hand, there almost seems to be a certain eagerness to pepper accounts about similar groups from Muslim backgrounds with the adjectives "Muslim" and "Islamic."

Constructing the Hostage

Cultural images of abductions of Northerners by Muslims have existed for a long time. Tales of "white slavery" involving the kidnapping of European women by Arabs and Turks have gripped the European imagination since the Middle Ages. In the present century, there have been innumerable romances written about white women abducted by swarthy noble savages from the desert; Hollywood films such as "The Sheik" (1921) and "The Wind and the Lion" (1975) replicated this theme on celluloid. In the Elvis Presley film "Haram Scarum" (1965), the hero was kidnapped by an Arab group, whose chief was called Sinan—the name of a leader of the medieval "Assassins." In such examples we have the manifestation of the Northern hero/victim suffering her trials as a hostage and eventually emerging triumphant over the violent and barbaric Muslim. News accounts of incidents in which Muslim groups take Northerners hostage appear to borrow from this cultural model.

The term "hostage" has come to have a very specific cultural connotation following the highly-publicized hostage-taking in Tehran in 1979-81, when 52 American members of the embassy staff were held prisoner by Iranian militants. Due to the length of the period (444 days), the poor handling of the incident by Washington and its intense media coverage the event had a strong impact on American public opinion. The episode was framed as "America held hostage" by the U.S. mass media, which depicted the entire nation as victimized by "Islamic terrorists." The defeat of President Jimmy Carter in the 1980 American presidential elections was attributed to the inability of his government to bring the hostages home. The Reagan administration was aware of the consequences of giving a hostage situation too high a profile and attempted to downplay the subsequent kidnappings of Americans in Beirut. And when Saddam Hussein initially refused to let Western expatriates leave Iraq following its August 1990 invasion of Kuwait, the Bush administration was reluctant to call them "hostages," as was the Canadian government four years later when its peacekeeping soldiers were held by rebel Serb forces in Bosnia. The term has come to be seen as a double-edged sword.

From the mid-1980s to the early 1990s the kidnapping of a series of Americans and other Westerners by Islamist groups in Lebanon was a major running story in the transnational media. Narratives placed the abductions within the interlocking cognitive models of the clashes between Islam and the West, terrorists and governments, and barbarism and civilization to make the long drawn out saga interesting for audiences. During this period there were a number of kidnappings around the world. However, the transnational media seemed to be focused primarily on the plight of the Westerners captured by Islamist groups in Lebanon—the captive Americans and Englishmen came essentially to embody the notion of Hostage in dominant discourses: the names of some of the captives became legendary—Terry Waite, Terry Anderson, David Jacobsen, Thomas Sutherland, Martin Jenco. Collectively and individually, they represented the heroic Western victim of the "Islamic terrorist." Canadian newspapers appeared to be getting their cue on this issue from American news services, with coverage of the saga seeming almost parallel in both countries.

The Canadians reported kidnapped abroad during this period included an engineer in Colombia, a nun in Lesotho, two businessmen in Brazil, and two tourists in Cuba. Among the other kidnappings that received some reporting in the Canadian press between 1985 and 1991 included those of an Ecuadorean president, a former Belgian prime minister, a Colombian political leader, the daughter of an Italian industrialist, an Italian businessman and his grandson, an American missionary and a Swiss tourist in the Philippines, the daughter of a Lebanese millionaire and a Spanish millionaire in Spain, a French woman and her three daughters by Palestinians, a group consisting of Colombians, West Germans, French and Swiss officials and journalists in Colombia, and eight Israelis in Kashmir. But the occasional space given to these and other hostages paled in comparison to Canadian mass media's sustained coverage of the Beirut abductions, especially those of Americans and British.[18] War-torn Lebanon, more than any other place, provided the stage for the enactment of the Western hero/victim's battle with the chaos resulting from the breakdown of civilization. Kidnappings of Westerners in other countries, even those by Arab or Muslim groups, did not seem to attract as much attention as those in Beirut because they apparently did not provide such a sharply-outlined mythological backdrop against which to portray the battle between good and evil.

There were occasional reminders that many non-Western people who had also disappeared from the streets of Lebanese cities were still unaccounted for and were probably also languishing as captives; however, the scale of this coverage was minuscule compared to that of the abducted American and European men. Also absent from the coverage of hostages were the thousands of Lebanese held in the "detention centres" in Israel's "security zone" in southern Lebanon. When lists of those kidnapped in Beirut were published in the print media they did not even make a passing reference to any Lebanese, reserving the term "hostage" for foreigners—mostly from the West. British news correspondent Robert Fisk asked in his *Pity the Nation: Lebanon at War,*

...why was it that Western hostages were called 'hostages'—which they were—while Lebanese Shia Muslim prisoners held in an Israeli-controlled jail in southern Lebanon were referred to by journalists simply as 'prisoners'? These Lebanese were also held illegally, without charge and—according to one of the militia leaders who controls their lives—as hostages for the good conduct of their fellow villagers in southern Lebanon.[19]

But these observations were rarely made in dominant media discourses. A chart published in *The Montreal Gazette* on June 22, 1987 titled "Hostages in Lebanon" listed only nine Americans, six Frenchmen, two West Germans, three British men, one South Korean, one Irishman, one Italian, one Indian, and one "Unidentified" person. And "A history of hostage-taking" in the August 10, 1991 issue of *The Ottawa Citizen*, which chronologically cited various abductions, seemed to imply that kidnapping in human history began in 1985 in Lebanon and that its victims were mainly Westerners. At the release of the last of these men, *The Montreal Gazette* published an article on December 5, 1991 from the Cox News Service, reminding readers that a "Saudi diplomat was first of 99 hostages." The article's penultimate paragraph did mention that "Lost forever in the madness of Lebanon are the thousands of Lebanese Christians, Muslims and Jews who were kidnapped during the civil war that lasted from 1975 until October 1990." However, it did not refer to them as "hostages."

Ironically, the Canadian press usually neglected to mention Henriette Haddad, who held dual Canadian and Lebanese citizenship and whose family and friends maintained that she had most likely been kidnapped while on a visit to Beirut in 1985. The story did not break until the fall of 1991 since the family had believed until then that her life would be jeopardized by publicity. However, even after coming to light, the Canadian mass media did not follow this case like they did those of the American and European men. The 64-year old Mrs. Haddad's story does not seem to have provided the dramatic edge that invokes the clash of civilizations. Despite having a Christian background, she was part of both the West and the East—this made it awkward for the dominant journalistic discourses to incorporate her into their polarized scenarios. She did not appear to rate a mention in the articles about the release of Westerners from Beirut in December 1991—apparently because, like so many of her fellow Lebanese victims of kidnapping, she did not fit into the dominant discourses' conception of "hostage."

The abductions by Islamist groups of Westerners was rarely discussed in the context of the North's intrusions into Muslim societies, which the former frequently cited as the reason for their actions. Massive military and financial support by the West for Israel, which has engaged in severe repression of Palestinians and Lebanese, was topmost among the grievances of militant Muslim groups against the West. A member of a terrorist organization holding Western hostages in Lebanon reportedly asked a visiting American Muslim:

> "...who is the terrorist? Your government, which has supported Israel to kill some 20,000 Lebanese and Palestinians and wounding some 30,000 of us and destroying one-third of southern Lebanon? Or the hostage-holders who have captured a few individuals, limited their freedom of movement and contact with the outside world, and yet feeding them and taking care of them as much as possible? The American government was the greatest terrorist in the world," he said, "notwithstanding the fact that America kills in a 'civilized' way, dropping its bombs by the most sophisticated airplanes, and notwithstanding that those decisions are made in a democratic way by the majority of the people and the decisions to give those airplanes to Israel are also made by Congress in a democratic fashion."[20]

This reasoning, flawed as it is, seldom appears in the dominant media coverage of "Islamic terrorism." Such resentment towards Washington is relatively recent in origin according to Walid Khalidi.[21] Unencumbered with a colonial past like that of Britain or France, the United States was looked upon favourably in Arab public opinion. However, since emerging as a global power in the wake of World War II it has increasingly tilted in favour of Israel and against the Arabs, thus largely alienating the latter.

The systemic violence of Israel and Western support for its government often becomes invisible in dominant discourses. The connection in Arab opinion between the Western arming of Israel and Israeli oppression of Arabs appears to be lost on Western perceptions of the conflict. It would seem completely inexplicable, therefore, that Arabs should take Westerners as hostages in their fight against Israel. Upon freeing British hostage John McCarthy, the Islamic Jihad group indicated in a letter why it was holding Westerners. Whereas it was rare for such material to be published in the mass media, *The Toronto Star* did print most of an English version translated from the original Arabic on August 13, 1991. It read in part:

> ...the question of the detainees [i.e., the Western hostages] was a reaction on the part of Muslim freedom fighters to all those [Israeli and American] practices and an endeavour to secure the release of our incarcerated fighters. This action will continue as long as they remain incarcerated.

As far as the group was concerned, the prisoners whom it was holding and those under Israeli control were all "detainees" and deserved similar consideration.

The interpretation of Islam by some militant Islamists leads them to believe that their religion provides the justification, indeed, the incentive to hold hostages and to attack people and property in ruthless manners. Their personal faith appears to make them fearless even to the point of being self-sacrificial. However, to refer to them as "Islamic terrorists," "Islamic extremists," or "the warriors of Islam" reduces the religion to the narrow readings of this small section of its adherents. It takes away from a large part of some one billion Muslims the ability to practice their faith without being tainted with the violence and conflict that the militants have imposed on Islam. In any case, this is not the only religion which has some followers who insist on burdening it with their own belligerency. Apart from Christianity, Judaism, and Hinduism, even the civil religion of the state has "true believers" who go beyond the bounds of humanity to pursue what they believe is best for the common good.[22] This has often involved violence (both direct and structural), which in some cases has been of such savagery that the governments responsible are viewed as sources of evil. The involvement of the United States in numerous conflicts abroad and its arming of client states, which have unleashed savage violence, has earned it the title of "the Great Satan" among certain Muslim groups. Dominant American discourses have in turn demonized these groups. The mirror-images that these antagonists have of each other are constructed in accordance with their respective historical and cultural perspectives. Inter-cultural communication between them remains problematic as long as the Other is viewed as the only transgressor and the Self as completely innocent.

NOTES

1. Benjamin Netanyahu, *Terrorism: How the West Can Win* (New York: Avon, 1987), p. 3.

2. Cf. Daniel Frank, ed., *The Jews of Medieval Islam: Community, Society, and Identity* (Leiden: E.J. Brill, 1995); Mark R. Cohen, *Under Crescent and Cross: The Jews in the Middle Ages* (Princeton, N.J.: Princeton University Press, 1994); and Ira Lapidus, *A History of Islamic Societies* (Cambridge: Cambridge University Press, 1988).

3. See his *The Jews of Islam* (Princeton, N.J.: Princeton University Press, 1985) and *Semites and Anti-Semites* (London: Weidenfeld and Nicholson, 1986). Also see his *Race and Slavery in the Middle East: An Historical Inquiry* (New York: Oxford University Press, 1990), a republication of an earlier work, for its purpose of debunking the perception that Islam promotes inter-racial harmony. Edward Said writes about him: "Lewis is an interesting case to examine further because his standing in the political world of the Anglo-American Middle Eastern Establishment is that of the learned Orientalist, and everything he writes is steeped in the 'authority' of the field. Yet for at least a decade and half his work has in the main has been aggressively ideological, despite his various attempts at subtlety and irony. I mention his recent writing as a perfect exemplification of the academic whose work purports to be liberal objective scholarship but is in reality very close to being propaganda *against* his subject material." Edward W. Said, *Orientalism* (New York: Pantheon Books, 1978), p. 316.

4. Bernard Lewis, "Islamic Terrorism?" in Benjamin Netanyahu, ed., *Terrorism: How the West Can Win* (New York: Avon, 1987), pp. 65-66.

5. Ibid, pp. 66, 67.

6. Lewis is not unfamiliar with Jewish history; see his *History—Remembered, Recovered and Invented* (Princeton, N.J.: Princeton University 1975). According to Gabriel Weimann, "One of the earliest documented examples of a terrorist organization is the Sicarii, a religious Jewish sect which was active in the Zealots' struggle in Israel in 66-73 A.D." Gabriel Weimann, "Mass-Mediated Terrorism," *Middle East Focus*, March 1986, p. 10. Yitzhak Shamir, a prime minister of Israel in the 1980s, stated in the summer 1943 issue of *Hehazit*, a journal of the Jewish underground in Palestine, "Neither Jewish ethics nor Jewish tradition can disqualify terrorism as a means of combat... We are very far from having any moral qualms as far as our national war goes. We have before us the command of the Torah, whose morality surpasses that of any other body of laws in the world: 'Ye shall blot them out to the last man.' We are particularly far from having any qualms with regard to the enemy, whose moral degradation is universally admitted here." "Shamir on Terrorism (1943)," *Middle East Report*, May-June 1988, p. 55. In more recent times, the movement founded by the militant rabbi Meir Kahane has been involved in terrorist incidents in the United States and Israel-occupied territories. In 1985, Jewish groups were deemed responsible for the largest number of terrorist incidents in the United States by the Federal Bureau of Investigation. Terrorist Research and Analytical Centre, "FBI Analysis of Terrorist Incidents and Terrorist Related Activities in the United States," *Terrorist Research and Analytical Center Report* (Washington, D.C.: U.S. Federal Bureau of Investigation, 1985). Yet, it was "Middle-East/Mediterranean terrorism," carried out mostly by Arab groups, that was selected by editors as the lead story of 1985 in an Associated Press poll. Noam Chomsky, "International Terrorism: Image and Reality," in Alexander George, ed., *Western State Terrorism* (New York: Routledge, 1991), p. 13. Dominant discourses did not label Israeli Prime Minister Yitzhak Rabin's assassination in November 1995 an act of "Judaic terrorism," despite his killer's connections to a militant Jewish religious group.

7. Bernard Lewis, "Islamic Terrorism?" p. 67.

8. See Farhad Daftary, *The Assassin Legends: Myths of the Isma'ilis* (London: I.B. Tauris, 1995) and Marshall G.S. Hodgson, *The Order of Assassins* (The Hague: Mouton & Co., 1955), pp. 133-37.

9. Daftary, *The Assassin Legends*, pp. 68-72.

10. Daniel Easterman, *The Last Assassin* (London: Grafton Books, 1991).

11. Elie Kedourie, "Political Terrorism in the Muslim World," in Benjamin Netanyahu, ed., *Terrorism: How the West Can Win* (New York: Avon, 1987), pp. 72-73.

12. See Mortimer Graves, "A Cultural Relations Policy in the Near East," in Richard N. Frye, ed., *The Near East and the Great Powers* (Cambridge, Mass.: Harvard University Press, 1951), pp. 70-78 an d T. Cuyler Young, "The National and International Relations of Iran," in T. Cuyler Young, ed., *Near Eastern Culture and Society* (Princeton, N.J.: Princeton University Press, 1951), pp. 188-204. This view has been revived in Samuel Huntington's scenario that brings together communist China and Muslim-majority countries in an alliance against the West. Toynbee remarked that "Communism has been called a Christian heresy, and the same description applies to Islam as well." Arnold Toynbee, *The World and the West* (New York: Oxford University Press, 1953), p. 18.

13. Benjamin Netanyahu, *Terrorism: How the West Can Win* (New York: Avon, 1987), p. 63.

14. Netanyahu immigrated to the United States as a child from Israel, to which he subsequently returned. Before rising to prominence in the Israeli government he was even more unrestrained in speaking about what he characterized as the inherent Arab "propensity to violence." Karen Seidman, "Arab 'Propensity to Violence' at Root of Middle East Conflict: Israeli Envoy," *The Montreal Gazette*, February 27, 1984, p. A4.

15. Jacques Ellul, *Propaganda: The Formation of Men's Attitudes*, translated by Konrad Kellen and Jean Lerner (New York: Alfred A. Knopf, 1969), p. 35.

16. See M. Mehdi Semati, "Terrorists, Moslems, fundamentalists and other objects in the midst of 'us,'" *Journal of International Communication*, 4:1 (1997), pp. 30-49 and Council on American-Islamic Relations, *The Usual Suspects: Media coverage of the TWA flight 800* (Washington, D.C.: CAIR,1997).

17. See Bernard Weinraub, "White House and Its News: Disclosures on Libya Raise Credibility Issue," *The New York Times*, October 3, 1986, pp. A1-A2.

18. Prominent journalists like Laurence Zuckerman, associate editor of the *Columbia Journalism Review*, made the case to keep the press's spotlight continually focussed on the Western hostages in Beirut. Laurence Zuckerman, "The Dilemma of the Forgotten Hostages," *Columbia Journalism Review* (July/Aug. 1986), pp. 30-34. Whereas numerous articles had appeared about the Western hostages, there was massive coverage of the release of the Terry Waite on November 19, 1991 and that of Terry Anderson on December 5, 1991, including lead stories, editorials, columns, analyses, and backgrounders. A survey by the International Institute of Communications of the news broadcasts of 87 television channels in 55 countries on November 19, 1991, reported in *The Economist* on February 8, 1992, indicated that the release of Thomas Sutherland and Terry Waite on consecutive days had dominated the air waves.

19. Robert Fisk, *Pity the Nation: Lebanon at War* (Oxford: Oxford Univerity Press, 1991), p. 435

20. Mohammad T. Mehdi, *Terrorism: Why America is the Target* (New York: New World Press, 1988), p. 77.

21. Walid Khalidi, "Toward Peace in the Holy Land," *Foreign Affairs* (Spr. 1988), pp. 771-89.

22. Stephen Emerson, "Capture of a Terrorist: The Hunter and Her Witness," *The New York Times Magazine*, April 21, 1991, p. 57.

CHAPTER 5

THE RITES OF REPORTING A HIJACKING

Myth, Drama, and Ritual

Media narratives are framed within society's myths. But journalists, like most other people, may not admit or even be conscious of adhering to any specific field of meanings. Nevertheless, subjectivity can detected in how the media operate—by identifying which kinds of people are routinely granted the status of authorized knowers, the assumptions of questions asked, what passes for explanation, the analytical concepts which serve to link events to causes, and what is considered newsworthy. Analysis of news coverage can be greatly aided by deciphering its dramaturgically and ritually-coded material. In addition to exploring the explicit content of texts, these qualitative methods delve into the layers of implicit meanings that reside in the production and presentation of news. This chapter primarily uses the analysis of ritual to deconstruct the operation of journalistic rites in producing news and dramatistic analysis to uncover how the constructions of the hero, villain, and victim ideologically slant the narrative.

One of the major incidents before the end of the Cold War that was reported within the conflict frame of "Islam versus the West" was the hijacking of a Trans World Airways plane by a Lebanese Muslim group in the summer of 1985. Analysis of a newsmagazine's coverage of the two and half week event yields an intriguing picture about the discursive means used to portray the struggle between the Western Self and the Muslim Other. This was among the major incidents that helped to prepare for the emergence of Islam as a post-Cold War enemy. In contrast to the large volume of content generated by daily reportage, the coverage of the incident by *Maclean's* magazine (which styles itself as "Canada's Weekly Newsmagazine") provides a manageable body of material for an intensive qualitative examination. Whereas weeklies by definition do not conform to the 24-hour news cycle, they operate in a newsworld where computer networks, television, radio, and daily newspapers determine the pace of information dissemination. The longer production processes and intervals between consecutive issues of weeklies make their contents prone to greater redundancy, and as a consequence they aim at providing lengthier and more analytical reports of current events. Nevertheless, the rites of news production remain largely the same as those of the more regular mass media, and they have similar forms of routinized newsgathering and news processing.

Owned by Maclean Hunter Limited at the time of the hijacking, the newsmagazine was only one of the numerous holdings of a media empire that controlled companies across Canada as well as in the U.S., Britain, Italy, France, Austria, Switzerland, and West Germany.[1] The publication was integrated into Western media networks as well as into the institutional structure of elite Western countries, and consequently had a stake in the preservation of that order. The conglomerate's 12 American holdings gave it a strong reason to identify with the U.S. when broader interests of that elite nation were threatened. Canada also has historical, cultural, economic, political, and military ties with its southern neighbour. And when the superpower's interests are attacked by a sub-national group in a developing country with whom Canadian elites have tenuous links, the newsmagazine's constructions of the event tend to favour the U.S.[2] Like most Canadian mass media, *Maclean's* subscribes to the global media narratives which determine the hegemonic placing of particular countries and groups of people in hierarchical orders. This analysis studies the magazine's cultural role in contributing to the consensus of dominant Northern discourses on Islam.

Maclean's began its coverage of the American airliner's hijacking in the fourth week of June 1985. The 17-day incident was reported in four issues dated June 24, July 1, July 8, and July 15. The space and number of articles devoted to the hijacking varied widely from week to week: June 24—an editorial and two articles covering four pages; July 1—six articles in nine pages, plus the magazine cover; July 8—one article of three pages; and July 15—one article of two pages. Whereas four write-ups were collaborative efforts by correspondents, stringers, and editorial staff, six were individually authored. Even in the latter case, the editor would ensure that the writing agreed with the magazine's overall framing of the series of occurrences. The newsmagazine's writers ritually framed information about events to fit the dominant cognitive model regarding such situations; there was little in the way of an alternative discourse. Several themes were immediately apparent in their reporting of the hijacking:

* the randomness and irrationality of terrorism;
* "Terrorism International" threatened Western civilization;
* the terrorism in Lebanon was "Islamic";
* America prepared for just retaliation.

The newsmagazine's production team immediately swung into action upon receiving early reports of the event. Kevin Doyle wrote in the editorial of the June 6 edition:

Writers, editors, designers and others *acting out of habit and instinct*, worked to prepare a cover story on the rapidly unfolding events and their profoundly troubling ramifications...Associate Editor Jared Mitchell wrote against a four p.m. Sunday press deadline to complete the main story from correspondents' reports and background information provided by Chief Librarian Roberta Grant. But by early afternoon it was clear that no one could possibly foresee the developments—let alone the outcome—of the affair. As a result, we decided to do what a newsmagazine can do best: *explain why* the tragic *epic* was unfolding [emphasis added].

The editor freely admitted, indeed boasted, of his crew's ability to act as a team and routinize its reaction to unexpected occurrences anywhere in the world. As Gaye Tuchman has shown, the process of news production is turned into a routine and a ritual by newspersons who impose modes of operation that order newsmaking into a regulated, day-to-day activity.[3] Even though this was not a daily newspaper there was still a deadline to be met; the saga could not be concluded and was to be continued in the following week. Since the newsmagazine was not able to report the events on a daily basis, Doyle stressed the interpretive role of the medium.

From the outset, the hijacking was constructed in dramaturgical terms: it was an "epic."[4] Possibly alluding (consciously or unconsciously) to the Mediterranean location of the incident, epithets and mythological images flowed thick and fast. Apart from helping re-enact the trial that the archetypal hero undergoes through abduction, the magazine's mythological framework also highlighted what was viewed as the basic irrationality of terrorism. The unwilling heroes/victims were thrust into battle with foes who were evil and did not abide by the rules of normal existence. Like Jonah trapped in the belly of a whale, the passengers strived to escape from the plane, ritually enacting the drama that established their heroic status. Focussing on the tribulations of the hostages, the narrative paid scant attention to the political, social, and cultural causes which had led to the hijacking.

Joseph Campbell, a renowned scholar of myth, notes that before a protagonist enters and exits the place of trial, she has to cross symbolic (but mandatory) thresholds. These boundaries are usually indicated in a narrative by certain images which signify transitions into another time and/or space.[5] The narration in the June 24 issue opened with:

Ordinarily, Trans World Airlines flight 847 is a short two-hour connector run between Athens and Rome. Indeed, last Friday's flight *began as usual*, with the plane's eight crew members greeting their 145 passengers for the pleasant two—hour crossing over the blue Mediterranean. *Then, shortly after the Boeing 727 lifted off the runway* at Athens International Airport, gunmen carrying 9mm pistols and Mills hand grenades stormed the cockpit threatening to blow up the aircraft...*With that, Flight 847 began a frightening odyssey around the Middle East*...[emphasis added]

It appears that as soon as the plane left *terra firma* and moved towards the heavens it passed from the concrete world into a mythological dimension, setting the stage for a re-enactment of the primordial battle between good and evil. The journey was described as an odyssey, like that of the heroic Odysseus who also faced trials while travelling across the Mediterranean.

Interestingly, the caption of the lead photograph of the airplane read: "TWA Flight 847 on the tarmac at Beirut's airport." It was not a Boeing 727 but "Flight 847" which was said to appear in the picture: the physical characteristics of the object had been overshadowed by the usually ephemeral "flight" in which the plane remained trapped even as it was at an airport. Despite being on the tarmac, it was not, so to speak, grounded in reality. A July 8 article quoted a passenger describing the 17-day event as "Fellini-esque" and "surrealistic." The journalistic narrative portrayed the hijacking as an incident that had removed the aircraft and its passengers to a twilight zone.

Upon the release of the American passengers at the end of the incident, there were reverse boundary rituals of traversing exit thresholds that had to be related as the heroes returned from their trial. During this period, most American hostages held in the Middle East passed through the U.S. military base in Wiesbaden, Germany, upon their release. Before they could return home they underwent what amounted to a cleansing rite. The July 8 article related: "Then the men moved to the nearby U.S. military hospital at Wiesbaden for voluntary medical check-ups and de-briefings." As David Chaney indicates, one of the major ritual functions of the media is to report on rituals[6], such as these purgative ceremonies.

Another theme that appeared in the magazine's coverage of the hijacking was that of the conspiracy of "Terrorism International" against the civilized world. The lead story's title in the first issue reporting the incident signalled how terrorism was going to be treated by the magazine. "A free-for-all week of terror" framed together the hijacking of the TWA airliner with a previous takeover of a Royal Jordanian Airlines jet by "Shi'ite gunmen" who demanded "that Palestinians abandon the Beirut camps"; the seizing by "a lone Palestinian gunman" of a Middle East Airlines plane; the explosion of a car bomb in West Beirut; the kidnapping of an American in that city; and the release of "21 Finnish soldiers belonging to the United Nations peacekeeping force" held captive by the "Israeli-backed South Lebanon Army" (which, although predominantly Christian, was described in the article as "Shi'ite")—without looking at the distinct roots of each occurrence. In the following issue, other incidents that had taken place in various parts of the world were also placed under the all-embracing rubric of "international terrorism":

[U.S. President] Reagan issued a blunt warning to the hijackers [of the TWA airliner]—and the world: "The war which terrorists are waging is not only a war against the United States. It is a war against all civilized society."

Wounded: Indeed, while the hijackers were parading their hostages for the world's press, terrorists on three continents confirmed the President's point.

In San Salvador left-wing guerillas sprayed an outdoor cafe with machine-gun fire and killed 13 people, including six Americans. In Frankfurt a new terrorist cell calling itself the "Arab Revolutionary Organization" claimed responsibility for a huge airport explosion that killed three people and wounded 42. In Nepal the death toll reached eight from a series of terrorist bombings in Katmandu and three other towns.

Disasters: Terror also struck on two other fronts during the weekend. In Tokyo, 358 passenger and 16 crew members escaped injury, but two baggage handlers died when a luggage container exploded after a Canadian Pacific Boeing 747 landed at Narita airport from Vancouver. And off the Irish coast, a grim search began for 325 passengers and crew members aboard the Air India's Bombay-bound flight 182 from Toronto and Montreal.

The global system of nation-states thus seemed to be under siege by the many-headed hydra named terrorism. Little attempt was made to discuss the different causes of the various incidents that took place in the week between the two editions of the newsmagazine. On the contrary, the intention appears to have been to provide examples which "confirmed the President's point" that there was a co-ordinated wave of senseless world-wide violence aimed at the foundations of global order.

Whereas the mass media may often contradict government statements, there is a high degree of alignment of views on issues such as terrorism. Philip Elliot suggests that journalistic rites hark to the ancient belief that sacred power is embedded in authority: they are a "rule-governed activity of symbolic character involving mystical notions which draws the attention of its participants to objects of thought or feeling which the leadership of the society or group hold to be of special significance."[7] On the other hand forces threatening the *status quo* are described in dark and mysterious terms. The selection of quotations from national leaders and those who imperil order in nation-states is carried out in manners which buttress dominant media discourses.

Although, according to the editor, one of the newsmagazine's functions was to "explain why the tragic epic was unfolding" very little inquiry was carried out into the reasons for Americans to be targeted by Lebanese hostage-takers. Apart from referring to attacks in Beirut on the U.S. marine compound and embassy in 1983 no mention was made of the history of American military actions in Lebanon before those events: the 1956 landing of U.S. marines in the country; the American military, political, and economic support of Israel, which invaded Lebanon in 1982 and continued to maintain a broad "security zone" on its southern border; the propping up in 1983 of the contested leadership of Amin Jemayel by American marines who were ostensibly on a peace-keeping mission; the aerial and naval bombing of Lebanese targets in 1983 by U.S. forces; and the widespread involvement of the CIA in the region.

Personalization was a key feature in the weekly's cultural construction of the hijacking. Instead of dealing with larger issues, the spotlight was instead placed squarely on individuals—the hijackers, the hostages, the political leaders. Stuart Hall writes that personalization is

...the isolation of the person from his relevant social and institutional context, or the constitution of a personal subject as exclusively the motor force of history .... Photos play a crucial role in this form of personification; for people—human subjects—are *par excellence* the context of news and feature photographs.[8]

The cover illustration of the July 1 issue (similar versions of which simultaneously appeared on the covers of *Time* and *Newsweek*) showed "TWA pilot John Testrake with gunman at Beirut airport" under the title "THE PAWNS OF TERROR." It was an iconographic and thus highly usable image of terrorism—depicting the weary, unshaven captain in the cockpit of the airplane with one of the hijackers in the shadowy background holding a gun. This was a picture of the heroic leader (who goes down with his ship in popular lore) as a prisoner of an evil terrorist, depicted lurking in the dark. That the protagonist was a white male from the West and the hijacker a dark-skinned "Islamic terrorist" reinforced the mythological portrayal of the struggle between good and evil.

Heroes are usually presented as upholders of national virtues or as suffering the trials of the entire nation. The primacy of the military hero in American folklore had been eclipsed from the mid-1970s to the late 1980s following the failed U.S. intervention in Vietnam. During this period, the hostage seemed to have appropriated this position. The victim of evil kidnappers who was facing the trials of the mythological hero was made to look exemplary by merely coping and surviving his ordeal. The potent symbolism of the hostage/victim and the leader/hero facing a crisis situation was combined in the person of captain Testrake. He had already become a key figure for those readers of the magazine who had listened to radio and television broadcasts of the hijacking. *Maclean's* reminded them in the June 24 issue of his "tense but calm" voice relating "a shocking description of a terrorist next to him in the cramped cockpit."

However, the captain seemed to be relegated to a back seat by the newsmagazine when he began to urge caution to the American government: the image of the courageous leader appeared to be dimming. The hero is useful to the propagandist only in so far as he reflects the ideals that are aligned with the interests of the hegemony. It is also noteworthy that another passenger, Allyn Conwell, who acted as the spokesperson for the hostages was also kept out of the limelight; whereas the American media were attributing Conwell's apparent sympathy for the Shia groups to "the Stockholm syndrome" *Maclean's* chose generally to disregard him. Philip Elliot indicates that in "the human interest accounts of incidents and their aftermath people are portrayed acting out their roles with their appropriate emotions as prescribed by the norms and traditions of their culture."[9] Inappropriate behaviour is criticized or screened out.

Another aspect of the personalization rite is to dwell on the fatalism of the situation: to ponder the question "why did this happen to innocent bystanders?" Ian Austen's piece in the July 1 issue, "Death of an American boy," is a clear example of this tendency. Twenty-three year old Robert Stetham, a U.S. navy diver who was killed by the hijackers, was described as " 'just the kind of kid you'd like to have as your son'—an all-American boy, raised in a leafy Maryland suburb, a straight arrow, proud of his family, his profession, his country." The message was that he was an inappropriate, unfair target—in the navy, but a mere "boy" performing a non-combatant "profession." (Stetham was actually a member of the elite commando unit, the Navy Seals.)

No mention was made by *Maclean's* of the sustained bombing in 1983 by the USS New Jersey of Lebanon, which may have been a major cause of the hijacking and the lone murder of Stetham. This act was carried out by Ali Hamadie, who was from "a Lebanese village shelled by the USS New Jersey and the village and its inhabitants were killed and wiped out."[10] Instead of exploring this possible motive for Stetham's killing, the magazine's narrative highlighted what it viewed as the irrationality and randomness of the act, and sought to transform the murdered man into a martyr. According to the July 1 issue, "U.S. Vice-President George Bush declared that the young petty officer was a victim 'of a cruelty that knows no boundaries and a barbarism that selects the blameless for punishment.'" The terrorists and their heroic victim were shown acting as cultural norms demands they should; a fellow female passenger was quoted describing the young American officer "as the bravest man she had ever met." This characterization of the hero/victim was reinforced by the caption of the picture illustrating his funeral ceremonies, "Burial ceremony at Arlington National Cemetery for murdered navy diver Robert Dean Stetham: the bravest man"; and a sub-heading printed in bold letters reiterated: "Brave."[11] Only the images of an absolute nature are appropriate in the rites of relating the war between good and evil. Jack Lule, who analysed *The New York Times*' coverage of the death of Robert Stetham, notes that,

> ...in victimage, might lie the meaning and social significance of news reports about terrorism. In their gripping portrayals of the victim's sacrifice to terrorism, the news reports offer the community the opportunity to participate in the great drama of home, despair, purpose, and pain, and in that drama, and in that participation, community can be created and confirmed.[12]

Commemoration of Stetham's martyrdom in the war against terrorism appeared to be an integral social rite that helped define the good side.

"Islam Versus the West"

The coverage by *Maclean's* of the TWA hijacking was placed within the familiar cognitive model of Muslims threatening Western people and property in a religiously-inspired frenzy that is the antithesis of the West's rationalism and order. Contrary to exploring the historical and political causes for the reprehensible actions of some Muslims against the North, it is simpler to mystify the situation by veiling it in the old polemical image of Islam as the source of violence and barbarism. This form of depiction is familiar, and perhaps even comforting, to audiences used to seeing the age-old relationship between Christian and Muslim societies as essentially conflictual. The entire colonial experience and the current resentment of overwhelming Northern cultural, economic and political dominance are often underplayed, generally being attributed to a medieval disdain for modernity among Muslims.

Operating within this frame, the title of a June 24 profile of the hijackers, all of whose demands were non-religious, was "Islam's Holy Warriors." This was followed by a longer piece in the following week's edition on "The radical origins of Islamic terror in Lebanon." Two photographs and their respective captions ideologically closed its basic themes: one showed "Lebanese Moslems praying toward Mecca: Shi'ite militancy and a generational gap" and "Amal fighter: inspired by the Ayatollah." The first picture was typical of those used by various Northern publications to portray increasing Muslim religious fervour—a simple act of communal prayer was recoded as evidence of Shi'ite militancy. This journalistic frame, disregarding the social bases for the acts of violence by Muslims, attributes them primarily to their religion.

However, upon a close reading of the actual demands of the hijackers, which the newsmagazine characterized as "forbidding," it becomes apparent that the former were really protesting against the violence that they saw being perpetrated in their country:

> The hijackers issued a forbidding list of demands: the release of 700 Moslem prisoners in Israeli jails; international condemnation of Israeli armed forces' behaviour in southern Lebanon before the troops' recent withdrawal; similar criticism of U.S. support for Israel and of a March 8 Beirut car bombing which killed 80 people and which some Moslems allege was carried out by a group trained by the U.S. Central Intelligence Agency. Finally, they demanded an end to four weeks of fierce fighting between Lebanese Shi'ites and Palestinians in refugee camps on Beirut's southern edge as well as continuing clashes between Shi'ites and Druze militiamen.

The above appeared in the initial issue covering the hijacking; these details of the demands were not repeated in the following three editions, which concentrated mainly on the Western hostages, the various Shi'ite groups, and the American government's reaction. Pertinent issues were thus buried in the speculations of "experts" and officials, reducing the incident to just another hostage-taking by irrational Islamic fundamentalists in the Middle East.

The relatively fresh journalistic model of "America held hostage" that had become the rallying cry of the U.S. media during the Iranian hostage-taking in 1979-81 appeared to provide the overall frame for what was happening in Lebanon in the summer of 1985. In the July 1 issue, the seemingly impotent position of Ronald Reagan was compared to that of his predecessor, Jimmy

Carter, who was President during the previous incident. And Nabih Berri, the leader of the Shi'ite Lebanese group Amal, was put in the shoes of the former Iranian Foreign Minister, Sadegh Gotbzadeh, who had been viewed as a "moderate"[13] in the Iranian government. A distinct demonology emerged in the magazine's portrayal of the Shi'ite groups in Lebanon. Occupying the nether extremes was the "shadowy" Islamic Jihad, which remained incognito but had claimed responsibility for several violent incidents. Slightly less mysterious was the Hizbollah which was among "the most radical Shi'ite factions." A notch higher was Islamic Amal, which along with Hizbollah "operates out of Syrian-controlled Beka'a Valley in eastern Lebanon...Both are dedicated to the creation of an Iranian-like Islamic republic in Lebanon, and both are generously funded by Tehran." Association to what dominant discourses had deemed as evil governments served to discredit further the Lebanese groups, while making them appear as puppets of external forces and as lacking genuine grievances of their own.

Then there was the more "secular," "nationalistic" Amal led by the "soft-spoken," "pragmatic," "moderate," and Western-educated Justice Minister Nabih Berri. More importantly, he had endorsement from the American government: according to White House spokesman Larry Speakes, "Berri is a leader of standing in Lebanon. He has the ability to make the release possible." Nevertheless, the "pro-Syrian" Amal was only the best of a bad lot. Its

> ...second-in-command Akef Haider dispenses the Shi'ite version of sweet reason in fluent French, English and Lebanese [sic—Arabic?]. Immaculately dressed, scarcely perspiring in the fetid, overcrowded basement of Berri's fortified headquarters, Haider discourses with equal ease about the difference between the Cartesian set of Western mind and the more fluid, abstract thinking of the Arabs...

> Berri and Haider are the public faces of Amal. Around them is a shadowy power structure of religious, political and military leaders backed by the omnipresent gunmen in black T-shirts and green combat pants, who are walking arsenals of handguns, automatic rifles, grenades and rocket launchers.

Amal's deputy commander was made out to be definitely dangerous if not somewhat unhuman and devil-like—he spoke too easily and did not even sweat! And behind the façade lay the "shadowy power structure" which was dark and violent. This was the picture of Lebanon in a state of anarchy.

The American government, on the other hand, was shown in the four *Maclean's* articles on the hijacking to be working in an orderly manner with clearly-defined hierarchies of various administrative structures. There were frequent references to "the President," "the White House," "the Secretary of State," "Pentagon officials," "U.S. security experts," and "agents of the CIA" who "resolve," "withstand pressures," "urge," "pledge," "request," "believe," "deplore," "express confidence," "sustain," "appeal," "retaliate," and "deploy." But the "hijackers," "radical Shi'ite factions," "Shi'ite terrorists," "Iran-inspired terrorists," "mysterious, deadly pro-Iranian movement," "militant sect," "splinter groups," "accomplices," "captors," "ecstatic supporters," "shadowy groups," "disciples," and "holy warriors" seemed to "chant," "harangue," "allege," "demand," "undermine," "violate," "seize," "kidnap," "assault," "attack," "muscle [aside]," "take over," "destroy," and "murder."[14]

Therefore, whereas the officialdom of the elite nation-state was depicted as being stable, legitimate, rational and justified in its actions, the Shia groups which opposed the Lebanese government were shown to be anarchical mobs who were blood-thirsty, power-hungry and fanatical. "Weighing the risks of reprisal" in the July 1 issue discussed the official debate in the United States about the options of "retribution"/"reprisal" (not revenge) and negotiation, sustaining the impression of a careful and rational process as opposed to the emotionalism that was the preserve of Lebanese Muslims. These allusions were visually reflected in the photographs illustrating the article: its lead picture, which showed "The U.S. aircraft carrier Nimitz deployed off the coast of Lebanon," clearly spoke of the glamour of high technology and of disciplined formations that were apparent in the sleek, straight lines of the vessel and its state-of-the-art warjets. Another photograph of the "Burial ceremony at Arlington National Cemetery for murdered navy diver..." depicted uniformed American navy personnel performing military funeral rites in a disciplined fashion, bespeaking order and honoured tradition. On the other hand, pictures of "Shi'ite gunmen in Beirut" portrayed a motley group of bearded men in no visible formation and without a common thread of clothing between them, reinforcing notions of their illegitimacy as a military force.

Finally, the American government had to be shown preparing for righteous retribution against those who had incurred its wrath. "Targeting the Terrorists" in the July 1 issue was a panegyric to the "American Special Operations D—the elite squad better known as Delta Force." Such commando groups have a legendary status in martial mythology since the Second World War: they exhibit unique capabilities and supreme courage, succeeding where larger military formations fail, and are often credited with changing the course of a battle in favour of the "good side." The reader was told that the "'mission impossible' professionals" of Delta Force had been recruited from the cream of the American military to "undergo demanding training courses in skydiving, underwater reconnaissance and instruction in how to kill an enemy silently in unarmed combat." They used the latest in high technology, which even allowed them literally to see through walls, further enhancing the image of these veritable supermen.

Despite its superior abilities this was a disciplined force that only acted when the American people allowed it, through their democratically elected president, to carry out its legitimate violence: "Declared a former CIA officer: 'there will be pressure on the President to hunt the terrorists down and kill them. Delta Force is up to that job.' " (Although this military unit was not deployed in Beirut to rescue the hostages, a 1986 Hollywood feature film called *Delta Force* was based on the 1985 TWA hijacking; it portrayed American commandos engaging and vanquishing Lebanese Muslim terrorists.) The elite nation-state had to be constructed by Northern integration propagandists as a strong yet just entity that acts in a rational and correct manner set out by a popularly chosen leadership. Adhering to the global media narrative's hierarchy of nations, the Canadian publication did not question the right of the American superpower to intervene in another country.

Alternatives Modes of Reporting

The coverage of the TWA hijacking by *Maclean's* was broadly similar to that in the American mass media. A quantitative study of the reportage of the event by the television networks ABC, CBS, and NBC revealed that:

> Topics which most often involved hostage stories were those about the plight of the hostages and U.S. government reaction to the crisis. Little attention was focused on less dramatic topics such as [the] history of Lebanon and conditions which may have given rise to the TWA hijacking.[15]

The newsweeklies *Time* and *Newsweek* had coverage that largely corresponded to that of *Maclean's*. Whereas the American magazines devoted more space than the Canadian weekly to the hijacking, qualitatively, the reporting was very similar. The same themes of "Islamic" barbarism versus Western civilization, the heroism of the navy diver Robert Stetham and of the airline captain John Testrake, the irrationality and randomness of terrorism, the correct responses of the United States and Israel, the infighting among Lebanese Shi'ite groups, and the U.S. military's preparations for "retaliation" appeared in American newsmagazines. *Newsweek*'s headlines included "An Odyssey of Terror," "Islam Versus the West," "Under the Gun," "Lebanon's Holy Warriors: The lowly Shiite Muslims seek power—and revenge," "Berri: I'm Against Hijacking," "TEN WAYS TO FIGHT TERRORISM: When to Retaliate—And How," "The Crisis Manager: McFarlane now faces his toughest test," and "STRIKING BACK: What Reagan Might Do," and those of *Time,* "The Roots of Fanaticism," "An Attack on Civilization," "Prime-Time Terrorism: The hostage crisis continues as the U.S. and Israel defy the hijackers," "We are continuously surrounded: the homesick hijack victims eat, sleep and wait," "The Dilemma of Retaliation."

Since a national news medium may "itself be a ritual or a collective ceremony"[16] that continually reaffirms national values and reproduces dominant discourses, is it possible for the population of a country to receive alternative views of events occurring in a culturally alien region of the planet? Despite advances in technology, the nature of global information structures make it difficult, although not impossible, for Northern publics to have efficient access to the media products from developing countries. Information on computer networks, although frequently drawing on dominant discourses content, also facilitates access to some other perspectives. However, despite the rapid growth of the Internet, print and broadcast media continue to be the major sources of news for most people. The alternative transnational press in the West run by immigrants from Africa, Asia, and Latin America, despite its modest circulation, is fairly accessible and provides perspectives that are not usually available in the mass media.

A brief examination of the reporting of the TWA hijacking by two such media organs, *The Middle East* and *Arabia* magazines, provides a useful comparison with *Maclean's* presentation. The monthlies published in London were relatively easily available in Canada in 1985 (*Arabia* has since folded). Both were owned by former Middle Easterners; although, apart from its editor-in-chief, the staff of *The Middle East* was mainly Western. Scanning through the June, July, and August 1985 issues of these newsmagazines, it becomes immediately apparent that the story which had monopolized the attention of Western mass media had been of secondary consequence to these publications. The major topics were Syria's growing influence in Lebanon and Amal's siege of Palestinian refugee camps. However, the two magazines had vastly differing views on these matters.

The Middle East's June cover story revealed the slots into which it put the various participants involved in the country's conflict. Israel, the United States, and the Phalangists were the villains in this publication's scenario, while Amal, the Druze militia, and Syria were portrayed in a more favourable light. The piece by Beirut correspondent Jim Muir and political editor Judith Perera opened with: "Death and destruction, misery and massacre are the obvious legacy of Israel's three years in Lebanon." The "excesses of [Phalangist military leader] Geagea and of the Israeli-backed South Lebanon Army (SLA)...have led to retaliation by Shiite and Druze militias." The Israeli invasion was also seen as being responsible for exacerbating the "intense sectarianism" and obliging the communities to "assert themselves." The newsmagazine depicted Shia militias as reacting to years of repression by Israelis and Phalangists. Similarly, the Druze were also shown as "being prodded into self-assertion by the excesses of the [Phalangist-dominated] Lebanese Forces." Thus began the fracturing of the national army along sectarian lines, according to *The Middle East*. The "moderate" image of Nabih Berri, in contrast to the "fundamentalist" Shi'ites, reappeared here:

> It was with great reluctance, therefore, that Nabih Berri, leader of the Shiite movement Amal, finally called his followers out of the Lebanese army in Feb. 1984. He had little choice. The forces of fragmentation were irresistible, and there was a power vacuum in the streets. If Berri had not acted, more radical Shiite groups like the pro-Iranian Hizbollah could have gained sway.

The bias is clearly apparent, but the critical reader could glean a wealth of information about the political situation in Lebanon unavailable in Western mass media organs.

It is also noteworthy that *The Middle East* spoke of the possible inauguration of a "new order" and the sweeping away of "political institutions based on a confessional system." We find in this a significant ideological difference from the major media, which did not even hint at a possible reformulation of the Lebanese state structure. But it is ironically the Shi'ites—the villains in the mass media's dramaturgy—who found it in their interest to bring about Lebanon's reunification, according to *The Middle East*. They, unlike the Maronites or the Druze who had carved out largely autonomous cantons for themselves, were scattered throughout the country and found it physically impractical to break away from it.

The primary frame within which the magazine placed the internal problems of Lebanon was the role of Syria as the emergent regional power. According to the August edition, it was Syria which would usher in the new Lebanese order, that had chosen the victorious Amal and Druze militias as allies, to which Phalangist forces were currently performing a "symbolic genuflection," and whose "pre-eminence in Lebanon is now grudgingly acknowledged even by Israel and the United States." This frame was even more obvious in that month's article titled "Assad's secret war," that dwelt on the Syrian president's use of proxies in Lebanon. The write-up by Judith Perera implied that the many-tentacled Syrian government may even have been responsible for the TWA hijacking, which it eventually helped end. Without giving names, she wrote: "sources point out that the original hijackers belonged to Islamic Jihad, a group which many in Lebanon believe to be a cover for Syrian operations, even though they are usually attributed to Iran. Far from being a condemnation of Damascus, the "great Syrian conspiracy" is made out by the political editor of the newsmonthly to be "an oblique tribute to Syria's success" in the region. This contrasted remarkably with coverage of the hijacking by *Maclean's*, in which Syria was hardly mentioned in the four issues under study.

Another article in the August edition of *The Middle East*, written by Magda Abu-Fadil in Washington, was critical of American media's portrayal of Shi'ism and Arabs. In "Ron-bo takes on the Shiites," she complained about the "spate of anti-Shiite jokes" by television comedians and disc jockeys who "fuelled the flames of hatred." But "the most visible sign of anti-Shiite and anti-Arab sentiment" was the view that "the Shiite mullahs of Iran, linked to the terror network in Libya and Syria, are the main threat to Western civilisation." She remarked that "there has been no shortage of analysis by self-appointed experts on terrorism, Islam and Shiite tendencies. Views have ranged from calls for diplomatic negotiations to free the hostages to denunciations of all Shiites as savages and bloodthirsty barbarians." On the other hand, she quoted a former U.S. ambassador to Egypt, a director of "hemispheric studies," and a syndicated columnist, all of whom warned about the dangers of Washington's ignorance regarding "Islamic fundamentalism" and who criticized the Reagan administration for joining "the bandwagon of Arab-bashing during the TWA hijacking episode." The newsmagazine's Washington correspondent, looking at American reactions to the hijacking from a Middle Eastern point of view, attempted to hold up a mirror to North American society. Even though the writer utilized only those pieces of evidence that illustrated her argument, she provided an alternative way of looking at the incident.

In contrast to *The Middle East*'s secular perspective, *Arabia*, which styled itself as "The Islamic World Review," took a definitely religious stance on reporting events. Its July and August issues focused on the fact that Muslims in Amal and in the Palestinian refugee camps were fighting against each other. It treated religious leaders—some of whose names rarely appeared in Western mass media—as primary sources for quotations. "Fallout from the camps explosion" in the July 1985 issue was a four-page piece largely based on the discussion of the situation by religious figures. A distinction, however, was made between the points of view of Sunni and Shi'ite leaders by the monthly's unnamed "special correspondent." The Sunni perspective was shown to be that which uniformly deplored the fact that Muslims were fighting Muslims. A Sunni religious leader was quoted as lamenting that Amal's siege of Palestinian camps was a cause for "celebration for the Phalanges and Israel, because Muslims are voluntarily killing Palestinians in their camps." The conflict was viewed here in terms of the "deterioration...of...Islamic values" rather than as a power struggle between co-religionists of two nationalities. (*Arabia* seemed to downplay the fact that Palestinian refugees in Lebanon, apart from Muslims, also included some Christians.)

On the other hand, the magazine was critical of the views of a prominent Shia leader, Sheikh Mohammed Fadlallah, who had proposed that the problem be dealt with in terms of "Palestinian political realities." In contrast to Fadlallah's implied support for Amal's actions, the magazine presented contrary views of another Lebanese Shia source (the Islamic Jihad) and an Iranian Shia leader—both of whom assailed Amal. The monthly spelt out its own position in "Amal in the political front line?" where it fundamentally disapproved of the Shia-based movement for the very reasons that *Maclean's* and *The Middle East* considered it "moderate." *Arabia* lamented the fact that Amal "has a sectarian structure with little concern about its members' Islamic commitments." Western readers looking for a religious perspective on the Lebanese situation would have thus found this magazine's approach useful, while becoming aware of its obvious tendencies to favour certain views.

The TWA hijacking shared only half a page of the four-page spread on Lebanon in the July issue. The unsigned "Who's human?...and whose rights?" read like an editorial on the American reaction to the incident. According to the newsmonthly, the positive fallout from the hijacking was that it focused the world's attention on the Arab prisoners in Israel. *Arabia* also criticized what it saw as the Americans

> ...viewing their side of the matter in terms of the need for more security at airports and more suppression of Muslims. Yet if there are any sensible people left in Washington, priorities should focus on more concern for justice and the display of firmness against the extreme militarism that is subsidised exclusively by the US. The Americans cannot foot the bill for Israel's Lebanon War, and even increase aid to Israel, and at the same time expect to escape the blame for the atrocities they have paid for.

These sentiments, commonplace in many quarters of the Middle East, were rarely presented to Western audiences by the mass media. Exposure to alternative media such as *Arabia* would have broadened the understanding of some of the root causes of terrorist attacks against Westerners in the region.

The monthly's editorial column, "Fathi Osman on Reflection," was revealing of the basic position taken by the magazine on terrorism. In the August issue, the editor attempted to view the legitimacy of the use of force from a Muslim perspective. He wrote that the appearance of terrorism in the contemporary world had coincided with the simultaneous growth in the "oppressive power of modern governments." Osman cited Koranic verses which, according to him, indicated that while it was permissible to defend oneself against evil, "requiting evil may, too, become an evil: hence, whoever pardons (his foe) and makes peace, his reward rests with God..." He wrote further that the "use of force is the last resort of oppressed Muslims when all other reasoning and peace means fail." *Arabia*'s interpretation of Islamic scripture contrasted remarkably with the monolithic images of "Islamic fundamentalism" prevalent in Northern mass media. Its narratives exposed readers to the heterogeneous nature of Muslim groups and individuals and to the view that, as in other religions, doctrine is used by various organizations to justify a number of positions.

Residents of the North seeking factual information about current events in Lebanon do have accessible to them a range of sources that present a variety of—though not all possible—perspectives.[17] In order to arrive at a picture truer than that available in any one source, one can pit the cultural constructions presented in various media against each other in a dialectical fashion. Such an exercise may reveal factual omissions, generalizations, contradictions, and even distortions. Slanted openings of articles, strategic sequencing of information, specific narrative styles, consistent application of negative or positive parts of speech to particular persons or groups, quoting only certain types of authority figures, favourable or unfavourable allusions, the use of particular photographs—the stuff of mystification—may become transparent to audiences when juxtaposed with variants. The predilection of a medium or an individual journalist for a free market, Marxist, secular, or religious stance may also become more apparent and enhance one's own reading of the situation and of its reporting.

NOTES

1. Dun and Bradstreet Ltd., *Who Own's Whom: North America, 1984* (London: Dun's Marketing Services, 1984), p. 253.

2. For analysis of the similarity of foreign coverage in Canadian and American press, see Walter C. Soderland, Ronald H. Wagenberg, and Ian C. Pemberton, "Cheerleader or Critic? Television News Coverage in Canada and the United States of the U.S. Invasion of Panama," *Canadian Journal of Political Science* 27:3 (Sept. 1994), pp. 581-604.

3. Gaye Tuchman, *Making News: A Study in the Construction of Reality* (New York: Free Press, 1978).

4. Journalists often referred to the 1975-1990 Lebanese civil war in dramaturgical terms; for example, an article published in the September 18, 1983 issue of *Maclean's* on the various

groups involved in the ongoing fighting was headlined "The performers in a recurring tragedy," and another in *The Ottawa Citizen* of April 23, 1990 on the release of an American hostage from captivity, was titled "Beirut's a stage: Western hostages become tragic actors in cruel theatre of the absurd."

5. Joseph Campbell, *The Hero with a Thousand Faces* (Princeton, N.J.: Princeton University Press, 1972), pp. 77-89.

6. David Chaney, "The Symbolic Form of Ritual in Mass Communication," in Peter Golding, Graham Murdock, and Philip Schlesinger, eds., *Communicating Politics: Mass Communications and the Political Process* (New York: Holmes and Meier, 1986), p. 116.

7. Philip Elliot, "Press Performance as Political Ritual," in Harry Christian, ed., *The Sociology of Journalism and the Press* (London: Constable, 1979), p. 147.

8. Stuart Hall, "A World at One with Itself," in Stanley Cohen and Jock Young, eds., *The Manufacture of News: Social Problems, Deviance and Mass Media* (London: Constable, 1973), p. 183.

9. Elliot, "Press Performance as Political Ritual," p. 161.

10. Mohammad T. Mehdi, *Terrorism: Why America is the Target* (New York: New World Press, 1988), p. 84.

11. Compare this with the similar narratives of *The New York Times* about another incident in October 1985, in which men identifying themselves as members of the Palestinian Liberation Front hijacked the cruise ship Achille Lauro and murdered Leon Klinghoffer, a 69-year old Jewish American who used a wheelchair. According to Jack Lule, an important theme in the newspaper's coverage was "… the portrayal of the victim as good, innocent, and heroic… Leon Klinghoffer was described as 'a determined man' who fought hard to recover from his stroke. The son-in-law called him 'a devoted husband, a loving father and a good friend.' A friend said, 'He was an unbelievably gentle man.' A neighbour testified, 'He always smiled, and he'd say hello.' And a niece was quoted: 'All he talked about was family and love.'" Jack Lule, "The Myth of My Widow: A Dramatistic Analysis of News Portrayals of a Terrorist Victim," *Political Communication and Persuasion* 1:2 (1988), 109-110.

12. Jack Lule, "Sacrifice and the Body on the Tarmac: Symbolic Significance of U.S. News About a Terrorist Victim," in Yonah Alexander and Robert G. Picard, eds, *In the Camera's Eye: News Coverage of Terrorist Events* (Washington, D.C.: Brassey's, 1991), p. 43.

13. When Western mass media label a leader of a non-Western country as "moderate" or "pragmatic" it usually implies that she is pro-Western, while "extremists" tend to be critical of the West.

14. Picard and Adams's study, which looks at the descriptions of terrorists and their actions in *The Los Angeles Times*, *The New York Times*, and *The Washington Post* between 1980 and 1985, reveals the prevalence of similar sets of words. Robert G. Picard and Paul D. Adams, "Characterizations of Acts and Perpetrators of Political Violence in Three Elite U.S. Daily Newspapers," *Political Communication and Persuasion* 4 (1987), pp. 1-9.

15. Tony Atwater, "Network Evening News Coverage of the TWA Hostage Crisis," *Terrorism and the News Media Research Project* (Boston: Association for Education in Journalism and Mass Communication, n.d.), p. 7.

16. Chaney, "The Symbolic Form of Ritual in Mass Communication," p. 117.

17. There are similar American magazines currently on the market such as *The Washington Report on Middle East Affairs* and *Minaret*; the websites of newspapers published in Muslim-majority countries as well as those operated by Muslim community organizations around the world are also sources of alternative information.

CHAPTER 6

DISPATCHES FROM THE HOLY LAND

Israel Through Biblical Lenses

Whereas most dominant Northern discourses tend to emphasize the secular character of Israel, the biblical claim of Jews to the Holy Land remains an implicit and powerful argument even against the rights of native Christians and Muslims whose ancestors had also lived there for thousands of years. The following sentence from a cover story by David Hayes in the August 1988 *Toronto Life* magazine, that discussed the media coverage of Israel, succinctly summarized this narrative: "Israel was created by survivors, its existence a debt that civilization repaid to the Jews because of their historical and spiritual roots in the region as well as their extraordinary suffering." Underlying this statement, which spoke volumes, were dominant discourses about the Jewish state. In saying that "Israel was created by survivors," the author invoked the script of the Jewish victim/hero who had escaped the Holocaust in Europe and (re)constructed the Jewish state by overcoming the savage land and its savage inhabitants. Israel's "existence [was] a debt that civilization repaid to the Jews because of their historical and spiritual roots in the region"—"civilization" seems limited here to the Eurocentric Christian world, which, within its particular biblical perspectives saw the Holy Land as the homeland only of Jewish victim/heroes. Northern support for the creation of Israel was also compensation for the Jews' "extraordinary suffering" in Europe. It was for Northern Christendom to give the Holy Land to Jews as recompense for its own misdeeds against them, thus disregarding the history and rights of other peoples (including indigenous Christians) who have lived on the same land.

A significant proportion of Northern Christians appears to believe in at least the moral if not divine right of Jews to possess a state in the Holy Land. References from the Bible are common currency among supporters of Israel from the American religious right. A mainstay in some Christian fundamentalist media is the theme of the coming Armageddon in the Middle East. They present the formation of the modern state of Israel as evidence that biblical prophecies can predict contemporary events. Northern publics have purposely been encouraged by such propaganda to blend tales from the Bible with the contemporary political realities of Israel. Quoting from the Book of Samuel, the *Zion Quarterly*, "a publication of Christian Friends of Israel," identified the contemporary conflict of Israelites and Palestinians as that which existed between the biblical Israel and the Philistines.[1]

Contemporary history is woven into an apocalyptic scenario that culminates in Christ's return. According to John Walvoord, author of *Armageddon, Oil and the Middle East Crisis*:

Israel and the nations of the world have been prepared for the final drama. Most important, Israel is back in the land, organized as a political state, and eager for her role in the end-time events.

Russia is poised to the north of the Holy Land for entry in the end-time conflict. Egypt and other African countries have not abandoned their desire to attack Israel from the south. Red China in the east is now a military power great enough to field an army as large as that described in the book of Revelation. Each nation is prepared to play out its role in the final hours of history.

Our present world is well prepared for the beginning of the prophetic drama that will lead to Armageddon. Since the stage is set for this dramatic climax of the age, it must mean that Christ's coming for His own is very near.[2]

Such arguments by some Christian fundamentalists, who forward sweeping divine plans for human destiny, serve to justify Israel's hegemony over its Arab residents and neighbours. The large corpus of reports detailing injustices suffered by Palestinians at the hands of Israelis is unable to counterbalance the weight of Bible-based prophecies and Holocaust-inspired guilt. Additionally, the rarely reported evidence of wide-scale and systemic Israeli destruction of the Palestinian agricultural infrastructure is eclipsed by the utopic myth of how Jewish settlers made the desert bloom.[3] The brutality of the terrorist acts by Palestinians reacting to Israeli repression serves further to entrench dominant discourses.

The religious image of the state of Israel appears to have been a factor even as decisions were being made by colonial authorities in London to prepare for its eventual establishment. Thomas Friedman relates that "Lloyd George, the British Prime Minister when the 1917 Balfour Declaration promising the Jews a homeland was issued, once told the Zionist leader Chaim Weizmann, the names Judea and Samaria, and Jerusalem 'are more familiar to me than the names of Welsh villages of my own childhood.' "[4] It appears to have been the deliberate policy of the Israeli government to exploit the dual feelings of romanticism and guilt that Northern Christian audiences had towards Jews after World War II. Abba Eban, a former Israeli cabinet member stated:

The entire region rejected us. We were forming a state for people who were not yet here. And we were not a majority in our country. We had to seize the ears of the world. We could not just rely on pure juridical arguments. We could not argue like Ghana. We had to make ourselves exceptional. So we based our claim on the exceptionality of Israel, in terms of the affliction suffered by its people, and in terms of our historical and spiritual lineage. We knew we were basically appealing to a Christian world for whom the biblical story was familiar and attractive, and we played it to the hilt.[5]

It thus appears that the Israeli government has consciously sought to blur history, fusing the identities of contemporary Jewish Israelis with biblical figures. The Northern Christian view of Israel, which was framed within the dual perspectives of the Bible and the Holocaust, seemed eager to embrace the carefully constructed image of Jews returning to reclaim the Holy Land as their rightful property.

Public relations techniques have been used since the establishment of the state to make this case to Northern Christian audiences. Art Stevens writes in *The Persuasion Explosion*,

In the early 1950s, when the newly formed State of Israel was struggling for recognition in the court of world opinion, America was largely apathetic. [Edward] Gottlieb who at the time headed his own public relations firm, suddenly had a hunch about how to create a more sympathetic attitude toward Israel. He chose a writer and sent him to Israel with instructions to soak in the atmosphere of the country and create a novel about it. The book turned out to be *Exodus*, by Leon Uris. His novel did more to popularize Israel with the American public than any other single presentation through the media.[6]

The novel and the subsequent film (which is frequently rebroadcast on North American television) narrated the story of a shipload of European Jews who sought to make the journey to Palestine in face of opposition from the British colonial authorities. It purposefully evoked the well-entrenched script of the exodus of the Hebrews from Egypt to the biblical land of Israel. Television dramas such as the late 1980s miniseries on the Arab-Israeli conflict titled "Sword of Gideon," with a cast including well-known American and British actors, have also reflected this tendency.

Such images of Zion have not only affected the thinking of the overtly religious among Christians. Teddy Kollek, a former mayor of Jerusalem, remarked about a particular site in the city: "In ancient times, it was believed that Jerusalem was the center of the world and that this hole was the center of the center—the very navel of the universe. Sometimes I have the impression that the foreign correspondents who reside here, and the hundreds more who visit every year, still believe that."[7] Most Northern news organs which have correspondents in the Middle East are based in Jerusalem: the effect of the Bible on their views about the city and Israel has often been manifested in their reporting of the Holy Land. Robert Lichter's study of media elite's attitudes support for Israel found that over 90 percent of those with Jewish religious affiliation "asserted a moral obligation to defend Israel, compared to 75 percent among Catholics and 71 percent among Protestants." Those with no religious affiliations were at 68 per cent,[8] thus indicating high overall support for Israel among American media elites. The tenor of their reporting on the Holy Land should therefore not come as a surprise.

Travel sections of newspapers respond to this desire of Northern Christians to re-trace the steps of characters from the Bible and others from Christian history. For example, a front page article in the May 16, 1987 Travel section of *The Montreal Gazette* was headlined "ISRAEL: Biblical co-ordinates can help you hike in the Judean desert":

> Pass the Mount of Olives and Gethsemane and take the Jericho Road outside Jerusalem. Turn right at the Dead Sea.

> Those biblical co-ordinates led writer Jonathan Auerbach to the lowest point on Earth, Israel's Judean desert, a breathtaking wilderness at the geological crossway of three continents that is one of the most historic, yet least-travelled, places in Israel.

Such scriptural references serve to eliminate distinctions between the religious world view and the contemporary political reality. They enhance the scenario in which Jewish Israelis are seen as acting out a heroic biblical drama in the places whose names come straight out of the Old Testament. The historical claims of the Palestinians to the same places are symbolically eliminated along with the erasing of their Arabic names. Whereas the Northern mass media have not adopted as normative the Israeli government's references to "Judea and Samaria," the use of the term "Temple Mount"—a primary focus of conflict between Jews and Muslims in Jerusalem—is generally preferred over the Muslim "Haram al-Shareef." This kind of usage tends to lend greater legitimacy to Jewish historical claims over this piece of land than those of Muslim Palestinians. (Similarly, the war fought between Israel against Egypt and Syria in October 1973 is usually called "the Yom Kippur War" in dominant Northern discourses, as opposed to "the Ramadan War"—which is common in Arab discourses—or even the more neutral "October War.")

Ironically, it was the overturning of a biblical image in the late 1980s that appears to have been key to a shift that took place in Northern sentiments about Jewish Israelis. Dominant discourses usually portrayed three million Israeli Jews as being a collective island surrounded by a sea of 200 million Arabs. The Israeli army had generally been personified as the biblical David threatened by the Arab Goliath. This was a key metaphor in the symbolic construction of the Israeli hero who triumphed in the face of seemingly insurmountable odds. While Israel's ruthless invasion of Lebanon in 1982 and the subsequent massacre of Palestinians in Sabra and Shatila by its Phalangist allies did raise eyebrows in Europe and North America, it was not until the brutal reaction to the *intifadah* over several years that pointed questions were asked about Israel's moral standing. The image of the Arab as Goliath suffered a serious blow when Palestinian boys began using home-made slings to throw stones at Israeli soldiers armed with deadly weapons. Adolescents from the

West Bank and Gaza seemed to be appropriating the role of David. The deadly reaction of the Israeli military to the *intifadah*, which was recorded by foreign television crews, was probably responsible for the drop in the almost unconditional support that Israel had received from the American public and government. Simultaneously, Palestinians lost some of the dark lines with which they had been drawn. The Northern mass media suddenly discovered that all Palestinians were not terrorists and that they could even sit down with Israelis to discuss peace. However, these alternative discourses have to work continually against the dominant constructions of the Jewish Israeli as hero/victim and the Palestinian Muslim as villain. They also have to contend with global discourses that portray the Muslim as a post-Cold War Other.

Transferring Anti-Semitism

Overlaid onto biblical readings that present Israel as the Jewish homeland is the powerful memory of the Holocaust during which a European state worked to eliminate Jewish presence through a policy of genocide. This had been preceded by centuries of aggressive anti-Semitism. North American and European governments had failed to come to the rescue of Jews who were being slaughtered *en masse* by Nazis during the Second World War. Dale Bishop notes that "The history of Western Christendom's treatment of the Jewish people and persistent persecution leading to attempted genocide, has created suspicion on one side, and overwhelming guilt on the other, of the Jewish-Christian divide. Christians need to accept a large measure of responsibility for the Holocaust, but accepting responsibility is different from being paralysed by guilt."[9]

The horror and guilt borne by Northern Christians for the Holocaust was vital in harnessing support for the creation of a Jewish state in Palestine in 1948. But, it was the exaggeration of Christian guilt for the consequences of the Nazi doctrine (which, ironically, was contemptuous not only of Jews but also of Christian sentiments) that seemed to engender the need to over-compensate by demonizing Palestinians. These feelings of remorse remain open for exploitation by Zionist propagandists when gentile criticism of Jewish actions against Palestinians threatens Northern support for Israel.

> Recall [former Israeli prime minister] Menachem Begin's reply to international outrage over the 1982 invasion of Lebanon: "Don't you dare moralize to us when you remained silent as six million Jews were sent to the gas chambers."

> Hence, the incessant interjection of the Holocaust and stories of alleged anti-Semitism or potential anti-Semitism on the news, editorial and feature pages. When all else fails, the six million victims of Hitler are invoked to confront and confound all who question or criticize Israel.[10]

The intensity of gentile guilt sustains the image of the Jew as the victim *par excellence*, giving the latter the moral right to victimize others without losing her own status as the perpetual victim. Whereas dominant Northern presentations of the Jewish Israeli are carried out within the heroic myth of carving out a nation out of a desert wilderness in the face of vicious Arab opposition, her past as a victim is brought to the fore whenever it is required to fulfil the propagandic function of maintaining her moral superiority.

Zionist propagandists presented Arab attempts to stop the establishment and expansion of the Jewish state within the frame of the Holocaust, which was all too fresh in Northern minds. Clothing Arab armies in Nazi garb elicited the kind of compassion that the fledgling state was seeking from the Christian West, even as it uprooted hundreds of thousands of Palestinians. The particular form of anti-Semitism that had developed over two millennia of Christian-Jewish relations in Europe was projected onto Arab Muslims, who have had a very different approach to accommodating minorities, particularly Jewish and Christian communities, into their body politic.

Non-Muslim and Muslim minorities did suffer several historical episodes of persecution under Muslim rule, usually during periods of instability. However, S.D. Goitein, whose life-long endeavour involved the translation and analysis of texts produced by medieval Jewish communities living under Muslim rule, noted that "When the known facts are weighed, I believe it is correct to say that as a whole the position of the non-Muslims under Arab/Islam [sic] was far better than that of Jews in Medieval Christian Europe."[11] There did not exist a theological sanctioning of systemic violence against minorities such as that which resulted from the Church Fathers' characterization of Jews as "Christ-killers." Medieval Muslim rule on the Iberian peninsula was also generally marked by an inter-communal harmony that strongly contrasted with the religious persecution during the Counter-Reformation. When Jews along with Muslims were expelled by Philip II of Spain in the 15th century, they sought refuge mainly in Muslim lands.

The Koran refers to Jews and Christians as *ahl al-kitab*, "people of the book," in recognition of the biblical prophetic tradition. In medieval Muslim polities they were treated as "protected peoples," *ahl al-dhimma*, who had autonomy to administer communal law. For the most part they were incorporated as a legitimate part of the Muslim state, in which they had rights and obligations that were different from those of Muslims. The *dhimmi* were taxed more heavily but were not obliged to participate in the military. There was little compulsion upon Jews and Christians to convert, although some did find that becoming a Muslim offered better opportunities of advancement in state bureaucracies. Some Koranic passages reflect the political conflicts that the prophet Muhammad had with Jewish tribes in Arabia who allied themselves with pagan Arabs seeking to destroy the nascent Muslim community. But despite these temporal differences Muhammad did not repudiate the teachings of the Hebrew prophets. However, contemporary events have led some Muslims to use the Koranic verses relating to Muhammad's conflict with Jewish tribes in their anti-Zionist propaganda. They have also borrowed some anti-Jewish arguments from Europe to support their arguments against Israel. Such a polemical approach, which runs counter to a millennium of generally harmonious relations between Muslims and Jews, have in turn provided fodder for those Zionist propagandists who seek to portray Islam as fundamentally opposed to Judaism.

There also appears to be a trend in some academic work that underplays the secure status that Jewish communities traditionally had in Muslim lands and projects the current tensions between Jewish Israelis and Muslim Arabs into the past. The work of Bernard Lewis is a case in point. His 1971 book *Race and Color in Islam* was republished in 1990 as *Race and Slavery in the Middle East*.[12] According to *The New York Times Book Review*, "Mr. Lewis equates the image of racial innocence with other Western myths of the Islamic world that his other writings have done much to shatter. One such myth was the notion of an Islamic world that accepted Jews and allowed them to practice their religion freely."[13] Working to correct the supposedly good image that Islam appeared to be acquiring in the North, Lewis seems to have seen it as his scholarly duty to put it back in its proper place. This tendency of Lewis is also apparent in his *Jews of Islam* (1985) and in *Semites and Anti-Semites* (1986), both of which seek to make links between European anti-Semitism and current anti-Jewish propaganda in Arab countries.

Edward Said notes that "Lewis everywhere restrains himself from making such inflammatory statements flat out; he always takes care to say that of course Muslims are not anti-Semitic the way the Nazis were, but their religion can too easily accommodate itself to anti-Semitism and has done so."[14] Lewis appears to see the dominant discourses on Muslim (mis)treatment of religious minorities as being threatened by alternative ones provided periodically in works such as those of Mark R. Cohen, A. S. Tritton, Philip K. Hitti, Walter F. Fischel, and S.D. Goiten,[15] and seems to be on a self-assigned mission to reaffirm the predominant view through continual repetition. His utterances and writings have received a higher profile in the mass media due to his vaunted standing as "the doyen of Middle Eastern studies."[16] Lewis's work also seems to have been appreciated in the North since it has helped to transfer some of the guilt for centuries of anti-Semitism and the Holocaust onto the Arab Muslim bent on the destruction of Israel. Well-established images of the Muslim as violent and barbaric have facilitated the placing of the mantle of anti-Semitism on her shoulders. The Arab-Israeli conflict has thus partially eclipsed centuries of persecution of Jews by Christian Europeans.

Media discourses also relate Islam to Nazism from time to time. During the Gulf War, the demonization of Saddam Hussein was accomplished by endowing him with Islamic characteristics as well as by turning him into a contemporary incarnation of Hitler. The speculation that Iraqi Scud missiles launched against Israel would contain poison gas was compared to Nazi gas chambers. The Montreal newspaper *La Presse's* review of a book on the veiling of Muslim women on November 17, 1996 linked Islamism to Nazism. The consequences of such discourses seem to be that the blame for most terrorist activities against Jews immediately falls upon Muslims, as in the 1994 bombing of a Jewish community centre in Buenos Aires. It was not until one and a half years later, having failed to find any evidence of a Muslim link, that Argentinean authorities arrested neo-Nazis, including members of the country's army.

Covering (up) Arab Christianity

The image of the Muslim as innately violent is integral to the dominant construction of interfaith relations in the Holy Land. Mainstream media seem to assume that an "Arab-looking" guerilla with a gun can be none other than a Muslim terrorist. That the person could possibly be of a Christian background often appears to be dismissed, even though Christian Arabs have engaged in a number of high-profile terrorist incidents. There seems to be a fixed idea in the minds of many Northern journalists about the visual appearance of a Muslim terrorist. For example, a December 26, 1983 article titled "The Suicide Terrorists" *Maclean's* captioned a picture of a dishevelled teenager wearing battle fatigues and holding an automatic rifle, "Islamic amal gunman in Beirut: 'human Exocet missiles' can attack anywhere." The image seemed to fit the stereotypical model of a "Muslim terrorist" so well that the editors appear to have overlooked that two crucifixes were hanging from the teenager's neck. In an apparent haste to illustrate the article with a file photo of an "Islamic gunman" the editorial staff seems to have disregarded the all-important detail.

Even though the gaffe could be excused as "an honest mistake" in the rush to meet a deadline, it was undoubtedly made possible by the cultural stereotypes that exist in Northern societies about Muslims. Whereas such an error cannot often be spotted by readers, this particular mistake underlines the extent to which they are dependent on the mass media to deliver the "facts" of events that they cannot personally verify. Each society's cognitive scripts provide its members with sets of stereotypes about various groups of people. Mainstream cultural workers in Northern countries—writers, artists, musicians, choreographers, film-makers as well as editors, producers, directors, photographers, studio technicians, and webmasters—operate within these scripts to reproduce the images conforming to dominant stereotypes.

The dominant image of the violent Muslim appears occasionally to prompt journalists to identify Muslims as perpetrators of violent acts for which they are not responsible. The syndicated American columnist William Pfaff constructed a scenario that encompassed the history of several Arab "Islamic states" in a column published on February 9, 1986 in *The Montreal Gazette*. Its lead inquired into the reasons why a group called the Lebanese Revolutionary Armed Faction was setting off bombs in Paris. In fact, the members of this terrorist organization were Lebanese adherents of the Greek Orthodox Church. Yet, this fact was not mentioned by Pfaff, who went on to make grand statements about a global "collision of two civilizations": "What began in 1948, in the conflict of Arabs with the new Israeli state, has grown in sinister progress to become a struggle of Moslems with Jews, of radicalized Moslems with moderate Moslems, of secular revolutionaries and Islamic integrists with non-Moslems, with one another and with the United States and the West." It appears that the columnist was looking for an appropriate lead to introduce and provide validation for his views, and had found it in the current activities of a Lebanese group which seemed to fit the mould of "Islamic terrorists." Middle Eastern Christians did not exist in this grand scenario. Similarly, the narrator of a television documentary titled "The Sword of Islam," produced by the British-based Granada Television in the late 1980s, asked "Why do young men kidnap and kill, fight and die in the name of Islam?" as the visuals showed the aftermath of a bombing in Paris carried out by the same Lebanese Revolutionary Armed Faction.[17]

"Arab" has been conflated with "Muslim" to such an extent that native Christianity in the Middle East has almost completely disappeared in dominant Northern discourses. Although the Christian communities within Muslim societies are the oldest in Christendom and have their own churches, festivals, and religious customs, they are largely invisible to the Northern observer. Edward Said notes that

> ...there are distinctly Christian traditions inside the Islamic world: I myself belong to one. But it would be grossly inaccurate to think of them as separate and outside Islam, which includes us all. This, I think, is the most important point of all: Islam is something all Arabs share in and is an integral part of our identity. I may be speaking only for myself, but as an Arab Christian, I have never felt myself to be a member of an aggrieved or marginal minority. Being an Arab, even for a non-Muslim, means being a member of what the late scholar Marshall Hodgson called an Islamicate world or culture.[18]

But in dominant Northern discourses there has been little room for Christian Arabs, who do not fit neatly into the polarized scenario of Islam versus the "Judeo-Christian" North. Mainstream reporting has seemed unable to rise above the binary world view in which Muslim and Christian cultures are completely separate, if not hostile to each other.

This perspective has made it easier to view the conflict between Arabs and Israelis as Muslims versus Jews. The existence of indigenous Arab Christians has been downplayed in dominant media coverage over the past few decades in favour of presenting a neat, dichotomized picture in which all Arabs are Muslims and all Israelis are Jews. Even though some 20 percent of Palestinians have a Christian background this fact is rarely reported, and the conflict in the Holy Land has been implicitly portrayed as one between Jewish Israelis and Muslim Palestinians. Muslim and Christian Israelis of Palestinian and other backgrounds also remain largely invisible in Northern mass media. One only seems to hear of soldiers of Muslim background serving in the Israeli army in occasional, negative circumstances.[19] Similarly, the significant involvement of Christian Palestinians in the Palestinian National Assembly or the Palestinian Liberation Organization is also rarely indicated. The Christian background of George Habbash, the leader of the Popular Front for the Liberation of Palestine was hardly ever mentioned.

One of the clearest tendencies of erasing native Christian presence in the Holy Land has occurred in the ritual reporting of the annual observation of Christmas and Easter in Bethlehem and Jerusalem, respectively. Prior to the peace agreement between Israel and the PLO, the media focussed primarily on pilgrims from North America and Europe; the participation of Palestinian Christians from these cities was rarely covered. When Palestinians were mentioned they usually appeared as intrusive elements.[20] A headline in the Christmas eve 1988 issue of *The Ottawa Citizen* read: "Christmas is cancelled: Bethlehem shuts down as Palestinian uprising frightens away potential tourists." The article seemed to imply that without foreign, primarily Western, pilgrims there could not be Christmas in Bethlehem. In this discourse, only the presence of the Northern witness enables significant events around the world to take place: December 25 seems to lose its sacredness in Christ's birthplace without the Northern gaze.

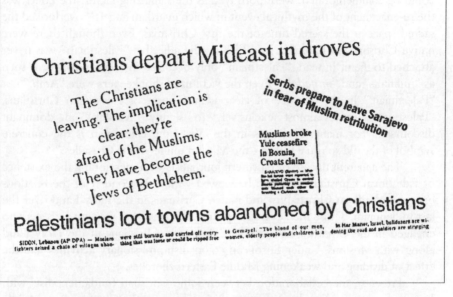

Illustration 4: Portraying Christians as victims of Muslims

The "Palestinian uprising" was the primarily negative factor here; although Israeli soldiers occasionally appeared in an unfavourable light, media narratives depict them as guardians of Christian pilgrims. The operative dramaturgy is that of the Muslim Palestinian terrorist/villain[21] threatening to victimize the Christian Northerner, who was protected by the Jewish Israeli soldier/hero. An article headlined "Pilgrims flock to Bethlehem service" in a December 26, 1991 issue of *The Toronto Star*, written by the paper's correspondent, stated:

> The Christmas spirit returned briefly yesterday to the birthplace of Jesus.
>
> For the first time in four years, the holy town of Bethlehem celebrated Christmas in a relaxed style with lights, international choirs and tourists from around the world.
>
> Israeli troops lined the streets yesterday and sharpshooters were posted on every rooftop surrounding Manger Square.

Outside the church [of the Nativity], most Arab shopkeepers closed their stores in response to a call by Palestinian militants to show the world that the *intifadah* is not over.

But many stores and restaurants adjacent to Manger Square remained open.

Israeli soldiers temporarily lifted a curfew on the West Bank residents of Ramallah and El Bira to allow Christians to attend Christmas services.[22]

"The Christmas spirit" had returned to Bethlehem because "international choirs and tourists from around the world" were present. Israeli soldiers, who temporarily cast a security net over Manger Square where the birth of Christ could be commemorated, were portrayed as the stabilizing factor: the effect was the re-enactment of the mythical event in which guardian angels[23] overlooked the sacred space at the sacred time of the first Christmas. Even though there were native Christians in Ramallah and El Bira, the adjective "Palestinian" was never attached to them. Instead, "Palestinian" only occurred in relation to words such as "militants" and "*intifadah*." Even the victimized shopkeepers were "Arab," not "Palestinian." In the absence of clear identification of Palestinian Christians, "Palestinian" came almost exclusively to signify "Muslim" in dominant discourses. "For many Christians in the West...the Palestinian is the concrete symbol of the old spiritual Other—the Muslim infidel of the Crusades."[24]

The apparent unease of Northern journalists with mentioning the existence of Palestinian Christians can also be viewed within the context of the relations between Northern Christianity and native Christians in the Holy Land over the last millennium. Those medieval European Christians from western Europe who engaged in the Crusades also attacked Orthodox Christians in the Holy Land along with Muslims. Under European colonialism, missionary activities had the effect of dividing and weakening Middle Eastern churches.

Presently, the collaboration between some Christian fundamentalists with Jewish fundamentalists have further harmed the interests of native Middle Eastern Christians. The latter have had to suffer a double indemnity—that stemming from the dominantly anti-Arab stance of the North and the suspicion in their own lands due to the inimical activities of foreign Christians.[25]

Problems between Jewish Israelis and Christians in the Holy Land are rarely covered, or when reported they lack the sustained focus given to Jewish-Muslim conflicts. Alfred Lilienthal commented on the coverage of a 1990 incident in which a Jewish religious group, using Israeli government funds laundered through a dummy Panamanian company, bought the lease of a Christian hospice located near the Church of the Holy Sepulchre:

The Easter Week takeover by singing and dancing Jewish religious fanatics marked the first non-Christian occupation [of the site] in eight centuries. It provoked a demonstration by Christian and Muslim leaders who, when they attempted to remove a Star of David installed over the entrance by the Jewish occupiers, were teargassed and dispersed by Israeli police.

After the initial occupation, most of the U.S. media dropped the story after reporting that "all but 20 Jewish settlers were ordered to evacuate" the hospice by an Israeli court. The fact that the 20, protected by Israeli police who prevent the former Christian occupants from entering even to remove their belongings, continue to occupy the building has gone unreported in mainstream American newspapers.[26]

Transnational media have generally remained reticent about Jewish takeovers in Jerusalem's Christian quarter. Such information would interfere with the primary dramaturgy in the Holy Land which presents the Christian as the victim of the Muslim terrorist and the ward of her Jewish Israeli protector.

Following the Israeli-PLO peace accord, it seems to have been somewhat more acceptable for journalists to write about the existence of native Christians in the Holy Land. However, this occurs frequently in contexts where they are portrayed as being threatened by Muslims. On 1991 Christmas eve, *The Toronto Star* ran a front-page feature headlined: "Christians depart Mideast in droves." Citing problems arising from the Arab-Israeli conflict as well as "Islamic fundamentalism," it related how native Christians were emigrating to North America and Europe. But, even though people living in the West Bank were mentioned in the article, the writer never referred to them as "Palestinian Christians." Similarly, on the previous day, the paper had carried a story with the following lead: "An Israeli family of Christian Arabs seeking asylum in Canada faces deportation to Israel where they fear Muslim extremists will kill them." However, the residual reluctance of Northern journalists to refer to "Palestinian Christians" appears to have begun diminishing by 1992. But they seemed to become visible only when threatened by Palestinian Muslims. This form of reportage usually coincides with the Christmas season; indeed, it appears to have become integral to the ritual reporting of the event.

A December 28, 1992 *Globe and Mail* article datelined Bethlehem and written by its Middle East correspondent dwelt on how Christian Palestinians felt sandwiched between the Israeli occupation, on the one hand, and "Islamic radicalism," on the other.

> Bethlehem endured its sixth Christmas under the strain of the Palestinian uprising amid growing fears that the Christian community here may never recover from the turmoil.

> ...in the West Bank, where Jesus Christ and Christianity were born, what little remains of the Palestinian Christian population is preparing to flee the vicious circle of military occupation and radicalism...

> Another Palestinian Christian, waiting for approval of his visa application to the West, said he worries that Hamas, the Islamic Resistance Movement, will take over the Palestinian community in the next few years.

> "A Palestinian state has never been closer to reality," he said, "but now it looks like it will turn out to be an Islamic state. I haven't prepared my kids for that."

Whereas "Palestinian" was previously linked with "Muslim," the notion of a future Palestinian state was now being placed within the framework of "Islamic radicalism." The 1994 Christmas eve edition of *The Ottawa Citizen* had a similar story by the Southam News' Middle East correspondent which was headlined, "Christian population continues to dwindle."

Whereas most Holy Land coverage during December 1995 was focussed on the hand over of Bethlehem by Israelis to the Palestinian Authority, *The New York Times* managed to highlight the dominant discourse. A Christmas eve article by André Aciman in the newspaper's weekly magazine surmised that "The Christians are leaving: The implication is clear: they're afraid of the Muslims. They have become the Jews of Bethlehem."[27] In this narrative, Palestinian Christians had lost their ethnicity: they had been brought into the "Judeo-Christian" fold in opposition to Palestinian Muslims. Even though indigenous Arab Christians became visible in media narratives, "Palestinian," once again, had come to denote only "Muslim." This is an example of how dominant discourses, upon their deconstruction by alternative perspectives, succeed in reconstructing themselves. The newspaper repeated the theme in a year-end feature titled "Palestinian Christians Feeling Like a Minority." This was echoed in a December 13, 1997 *The Ottawa Citizen* headline: "Christians now a minority in Bethlehem: West Bank instability hurts Christmas in Christ's birthplace." Given the traditional journalistic model, "West Bank instability" in dominant interpretations would refer to problems created by Muslim Palestinians. However, the actual text of the article by Samar Assad of the Associated Press, attempted to outline the complex social dynamics of Bethlehem. Whereas it stated that young Muslim men had made Christmas-time celebrations rowdier, it also indicated that the Palestinian Authority had ensured that Christians retained political power in the city even though their numbers had dwindled. The article related that the primary cause of Christian emigration over a number of decades was not Muslim presence but the economic stagnation brought about by the long-standing Israeli occupation.

Another write-up in *The Ottawa Citizen* of April 11, 1998 headlined "Three faiths flock to Jerusalem" seemed to promise a harmonious framing of the simultaneous commemoration of Easter, Passover, and the Muslim festival of Eid al-Adha in the city holy to the three religions. However, the second paragraph read, "Israeli soldiers, cradling assault rifles, lined the narrow alleyways of the old city on heightened alert for possible revenge attacks by the Muslim militant Hamas group following the mysterious death of master bomb maker Muhyideen Sharif." The article drew from Reuters and Associated Press (AP) copy, and carried an AP photograph at the top of the page (A6) that was captioned "With Israeli soldiers standing guard, Christian pilgrims and actors play out final steps of Jesus along Jerusalem's Via Dolorosa leading to his crucifixion." A front page picture by Agence France Presse in *The Globe and Mail* of the same day was titled "Guarded devotion"; its caption read, "A pilgrim carries a wooden cross past Israeli guards yesterday in Jerusalem's Old City as part of the Good Friday procession of penitents on the traditional route of Christ to his crucifixion. Security was heavy because of threats of attack from the Islamic group Hamas." Once again, the traditional media dramaturgy of the Palestinian Muslim villain, the Israeli Jewish hero, and the Western Christian victim was given prominence on the stage of the Holy Land—the indigenous Christian was no where to be seen.

The role of the establishment of the Jewish state in 1948 in the large-scale emigration of Israeli Arab Christians was largely avoided by dominant media discourses until the lead-up to the visit of Pope John Paul II in March 2000.[28] A February 5, 2000 feature titled "Holy Land Christians keep keys to kingdom" written by *The Ottawa Citizen*'s religion writer, Bob Harvey, pointed out that most pilgrims who visited the Holy Land were unaware of the existence of this Christian community which had existed for centuries. The community viewed Western Christians as having turned their backs on it.

In 1948, 722,000 Palestinian Arabs, including 55,000 Christians, fled what became the state of Israel. "It was a much more painful experience for Christians (than Muslims)," says Nora Carmi, a staff member at Sabeel, a centre for Palestinian liberation theology in East Jerusalem.

"We saw the Western Christian world trying to justify Israel's claims to the land by referring to our Holy Book. Many of the older generation still can't go to church and say the Old Testament is the word of God.

"As refugees, we had lost almost everything we owned, and we had the same question as the Jews had during the Holocaust: 'God, where are you?'," said Mrs. Carmi.

This discourse has been virtually absent in dominant media narratives, and still appeared only on page E18 of the newspaper.

Even though alternative narratives do appear from time in the back pages of newspapers, the enactments of the dominant discourse continue to be placed in the front sections. The harsh reaction of the Israeli military to the *intifadah* and the signing of the peace agreement had caused a reassessment of the primary frames of mass media coverage in which Jewish Israelis were heroes and Palestinians were villains. The partial recasting of the Palestinian as a victim seems to have allowed for reporting on native Christians in the Holy Land. Previously, the Palestinian was epitomized by the depiction of Yasser Arafat as the Muslim arch-terrorist: there was little room for indigenous Christians in that dramaturgy which essentially presented Muslim terrorists in mortal combat with Jewish Israeli commandos. But although the Palestinian Christian has become more visible in media content, she often appears as the victim of the Palestinian Muslim, in a reconstruction of the age-old "Islam versus Christendom" frame.

NOTES

1. Robert Franklin, "The Intifada: Five Years After," *Zion Quarterly: A Publication of Christian Friends of Israel*, 1 (1993), pp. 1-6.

2. John F. Walvoord, *Armageddon, Oil and the Middle East Crisis: What the Bible Says About*

the Future of the Middle East and the End of Western Civilization (Grand Rapids, Mich.: Zondervan Publishing House, 1990), p. 228.

3. According to the Palestine Human Rights Information Centre in Jerusalem, Israeli occupation authorities had demolished 1,860 Palestinian homes, uprooted 103,120 trees, and confiscated 97,674 acres of Palestinian land in the West Bank and Gaza by 1991. Palestine Mission to Canada, "Palestine Highlights," *Palestine Newsletter*, June 28, 1991, p. 2.

4. Thomas L. Friedman, *From Beirut to Jerusalem* (New York: Anchor Books, 1990), p. 428.

5. Ibid, p. 438.

6. Art Stevens, *The Persuasion Explosion: Your Guide to the Power and Influence of Contemporary Public Relations* (Washington, D.C.: Acropolis Books, 1985), p. 52. For a discussion of strategies employed by the Israel lobby in the U.S. to influence the media's views and reporting about Israel, see Robert I. Friedman, "Selling Israel to America: The Hasbara Project Targets the U.S. Media," *Mother Jones*, Feb./Mar. 1987, pp, 21-26, 52. Also see Paul Findley, *They Dare to Speak Out: People and Institutions Confront Israel's Lobby* (Westport, Conn.: Lawrence Hill and Co., 1985).

7. Friedman, *From Beirut to Jerusalem*, p. 427.

8. S. Robert Lichter, "Media Support for Israel: A Survey of Leading Journalists," in William C. Adams, ed., *Television Coverage of the Middle East* (Norwood, N.J.: Ablex, 1981), pp. 44-45. For a more comprehensive discussion of the adherence of American journalists to religious world views, see Mark Silk, *Unsecular Media: Making News of Religion in America* (Chicago: University of Illinois, 1995).

9. Dale L. Bishop, "The Churches and the Middle East," *American Arab Affairs* 20 (1987), p. 126.

10. Alfred M. Lilienthal, "As Criticism of Israel Builds, U.S. Media Revisit the Holocaust," *The Washington Report on Middle East Affairs*, September 1990, p. 25.

11. S.D. Goiten, *Studies in Islamic History and Institutions* (Leiden: E.J. Brill, 1966), p. 84.

12. Bernard Lewis, *Race and Slavery in the Middle East: An Historical Inquiry* (New York: Oxford University Press, 1990).

13. Marvin Zonis, "Veiled Prejudice," *New York Times Book Review*, August 5, 1990, p. 7.

14. Edward W. Said, *Orientalism* (New York: Pantheon Books, 1978), p. 317.

15. Mark R. Cohen, *Under Crescent and Cross: The Jews in the Middle Ages* (Princeton, N.J.: Princeton University Press, 1994); A. S. Tritton, *The Caliphs and Their Non-Muslim Subjects* (London, 1970); Philip K.Hitti, *History of the Arabs* (New York: St. Martin's Press, 1970); Walter F. Fischel, *Jews in the Economic and Political Life of Mediaeval Islam* (London: Royal Asiatic Society for Great Britain and Ireland,.1968); and S.D. Goiten, *Studies in Islamic History and Institutions* and *A Mediterranean Society* 5 vols. (Berkeley: University of California, 1967-88).

16. Zonis, "Veiled Prejudice," p. 7.

17. It is not only in Muslim-Christian confrontations that the Muslim is systematically portrayed as villain: *John Kettle's FutureLetter*, an influential Toronto-based newsletter that forecasts socio-economic trends, stated in its January 12, 1990 issue in reference to the contested site of the Babri Mosque in India, "The fanatical Muslim attempt to appropriate a Hindu shrine in northern India on the grounds that it had once been the site of a Muslim temple caused western heads to shake." Despite wide coverage of the event, it is remarkable how the work of the Hindu nationalist movement in India to destroy the historic mosque in Ayodhya was turned around to lay the blame on the familiar fanatic, the Muslim.

18. Edward W. Said, "The Phony Islamic Threat," *The New York Times Magazine*, Nov. 21, 1993, p. 64.

19. For example, on May 25, 1987, *The Montreal Gazette* carried a Los Angeles Times news service article titled, "Soldier jailed 7 years is innocent" on page F8. This was a story about an Israeli soldier from the Circassian Muslim minority. Bedouins and members of the Druze minority in Israel have also served in the country's armed forces.

20. Muslims are also frequently depicted by the mass media as disrupting sacred Jewish rituals. For example, on Friday April 12, 1996, the Canadian Broadcasting Corporation's Jerusalem correspondent, Anna-Maria Tremonti, reported on Hizbollah's and Israeli's reciprocal bombings of each other's territory. She brought the audience's attention to the fact that the Islamist group's attacks (which did not cause casualties) had occurred as Jewish Israelis were preparing for the Sabbath. But she neglected to mention how the much more severe Israeli shelling had also disrupted the weekly communal prayers for Muslims on that Friday, apart from killing 75 civilian men, women and children who were taking shelter in a UN compound.

21. Muslims are also often portrayed interrupting Christmas festivities with their violence. *John Kettle's FutureLetter*, in its 1995 New Year's Day issue, described the hijacking of an Air France airliner in the third week of December 1994 by some Algerian Islamists as "the Christmas hijacking." In December 1991, *The Ottawa Sun* had an editorial a cartoon based on a Christmas scene based on traditional portrayals of the three wise men of the East bearing gifts for the Christ-child. It portrayed Qadhafi a gift-bearer, sitting on a camel and holding a package labelled "LIBYAN FRANKINCENSE." A man dressed in traditional robes was shown shouting, "... SOMEBODY RUN THE FRANKINCENSE THROUGH THE METAL DETECTOR!" The implication was that Muammar Qadhafi, the leader of a mainly Muslim country, was attempting to smuggle a bomb into the manger where the founder of Christianity was born. Regardless of the real involvement of Qadhafi in sponsoring terrorist activities, such symbolic representations serve to present Islam as a fundamental threat to the religious bases of Northern civilization.

22. Also see Associated Press, "Bethlehem pilgrims celebrate Christmas," *The Montreal Gazette*, December 24, 1986, p. B1; Associated Press and Reuters, "Pope prays for peace during Easter strife," *The Ottawa Citizen*, April 4, 1988, A6; Associated Press, "Bethlehem won't celebrate Christmas," *The Ottawa Citizen*, November 29, 1988, p. A6; "Israel: Christians mark Easter rites," *The Ottawa Citizen*, March 3, 1991, p. A10; Arthur Charity, "Christmas in Israel," *The Ottawa Citizen*, December 23, 1991, p. A9; Associated Press, "Little joy found in Bethlehem," *The Ottawa Citizen*, December 23, 1992; and "Peace reigns for Christmas: Warring factions across the world put differences aside temporarily," *The Ottawa Citizen*, December 26, 1992.

23. When New York's Cardinal O'Connor visited the Wailing Wall in January 1987, *The Montreal Gazette* printed a large picture of him and two other Roman Catholic churchmen praying at the holy site on the front page of its World section. An Israeli border policeman who appeared in the foreground was described in a prominent inset title as *"The guardian angel."*

24. Shiraz Dossa, "Auschwitz and the Palestinians: Christian Conscience and the Politics of Victimization," *Alternatives* 13:4 (Oct. 1988), p. 516.

25. Bishop, "The Churches and the Middle East," pp. 123-27.

26. Lilienthal, "As Criticism of Israel Builds, U.S. Media Revisit the Holocaust," p. 26.

27. In a letter published in *The New York Times Magazine* on January 14, 1996, Mark Levine, a professor of religious studies, wrote that Aciman's "article is so full of traditional Orientalist clichés and anti-Arab remarks that I plan to use it next term as an example of how religion, politics and bigotry still substitute for substantive discourse on the Middle East."

28. For example, "Palestine's shrinking Christians," *The Economist*, December 18, 1999, p. 40 and Nomi Morris, "Christianity fading from Israel: Pope's visit underscores the religion's diminishing status in land of its birth," *The Ottawa Citizen*, March 18, 2000, p. C7.

CHAPTER 7

CONSTRUCTING A POST-SOVIET THREAT

"Shi'ite Peril"

Following its defeat in Vietnam in the mid-1970s, the U.S. largely restricted itself to supplying various Southern client states involved in war with arms and sending small contingents of military "advisers." However, since 1985 it has carried out direct attacks in Lebanon, Libya, Grenada, Panama, Iraq, Sudan, and Yugoslavia. Although the United States has emerged as the dominant global force, it appears to have adopted a post-Cold War foreign policy of not contesting Russian interventions in former southern Soviet republics such as Azerbaijan, Georgia, and Tajikistan. Moscow's brutal campaigns in 1994-95 and 1999-2000 to stem the rebellion in the southern Russian federation republic of Chechnya, apart from prompting some Western diplomatic protests, were treated as an internal matter. Such incursions are viewed as legitimate in dominant discourses that present Northern states as guardians of the global order, which terrorist elements from the South periodically threaten. Integration propagandists engineer world-wide consensus on the legitimacy of the global hegemony of Northern powers by naming Southern terrorism as a global problem, by defining its causes as "Oriental irrationality," and then prescribing Northern military action as a solution.

Since Northern ideologues have identified "Islamic fundamentalism" as manifesting a major global opponent, certain Muslim-majority countries have become key targets of the growing Northern aggressiveness. However, the identification of "Islam" as an ideological and military rival is not a recent development. In a post-World War II assessment of the new global role of the United States, communism and Islam were seen as being the principal forces "contending with the American idea."[1] Nevertheless, the Muslim threat seemed to have remained largely dormant during the period when dominant discourses viewed the entire world as being either in the American or the Soviet camp. The ideological need to run an active propaganda campaign against Islam was generally absent during the Cold War, and the cultural memory of the intermittent war with the Muslim Other from the seventh to the early twentieth centuries remained largely latent. Old stereotypes of Muslims continued to surface occasionally in cultural productions, but did not appear in a coherent propagandic attack. In any case, Muslim countries lay largely defeated and colonized, and their political elites were eagerly adopting Northern ways of thinking and acting.

It was with the overthrow in 1979 of the Shah Mohammed Reza Pahlevi of Iran and the assassination in 1981 of Egyptian president Anwar Sadat (both allies of the West) by Islamist forces that "Islam" began to re-emerge as a principal bogeyman. The forcible, non-apologetic reassertion of traditional Muslim symbols by the revolution in Iran and its overt opposition to dominant global discourses seem to have spurred this trend. As the Iranian leadership decried Washington as the "Great Satan," American propagandists produced a similarly demonic picture of the theocratic government in Tehran. In their reciprocal images, both Americans and Iranians have characteristics abhorred by the other—moral decadence and cultural imperialism, on the one side, and religious fanaticism and barbarism, on the other. While Iranian antipathy extends to several Northern governments, it has remained focussed primarily on Washington. Similarly, American acrimony towards "Islamic fundamentalism" encompasses its manifestations in various Muslim societies but reserves a particular distaste for Iran. The struggle of "Islam versus the West" has tended at times to become exemplified in global discourses as that between Iran and America.

Mainstream reporting rarely subjects Iran's domestic and external power struggles, which its own leaders have tended to dress in "Islamic" garb, to rigorous political or economic analyses. The "barbaric" and "irrational" behaviour agrees so well with cognitive models about how Muslim fanatics are supposed to act that there generally seems no need even for the kind of pseudo-scientific explanations often used in rationalizing similar political conflicts in North America and Europe. Without awareness of the socio-cultural and religious contexts of events in Iran, readers could only surmise that irrational "Islamic" tendencies which had supposedly been eradicated by programs of modernization/Westernization, were once again rearing their heads in the form of "Shi'ite fundamentalism." The latter seemed to be a particularly virulent form of Islam: a columnist declared in The Atlanta Journal-Constitution, "Where there are Shi'ites, there is trouble."[2]

Those Northern journalists who want to make a distinction between a "bad Muslim" and a "good Muslim" have often used the cognitive model of the "ancient Shia-Sunni feud." In its August 17, 1987 issue, Time magazine published a short backgrounder on confrontations between Shi'ites and Sunnis to accompany a cover story on the Iran-Iraq War (1980-88) titled "Iran Vs. The World." Headlined "The Unending Feud: Shi'ites vs. Sunnis," the piece implied that there had been continual fighting between the two branches of Muslims since the death of the prophet Muhammad 14 centuries ago. (In reality, the Twelver branch of Shi'ism, which is in the majority in Iran, was quiescent for most of its history.) The article portrayed Sunnis as engaging in "private meditative piety" and Shi'ites as being "more likely to indulge in displays of religious ardor." Iraq, Kuwait and Bahrain were depicted as being destabilized by their Shi'ite minorities. This remarkable bit of generalization, prompted by a combination of ignorance and ideological motivation, attempted to create mass portraits of good and bad kinds of Muslims who were engaged in a millennial struggle manifested at that time in the Iran-Iraq War.

This frame recurs from time to time. The caption illustrating a picture of a pilgrimage scene in Mecca in a feature article on Saudi Arabian politics, reprinted in *The Ottawa Citizen* from the New York-based *Worth Magazine* on January 6, 1996, stated: "Saudi Arabia is home to Mecca's Grand Mosque, right, one of Islam's holiest shrines [.] For centuries Muslims have slaughtered one another in the name of Mohammed. Most Saudis are Sunni Muslims. The other main group is the Shi'ites." These apparently unrelated sentences seemed to fulfil the function of linking one of the most significant communal rituals of Islam to strife among its adherents. With this reconstruction, the annual pilgrimage to Mecca (*hajj*)—viewed by Muslims as a symbol of unity among the world-wide community of Muslims (*ummah*)—became an icon for the "ancient Shia-Sunni feud."

The general tendency in dominant Northern discourses to attribute various manifestations of militant Islamism to the "Shi'ite peril" has remained entrenched even after the publicity that has attended the conflicts in countries like Egypt and Algeria where the Islamists are Sunnis. When the Algerian Islamist party Front Islamique de Salut won the first stage of national elections in 1991, a December 28 *Globe and Mail* editorial expounded: "the Sunni Islam pract sed in Algeria is a more moderate, less hierarchical form of Islam than the Shiite branch followed in Iran." The subsequent ferocity of Algerian Islamists, following the annulment of the election results by the government, largely put such characterization to rest in the Algerian context. Nevertheless, the cognitive model ascribing fanaticism to Shi'ites remains dominant.

Illustration 5: Narratives about warring Muslims

In a March 13, 1995 article titled "Muslim clerics preach tolerance in Central Asia," *The Globe and Mail*'s Moscow correspondent wrote, "Most of the people in Central Asia are Sunni Muslims who have found no attraction in fundamentalism." Such discourses seem to imply that "fundamentalism" only exists among Shi'ites. Shi'ism is even linked to fanatical tendencies outside Islam: the Christian right has been described as "Shi'ite Christianity" in the language of American liberalism.[3] Having removed Shi'ism from its historical and cultural contexts, Northern propagandists can turn it into a synonym for religious extremism in general.

As the Cold War was drawing to a close, a debate was raging between those Northern integration propagandists who continued to couch international conflicts within the framework of the NATO-Warsaw Pact struggle and others who were beginning to see Muslims as the new Other. This discussion among participants in dominant discourses was reflected in the columns of two writers in *The Calgary Herald*, Horst Heise and Roy Farran, both of whom commented on the role of Iran in global politics in the August 11, 1987 issue of the newspaper. The former painted a sweeping geopolitical "worst scenario" in which the Soviet Union would emerge triumphant over the Middle East region and the West:

> Moscow welcomed Khomeini's revolution because it ended Iran's alliance with the U.S. But it is very concerned that the mullah's fundamentalism could jump the border and infect its own Moslem population. Therefore the Soviets' interest in keeping Iran's war with Iraq going.

> From this follows that a weak Iranian compromise government—in which the communists or their fronts would play an important role—would be the preferred outcome.

> Farther ahead, a mix of routine Soviet tactics applied to Iran...could give Moscow all it needs for exercising control over the region. No shots need be fired, and the Arabian [sic] states likely would fall in line.

> It would endear Gorbachev to the Arabs who—while quite nervous about Moscow's intent—value clever power politics and resent Washington's preference of Israel over them.

> In return for diplomatic ties Moscow could pose as the Arab states' protector against Khomeini's fundamentalist threat—in short become the effective guardian in the Gulf; as well as of stable oil prices.

> It will take very clever Western diplomacy to better Moscow's—and the unpredictable Khomeini will make this tough to do.

In this remarkable bit of Orientalist sophistry, reminiscent of the heyday of the Cold War when the world was viewed as a red and blue checker-board, Heise presented the Muslim states as pushovers who were manipulated by "clever power politics" of the "Evil Empire." The West was thus required to better this by being "very clever" in order to win over the Arabs who would easily "fall in line" under a moderate amount of pressure; they were also seeking a protector against the "unpredictable" Khomeini's infectious "fundamentalist threat."

On the other hand, Farran, expressing the emerging Northern discourse on the Muslim Other, argued that the West and the Eastern bloc should both view Iran as a common threat in the post-Cold War era:

> Within the Moslem faith, including its interface with Western civilization, there are undercurrents as profound as in the days of Mohammed himself.
>
> The huge and expanding church is in conflict within itself between Sunnis and Shias, between moderates and puritans, between zealots and rationalists.
>
> The world, including both America and Russia, must now face the fact that Iran is a maverick. It sees itself as the lone defender of moral principle against the devil as manifested through western lifestyles, the State of Israel, the Iraqi government and many fellow Moslems.
>
> Whether the reign of the mad mullahs would come to an end with the death of Khomeni is doubtful. But what is now very likely is that the fanaticism would not subside if the Ayatollah's army were victorious.
>
> Bill Casey of the CIA and Admiral Poindexter of the security staff in the White House were living in an earlier world where every war was seen as part of the super-power struggle.
>
> All the petty attempts by Democrats to discredit the outgoing Republican president [Ronald Reagan] must take second place to this, the biggest threat to world peace since Vietnam.

According to Farran, the Americans should stop fighting with the Soviets and the Democrats with the Republicans, and all of them should recognize the real enemy: Shi'ite Iran, which had brought back the global "turmoil" present "in the days of Mohammed himself." Civilization itself was threatened with a fanatical and medieval barbarism of a Muslim world "in conflict with itself." Thus the North had to side with the "good Muslims" in Iraq (Sunni, moderate, rationalist), who were doing battle with the "bad Muslims" in Iran (Shi'ite, puritan, zealot), to defeat the "threat to world peace."

Dominoes In the Middle East

Since integration propagandists had succeeded in painting Iran as the villain and Iraq as the hero/victim during the Iran-Iraq War, it became easier for the United States government to justify deliveries of armaments to the anti-Israeli, Soviet-supported dictatorship in Baghdad. While creating temporary uproar, neither an Iraqi warjet's attack on the USS Stark in the Persian Gulf in May 1987 (killing 37 American sailors) nor the chemical bombing by the Baghdad government of its Kurdish minority in March 1988 (killing thousands of civilians) seemed to raise the kind of outrage reserved for similar incidents by enemy governments.

The mass media also generally portrayed Iraq as bravely defending the Persian Gulf kingdoms and emirates from the virulent influence of "Shi'ite fundamentalism." A June 27, 1987 *Maclean's* article on Iran's ambitions of spreading its revolution in the region emphasized the model of the Shia-Sunni conflict over the territorial nature of the war between Iran and Iraq—an approach which seems ironic in light of Iraq's 1990 invasion of Kuwait: "Should Iraq ultimately lose the war the neighbouring Kuwaitis are clearly concerned that they would be next in line. The Sunni-ruled state has contributed millions of petrodollars to Iraq's war effort, making it a logical target for Iranian subversion." In this version of the domino theory, previously applied in the context of the spread of communism, Iraq was presented as the champion of Sunni kingdoms.

During this period the use of religious symbols by the Iraqi government was generally underplayed by Northern mass media, while similar tendencies by the Iranians were highlighted. But in the Gulf War, when Northern forces were arrayed against Iraq, the focus seemed to be on emphasizing the "Islamic" nature of the Iraqi regime and society. The religious posturing by Saddam Hussein was given considerable coverage and cameras seemed to seek out his supporters who were in "Islamic" garments.[4] At the height of the conflict *Maclean's* ran a cover story in its February 11, 1991 issue titled "The Gulf War and Islam," which discussed populist Muslim support for Hussein. Other publications also highlighted the perceived lack of rationality and logic among those who supported the Iraqi leader—this was blamed on Islam and the Arab character. An article in *Time* on August 27, 1990 expounded: "Logic in the Arab world is often eclipsed by emotion. Saddam's populist message against corrupt regimes kept in control by American and Zionist powers, and the swagger of a leader who can and will fight them, has had an intoxicating effect on the dispossessed across national boundaries." And another in the London-based *Spectator* of March 16, 1991, titled "Let's not leave it to the Arabs," stated: "The hatred of the West current in certain Arab circles, being visceral rather than rational in nature, simply has to be accepted as a way of life." Such typifications that present Southerners as primarily ruled by emotion in contrast to Northerners who calmly apply logic to deal with difficult situations are characteristic of traditional Orientalist narratives.

In an analysis of American media coverage of the Gulf War, Parker Payson notes how generalizations about Muslims and Arabs made up for the lack of interviews with Iraqis themselves. Speculation about "the Muslim mind" helped create an us-versus-them attitude. He gives the following example: "Leon Katzen, writing in the *Rochester-Gannet Papers*, argues that "Peace in the Middle East…cannot be achieved until the people of the West (including the Israelis) understand the Muslim mind," which, according to Katzen, is "manipulated by clerics calling for all Muslims to kill non-Muslims."[5] Mashoed Bailie and David Frank provide a transcription of an on-camera conversation between NBC news anchor Tom Brokaw and "expert" Edward Peck during the Gulf war:

Peck: I would tend to think that one of the things he[Saddam Hussein]'s going to do first, when he comes out of his bunker, is call on the Arab world to rise up and support him, and call on Muslims everywhere to do the same thing. I'm certain that Saddam Hussein can count on a very strong and very violent reaction from Muslims virtually everywhere.

Brokaw: And what are the prospects of that succeeding with the Arab masses, to say nothing of the other marginal leaders there?

Peck: I think it's going to succeed very well, well fairly well. And that's not something that pleases me of course...I think there's going to be a very strong emotional reaction on the part of all Arabs...when they know the United States has struck co-religionists, co-Arabs, co-ethnists, if you will.[6]

Generalizations flowed thick and fast: "the Arab world," "Muslims everywhere," "Arab masses," "all Arabs." There seemed to be little attempt at nuance here or to understand the diversity of millions of people spread along a vast area of the globe. Even though a large proportion of Iraqi immigrants to Canada is Christian no mention was made of them in an article in *Maclean's* issue on "The Gulf War and Islam" which dealt with the impact of the war on Canadians of Arab origins, nor generally in other mass media reportage. Also, in keeping with the portrayal of Iraq as an "Islamic" country, the mass media rarely alluded to the fact that the chief spokesperson and foreign minister of the Iraqi government, Tariq Aziz, was Christian. Dwelling on such details would have detracted from exploiting traditional Northern hostility towards the Muslim Other in the construction of Saddam Hussein's government as the demonic enemy.

The image of Iran as a fanatical, fundamentalist "Islamic" country appeared to have merged with that of Iraq in the course of the Gulf War. This seemed to be manifested verbally during the Gulf War in frequent slips of tongue by broadcast journalists who said "Iran" when they meant to say Iraq, and "Iranians" when they meant Iraqis. "One television producer, indeed, is said to have ordered a standardising of the house style: 'we've got to decide if we're calling it Iraq or Iran.'"[7] A scenario drawn up by the above-mentioned January 6, 1996 article from *Worth Magazine* reprinted in *The Ottawa Citizen* saw the two "Islamic" demons, Iran and Iraq, joining forces to cause global disaster; it would be instigated by a Shi'ite rebellion in Saudi Arabia:

Imagine the domino effect at work in the Middle East. Saudi Arabia is under siege, mass confusion reigns in the Western democracies, and so Iran and Iraq hurriedly kiss and make up. The U.S. policy of isolating them is already pushing them together.

So if Iran and Iraq can pull the new Saudi Arabia to their side, then Kuwait is going to fall, and so will the United Arab Emirates.

This powerful new oil cartel could renounce its debts to the evil West, causing the price of oil to shoot through the roof.

With billions of dollars in loans suddenly becoming nonproductive, our banking system will be thrown into a state of bedlam.

Bank stocks will collapse, and nobody will know whether to buy oil stocks or to sell them. Automotive stocks worldwide will plummet.

East and west, north and south, stock markets will close for days that stretch into weeks.

The language of popular economics is used to create images of a world-wide financial apocalypse. Cold War logic also plays a role in the construction of Muslim "oil states" falling like dominos. The appeal of such scenarios, which are frequently reprinted and rebroadcast by the transnational media, lies in the confirmation they provide for cognitive scripts about how Muslims act. (It is unimaginable that journalists would have a similarly free rein to ruminate about the dangers that the United States may pose, as a single superpower, to the rest of the world—especially to the South.)

Paradoxically, while the images of Iraq and Iran were being merged in Northern discourses, the "good Muslim/bad Muslim" dichotomy seemed to have been overturned in referring to the Sunni Saddam Hussein and the Shi'ite population of southern Iraq. Although the latter group was abandoned at the end of the Gulf War by the United Nations Coalition, which had encouraged it to rebel against the Baghdad government, its status as a victim of Saddam Hussein was temporarily revived in 1992 during George Bush's (unsuccessful) campaign for re-election as president. Having maintained the existence of Hussein as a necessary Other, the Bush administration, along with its allies in Europe, could be seen heroically coming to the rescue of the Iraqi Shi'ites. But integration propagandists were careful to indicate that these Shi'ites, despite having ties to those in Iran, were seeking a greater role in the Iraqi government and not a separate "Islamic" state. An article reprinted from *The Washington Post* in *The Ottawa Citizen* of August 29, 1992 emphasized that this issue

...becomes particularly important now that the United States and its allies are engaged in aerial intervention in the name of protecting Shiites in southern Iraq, where most of them live.

"The Shiites do not want to separate because they feel they are the core of Iraq," said Graham Fuller, a Middle East analyst with the Rand Corp. "There is no question of Shiites separating or joining Iran."

The ease with which the dramaturgical role of the Shi'ite could be transformed from villain to victim seems intriguing. Central to such manipulations are the ideological reasons that underlie them—these often have little relation to the actual situation of the people accorded these roles. The apparent purpose here was how to emphasize the stature of George Bush as a statesman, a key feature of his election campaign; once he had lost the election, the Iraqi Shi'ites once again vanished from the attention of the mass media.[8]

Containing Islam

John Esposito indicates in his book *The Islamic Threat: Myth or Reality?* that the "threat vacuum" following half a century of confronting the Soviet Bloc "has given rise to the search for new enemies."[9] At the end of the long standoff between the West and Eastern Europe there has appeared, apart from the many territorial and ethnic conflicts around the world, a global conflict model that pits the North against the South.[10] This perception of reordered alliances seems to have begun developing after Mikhail Gorbachev signalled his intentions in the late 1980s to bring the Cold War to an end. As former communist states seek to join Western multi-state organizations such as the G-7, NATO and EU, some opinion leaders view them as increasingly aligning themselves together with the West and in opposition to the South. Now with Marxism in general retreat, and notwithstanding the occasional bouts of China bashing[11], "Islam" seems to be the only other global ideology standing in the way of the complete triumph of Western capitalism.

Certain media commentators saw the Gulf War as an inevitable first battle in the emerging conflict between the North and the South. In the New World Order, North America, Europe and Australasia would close ranks and arm themselves to fight against other continents. Peter Newman, a columnist for *Maclean's* magazine, wrote in the January 28, 1991 issue:

> ...there are many Saddam Husseins; Canada may have to become more military as the cost of survival in this dangerous age. That was all supposed to have become ancient history with the end of the Cold War, but it turns out that both sides were arming for the wrong battle. It will be the regional warlords in the Middle East, South America and the Far East who will be managing the world's agenda in the 1990s.

And Peregrine Worstone of the London *Sunday Telegraph*, stated in an article reprinted on January 25, 1991 in the Toronto-based *Financial Post*'s "Insight" section,

> The riches of the First World provoke passionate envy in the Third World, and so do all the other appurtenances of civilization. We are envied both materially and non-materially, and the Third World would dearly love to pull us down. Nothing blocks this aim except Western strength. And it is this Western strength which must on no account be trammelled.
>
> The aim must be for America to win an overwhelming victory; for Western technology to prove devastatingly, chasteningly superior.
>
> *...it is beginning to look as if Saddam has given the West a chance once again to establish its unchallengeable pre-eminence in a manner impregnable at once to moral obloquy and military resistance.*
>
> Not only will our arms have prevailed in a most spectacular fashion. So also will our ideals [emphasis added].

The Gulf War seemed to have prompted the surfacing of a neo-colonial attitude that made it acceptable for the West to launch a massive assault on a developing country. Whereas such overt constructions of the war as a North-South conflict were not common, they seemed to be implicit in much of the conflict's media coverage. It was generally portrayed as a showdown between Western civilization, evidenced in its technological and moral superiority, and Islamic barbarism, personified in the crude violence of Saddam Hussein.

World War I	Allies	Germany/Austro-Hungary/ Ottoman Empire
World War II	Allies	Hitler/Axis powers
Cold War	NATO / "the West"	Warsaw Pact/"the East"
Gulf War	NATO-dominated UN Coalition / "Allies"	"Hitler" (Saddam Hussein) / the Muslim East

Table 1: The Allies and their enemies

The image of the military Other has accommodated different enemies in various periods. Tuen van Dijk notes that the "final nodes" of propagandists' scripts "are empty (default values), so that they can be applied to different situations by filling in such terminal nodes with specific information."[12] In World War II's operative script a number of nations came together to defeat evil. This script was successfully reused during the Cold War when the post-1945 Western alliance of countries engaged in ideological battle and in military conflicts against another grouping in Eastern Europe. The bipolar global conflict between NATO and the Warsaw Pact, the former led by the United States and latter by the Soviet Union, replaced that between the Allies and the Axis powers. With the impending demise of the communist bloc, the same script was applied to the Gulf War. In dominant discourses, the United Nations Coalition led by America became "the Allies" and Saddam Hussein was cast in the role of the nefarious Hitler.[13]

Former Israeli Prime Minister Shimon Peres has described "Islamic fundamentalism" in the following manner: "It has many of the characteristics of communism. It is fanatic, it is ideological, and it claims like communism, that the ends justify the means…[but] most of all, it has the same inclination to export its ideas."[14] Barbara Amiel, a prominent columnist on both sides of the Atlantic, wrote on August 15, 1990 in The Ottawa Sun that "A militant Marxist Islamic Middle East could be one of the most threatening things to world peace. We may have to face the inevitable consequences of pan-Arabism and pan-Islam and realize that, in one sense, all Arabia [sic] may be our enemy and we simply cannot go on arming, equipping and encouraging any of these people." The facility with which the Cold War script was adjusted to accommodate what integration propagandists presented as a new global conflict with the Muslim Other is amazing. As if to confirm the practical ease with which this can be done, a *Globe and Mail* headline exclaimed during the Gulf War: "Cold War battle plan transferred to gulf." Iraq filled this script's terminal node, which had previously been occupied by the Soviet Bloc. Other propagandists extended the nodes to present the scenario of a world-wide conflict. The title of an article by Robert Kaplan, initially published in *The Atlantic* and reprinted in the *Globe* on August 7, 1993, read "The cross and the crescent: A cultural curtain is descending in Bosnia to replace the Berlin Wall, a curtain separating the Christian and Islamic worlds. (Kaplan also published his views in a 1996 book titled *The Ends of the Earth*.) An article in the 1995 New Year's Day issue of *John Kettle's FutureLetter* assessing "the Islamic threat" highlighted the predictions of "intelligent" and "practical people" such as former U.S. Secretary of Defence Caspar Weinberger and writers for *The Economist*, *Life*, and *The Globe and Mail* who warned that the next "millennial collision" would be between Muslims and the "industrialized free world." Dominant discourses perpetuate themselves intertextually through continual self-reference, particularly within the mass media, thus imparting the semblance of uncontested truth.

Various international studies scholars such as John Esposito, Fred Halliday, James Piscatori, John Sigler, Jochen Hippler, and Andrea Lueg have sought to analyse the "Islamic threat" and have concluded that Northern fears are largely unfounded.[15] However, in an influential *Foreign Affairs* article Samuel Huntington predicted a future in which the West will be embroiled in a global struggle against "the Rest." In this, "a central focus of conflict will be between the West and several Islamic-Confucian states."[16] Huntington even proposed a short-term strategy whose aims, among other things, are "to limit the expansion of the military strength of Confucian and Islamic states" and "to exploit difference and conflicts among Confucian and Islamic states."[17]

Apparently borrowing from Huntington, *The Economist* on January 8, 1994, made predictions about the reordering of the world's patterns of power in which the United States, Europe, Russia, China, and an imaginary "Islamic power" would be the major players.

> [A]n Islamic power, may never come into existence; but if it did, it would doubtless give the gun priority over the purse. A new state created out of countries in the western part of the Muslim world, professing the principles of Islam, would have a clear-cut ideology in open competition with that of the modern West. If most of its people were Arabs, it would possess the further unifying force of a shared language. And it would have the power of oil, which could be denied to its adversaries or sold for buying the weapons with which to fight them.
>
> This pugnacious new arrival would confront two ready-made enemies. One

would be Europe, its centuries-old quarrel with western Islam still liable to flare up over places like Bosnia. Then would come Russia, whose border with Islam in central Asia remains a blur. It is by no means impossible that a new Islamic power would get into a fight with both Europe and Russia—and, if it did, it might look for an ally to China, which also has a border quarrel with Russia.

The magazine used entrenched stereotypes of Islam to construct this scenario: violent tendencies, historical feuds, a monolithic following, anti-modernist ideology, and oil wealth. The Northern mega-states would enter into conflict with Southern ones. This linking of China with the "Islamic power" allows the revisiting of the communist-Muslim nexus in another way.[18] In an alternative vein, William Dalrymple in an *Observer* (London) article of April 21, 1996, criticized Huntington's alarmist predictions and favoured Halliday's "balanced and sober analysis of this new anti-Islamic tendency."

A cover story in a later March 18, 1995 issue of *The Economist* did attempt to make distinctions in the various manifestations of "the Islamist movement," and concluded that:

Islamic fundamentalism is certainly not like communism, something to be resisted tooth and nail. It may be more like socialism, an -ism with many facets, some entirely compatible with liberal democracy, some more hostile to it, some perhaps wholly at odds with it. Living with Islam involves discrimination, as well as vigilance.

However, the front-page photo accompanying the write-up, titled "Living with Islam," was of a lone man prostrating in prayer towards a wall on which rested an assault rifle. An abridged version of this article was reproduced on March 20 in *The Globe and Mail*, where it was headlined "Living with radical Islam: Welcome the good, resist the bad." As with *The Economist*, its illustration provided a violent image of Islam: a drawing of a *muezzin* calling the faithful to prayer, but with his uplifted left hand transformed into a blazing minaret. Therefore, even though the text of the article did not present a monolithic view of Muslim societies the accompanying visuals in both the British and Canadian publications adhered to the primary stereotype of the "violent man of Islam"—an image that would undoubtedly influence the reading of the text.

The mass media have also made justifications for the continued spending on military-industrial complexes and other institutions from the Cold War era. The headline for a *Newsweek* write-up on July 12, 1993 read: "A New Kind of Containment: Stopping a resurgent Iraq—and Iran, too—will require a heavy U.S. military commitment". Containment had been a key strategy against the Soviet bloc during the Cold War. An article from the *Congressional Quarterly* on the Central Intelligence Agency, which was distributed to newspapers by the Scripps Howard News Service, advised both politicians and the mass readership that:

Today, the greater political threat is a long way from Moscow—in newly independent republics like Kazakhstan, where hundreds of former Soviet nuclear weapons are stored, in the streets of Medellin, Colombia, where the drug cartels are based, and in the mosques of Iran, where the seeds of Islamic fundamentalism are sown.[19]

The CIA, which had hitherto spent billions of dollars on activities against the Other in the form of the Eastern bloc, must now shift its sights southwards to find a new *raison d'être*. This is not a difficult case to make to audiences which already adhere to negative cognitive models of the South and of Islam. In fact, soon after the collapse of the Soviet Union, intelligence services of the former enemies began collaborating together by sharing vital military information about countries like Iraq, a client state of Moscow.[20] (The CIA is also making the case that its ranks, which have been reduced following the Cold War, should be reinforced to fight "the war against terrorism."[21])

Illustration 6: Constructing Islam as post-Cold War Other

In search of a new role in the post-Cold War era, NATO was re-packaged by the organization's former secretary-general, Willy Claes, as a bulwark against "Islamic fundamentalism" which he said "is just as much a threat to the West as communism was."[22] These remarks were made to the German daily *Süddeutsche Zeitung* in February 1995 and carried by news agencies to media outlets around the world. The underlying message was that since the Soviet bloc had ceased to exist, the military organization could expand to include some of its former communist rivals from Eastern Europe and turn its guns to aim at the southern front.[23] The U.S. government has been attempting to make the case for justifying the increasing costs of its involvement in NATO. With the virtual disappearance of the communist spectre, the primary danger is being constructed as emanating from "rogue states."

In a December 1997 speech to a NATO gathering in Brussels, American Secretary of State Madeline Albright said, "During the Cold War, we were brought together by our overriding interest in containing the Soviet Union. Many people believe we no longer face such a unifying threat, but I believe we do." This new threat is a "combustible combination of technology and terror," coming from "Eurasia and the Middle East." In this discourse the "war against terrorism" becomes the *raison d'etre* for sustaining high levels of funding for participation in NATO and even for converting military technologies developed under the Cold War era's Strategic Defence Initiative ("Star Wars") to fight "rogue states." This has involved the adoption of the policy to use nuclear weapons to counter a perceived threat of chemical or biological weapons by pariah regimes. The reporting of Albright's speech by *The Globe and Mail*'s Washington correspondent, Paul Koring, on December 18, 1997 was an example of informed journalism that placed the event into the framework of evolving geopolitical dynamics. He brought to light the attempt by NATO to reinvent itself since the collapse of its primary threat, and the ensuing debate between the U.S. and the UK on the one side, and other European NATO partners on the other, about the extension of the alliance's role beyond Europe. However, the dominant discourse reasserted itself in the headline that read, "NATO should fear Mideast, Eurasia Albright warns," thus subverting an alternative approach on reporting global conflict.

Even before the Soviet threat had begun to diminish, some mainstream journalists were looking for other justifications to keep the military-industrial complexes functioning at full steam. Seeking additional legitimation for the "Star Wars" project, William Safire of *The New York Times* brought up the scenario of nuclear terrorism in an article that was republished in *The Montreal Gazette* on October 16, 1984: "The real threat of the future may not be from 'a rational superpower' but from fanatics in the Middle East...the Third World War may not be the Soviet Union verses the free world, but terrorism versus civilization." One could engage in diplomatic relations with a rational dissident from the North such as the USSR, but not with an irrational Middle East.

In a survey of predictions by scholars "about what life will be like for the next generation," a *Maclean's* article in the September 11, 1989 issue said,

> Some experts...expressed that the growth of Islamic fundamentalism may...represent a threat to the world at large. Dalhousie[University]'s [Denis] Stairs said that Islamic fundamentalism, which rejects the Western scientific view of man, may be prevented by its very nature from "being accommodated to the engines of the modern world." As a result, some Islamic groups may suffer from alienation and turn to extreme forms of terrorism.

Having decided that there exists a monolithic entity called "Islamic fundamentalism, which rejects the Western scientific view of man," the foreign affairs "expert" does not seem to believe it even worth the trouble to attempt to establish a dialogue with any of the Islamists. It appears more comfortable intellectually to adhere to the script in which the gap with an absolute otherness which cannot be bridged. Similarly, an article from *The New York Times* reprinted in *The Ottawa Citizen* stated on August 23, 1994,

"The nature of terrorism is entirely different in the 1990s than it was in the 1970s," said John Christie, the British publisher of the *Gulf States Newsletter*, which has extensively examined the phenomenon. "What you have now is a unique threat from Islamic fundamentalist groups, supported by Iran and other countries, that want to turn the clock back. They are fanatical, they see the West as evil, and they have unlimited access to money."

In creating such a dark image, one wonders whether the likes of Christie and Stairs are not just as fanatical in their apparent insistence in seeing all Islamists as unbending militants and whether they are not projecting a mirror-image of "the Great Satan."

Such millennialist scenarios also appear in television dramas. A December 1999 episode of the American television series "West Wing," which dramatized life in the White House, depicted Pakistan and India going to war. In the plot, a British diplomat with experience in both countries tells the U.S. president that the conflict is based on religion, not history or geography, and unlike the U.S. and the Soviet Union during the Cold War, the Muslim-dominated Pakistan and the Hindu-dominated India would have no compunctions about using nuclear weapons. The episode ended with a character reading a passage from the Book of Revelations that foretells Armageddon.

Daniel Benjamin and Steven Simon, both former counterterrorism officials in the U.S. National Security Council, stated in a *New York Times* op-ed published on January 4, 2000 that even though the new Muslim terrorists are "rejected by most modern Islamic authorities," they are motivated "by a world view in which they are the vanguard of a divinely ordained battle to liberate Muslim lands." The form of terrorism just seems to be getting worse with time, according the media's experts. Rather than disappear in the new millennium, it has mutated into a greater evil. An article titled "The Future of Terror" in the second *Newsweek* issue of the new century stated,

> Throughout the cold war, terrorist groups usually had concrete demands: U.S troops out of Europe, say, or the destruction of Israel. Terrorist groups like the Irish Republican Army and the Palestinian Liberation Organization had political agendas and hopes of achieving legitimacy. Their ambitions set limits on the death and destruction they wrought...But the new breed of terrorists has murkier goals. They seem more interested in killing than in publicity...They are taught by their imams that Americans are infidels, and that if they kill them they will go to paradise," said Roland Jacquard, a well-known authority of international terrorism.

In a revision of the dominant view about the terrorists of the past, the IRA and PLO's killers were made out to be rational terrorists who had limits to their violence. The post-Cold War narratives which seem bent on creating images of a fanatical violence driven by mindless evil, rarely recite the litany of abuses related to America's role in the world or that of the repressive structures instituted by colonialism.

Sustained media depiction of conflicts between Northern interests and "Islamic" elements in Iran, Iraq, Libya, Algeria, Egypt, Lebanon, Turkey, Bosnia-Herzegovina, Azerbaijan, Tajikistan, Chechnya, Afghanistan, Pakistan, Malaysia, the Philippines, Indonesia as well as in Muslim communities living in Europe, North America and Australasia, has supported the cognitive model of a global struggle reminiscent of that between NATO and the Warsaw Pact. However, from time to time articles do appear in the press, usually penned by guest writers[24] but also occasionally by staff members of newspapers,[25] commenting on these ideological constructions. The attitude of Northern powers towards Muslim countries has appeared to be systematically harsher than that towards non-Muslim countries, noted columnist Gwynne Dyer in a rare manifestation of an alternative media discourse, in the March 16, 1992 issue of *The Toronto Star*: "It's not exactly a conscious plot, but then these things rarely are. It's more a matter of cultural reflex and ancient prejudice, reinforced by that well-known phenomenon whereby people's ideas mysteriously coincide with their interests... There is a pattern emerging, a get-tough-with-Muslims pattern." Interestingly, a February 6, 1995 *Globe and Mail* editorial criticized NATO secretary-general Willy Claes's comments about the "Islamic" threat, cautioning against stereotypically seeing "Muslims as hard-eyed fanatics lobbing bombs at the cathedrals of capitalism." However, a serial "survey of modern Islam" produced in May that year by the daily's roving correspondent, Patrick Martin, was packed with fearful images of "Islam's battle with the existing world order." The feature articles were headlined "Death holds no fear for Muslim militants" (May 12), "Islamic challenge fierce in Africa" (May 15), and "The empire strikes back: Islam's threat to Turkey" (May 23). Such narratives, which present "Islam" as the epicentre of Southern instability and violence against the post-Cold War global order, continue to be dominant.

Indeed, for some, the Cold War seems to have become an historical anomaly compared to the millennial struggle between Christians and Muslims. The January 6, 1996 article reprinted by *The Ottawa Citizen* from the New York-based *Worth* magazine stated, "In our western shortsightedness, we think modern history is the 50-year story of the Cold War. That was an interesting, important struggle, but it's only a sideshow compared with the main conflict of the past 1,300 years—the one between Islam and Christianity." This brings us full circle: integration propagandists who are constructing Islam as the new peril seem to be in the process of erasing the memory of the Cold War. In proclaiming Mikhail Gorbachev its progressive "Man of the Decade," *Time* magazine in its 1990 New Year's day issue could begin to publish articles which deconstructed the dominant Western discourses' demonization of the red menace: "Gorbachev is helping the West by showing that the Soviet threat isn't what is used to be—and, what's more, that it never was."

Ten years later, the 2000 New Year's day edition of *Newsweek* stated in a look forward into the new century that even though communism and Nazism, the scourges of the twentieth century, were gone, religious fundamentalism was an "ism" that remained. Whereas the article did indicate that "many of the fears of Islamic fundamentalism are overblown," it was illustrated with pictures of Sigmund Freud, Karl Marx and Ayatollah Khomeini and the accompanying caption read, "FALL AND RISE: Freud and Marx no longer inspire wide-eyed loyalty. But Khomeini-style fanaticism remains potent." As is often the case, the dominant discourse asserts itself in the more eye-catching aspects of write-ups, namely, illustrations and headlines.

Although there is a dominant tendency to present Islam as a primary Other, the depiction of the relationship between Northern and Muslim societies is ambiguous compared to the generally polarized portrayal of NATO and the Warsaw Pact. The renewed image of Islam as enemy has developed in dominant global discourses despite the military cooperation between the U.S. and governments of countries with Muslim majorities like Egypt, Turkey, and Indonesia, and even that with conservative states such as Saudi Arabia and Kuwait. Integration propagandists can rely on the strength of the traditional Northern antipathy against Islam as well as on the inability of the "current affairs man" to discern contradictions in propaganda.[26] The presence of the military forces of various Arab and non-Arab Muslim countries during the Gulf War on the side of the American-led United Nations Coalition was primarily symbolic in a conflict that was won by the overwhelming technological superiority of Western forces. In fact, *Time* magazine unabashedly declared on November 12, 1990: "They Don't Need to Fight: The Islamic allies deployed in the Arabian desert have already done their job even if they never fire a single shot."[27] But at the populist level in various Western societies the conflict was seen as a war against all Arabs and Muslims, not just Iraq.

> When the Canadian government went to war against Iraq, many Canadians of Arab or Muslim background found that they were being identified with the enemy. On the street, in workplaces, in schools, and in the media they became targets of ignorance, hostility and paranoia.

> Many key institutions in Canadian society identified Arab and Muslim Canadians with the enemy government of Iraq. The media sought out individuals who criticized the government's decision to go to war with Iraq and treated them as extremists.[28]

Even though government statements were made affirming the loyalties of citizens of Iraqi origins to their adopted countries in the West, populist discourses often blurred distinctions, making all Iraqis, Arabs and Muslims a common embodiment of the enemy. For many, this was a war to contain a global problem named "Islam."

NOTES

1. Mortimer Graves, "A Cultural Relations Policy in the Near East," in Richard N. Frye, ed., *The Near East and the Great Powers* (Cambridge, Mass.: Harvard University Press, 1951), pp. 70-78.
2. Edward W. Said, *Covering Islam: How the Media and the Experts Determine How We See the Rest of the World* (New York: Pantheon Books, 1981), p. 81.

3. New Oxford Review, Advertisement, "The End of the Reagan/Bakker/Falwell Era & the Future of Religion," *Harper's Magazine* (Apr. 1988), p. 22.

4. Cf. The Independent news service, "Asians line up to fight for Iraq," *The Ottawa Citizen*, January 23, 1991, p. A7; Peter Bakogeorge, Southam News, "Attack feeds Muslim anger," *The Ottawa Citizen*, January 25, 1991, p. A2; Stephen Vizinczey, "Bring on the Israelis," *The Globe and Mail*, January 31, 1991, p. A6; James Deacon, "The Will to Fight—and Die: Hussein Calls for a Holy War," *Maclean's* , February 11, 1991, p. 39; D'Arcy Jenish, Islam and the Gulf War: Why many Moslems Support Iraq, *"Maclean's*, February 11, 1991, pp. 34-37; and Judith Miller, New York Times news service, "Inside Saddam's Head: A messianic streak and a touch of history characterize Iraqi leader's conduct," *The Ottawa Citizen*, February 2, 1991, p. A2. To its credit, *Time* published a short article by Richard N. Ostling on "Islam's ideas of 'Holy War'" on February 11, 1991, p. 51, which briefly attempted to compare jihad to "just war" and to explore its history as well as its exploitation by various Muslim leaders. However, as in other examples of alternative discourses, it was lost in the barrage of material that emphasized the "Islamicness" of Saddam Hussein's actions.

5. Parker L. Payson, "The Gulf War: Trimming the Truth," *The Washington Report on Middle Eastern Affairs*, 40 (Mar. 1991), pp. 70-71.

6. Mashoed Bailie and David A. Frank, "An Occidental Construction of the Orient: Media, Madness, and the Muslim World," in Janet Wasko and Vincent Mosco (Toronto: Garamond, 1992), p. 84.

7. John Simpson, "The Closing of the American Media," *The Spectator*, July 18,1992, pp. 8-9.

8. The Kurds in northern Iraq were later manipulated in a similar manner by the American government. In a variation of the 1992 campaign, President Bill Clinton ordered the bombing of Iraqi targets during the run-up to the 1996 election in supposed retaliation for Baghdad's support for one Kurdish faction against another. However, after the election was over the U.S. government seemed to make little effort to forestall the triumph of the faction it had previously opposed.

9. John L. Esposito, *The Islamic Threat: Myth or Reality?* (New York: Oxford University Press, 1993), p. 7.

10. Samir Amin, "The Real Stakes in the Gulf War," in Dave Broad and Lori Foster, eds., *The New World and the Third World Order* (Montreal: Black Rose Books, 1992), pp. 69-80 and Andre Gunder Frank, "A Third-World War: A Political Economy of the Persian Gulf War and the New World Order," in Hamid Mowlana, George Gerbner and Herbert I. Schiller, eds., *Triumph of the Image: The Media's War in the Persian Gulf—A Global Perspective* (Boulder, Colo.: Westview, 1992), pp. 3-21.

11. For example, Richard Bernstein and Ross H. Munro, *The Coming Conflict with China* (New York: Alfred A. Knopf, 1997).

12. Tuen A. van Dijk, *News Analysis: Case Studies of International and National News in the Press* (Hillsdale, New Jersey: Lawrence Erlbaum: 1988), p. 21.

13. Occasionally, other images from the World War II are also be used in the ongoing clashes of Western powers with Saddam Hussein; for example, the London tabloid *News of the World* had the large front-page headline "RAMADAN BUSTERS" on December 20, 1998, following U.S. and British aerial bombing of Iraqi targets. The reference to the Muslim holy month referred to the preceding speculation regarding the reaction to attacking a Muslim-majority country at that time; the headline also played to the popular lore in Britain about the legendary "dam busters" of the Royal Air Force who prevailed over the Nazi military in the Second World War.

14. Maher Hathout, "The 'Danger' of Islam: Now that the Spectre of Communism Has Faded, Islam Has Become the New 'Danger' to America," *The Minaret* (Jan./Feb. 1993), pp. 15-17.

15. Esposito, *The Islamic Threat*; Fred Halliday, *Islam and the Myth of Confrontation: Religion and Politics in the Middle East* (London: I.B. Tauris, 1996); James Piscatori, ed., *Islamic Fundamentalisms and the Gulf Crisis* (Chicago: American Academy of Arts and Sciences, 1991); John Sigler, "Understanding the Resurgence of Islam: The Case of Political Islam," *Middle East Affairs Journal* 2:4 (1996), pp. 79-91; and Jochen Hippler and Andrea Lueg, eds., *The Next Threat: Western Perceptions of Islam*, translated by Loula Friese (London: Pluto Press, 1995).

16. Samuel P. Huntington, "The Clash of Civilizations?" *Foreign Affairs*, (Sum. 1993), p. 48. The article was later expanded into a book titled *The Clash of Civilizations and the Remaking of World Order* (New York: Simon and Schuster, 1996).

17. Ibid, p. 49.

18. The context in which dominant Northern discourses blend Islam and communism sometimes falls outside geopolitics; for example, an editorial in the September 6, 1995 issue of *Le Devoir* (Montreal) on the authoritarian stance on women's issues in Muslim-majority states and China carried the headline: "Entre l'islam et le communisme." American television dramas sometimes bring in Cuba as the communist element allied with Muslims. For example, an episode of the dramatic television series JAG, broadcast in March 1996, had the governments of Iran and Cuba conspire together against U.S. interests.

19. Rodman Griffin, Congressional Quarterly, "'The Company' seeks a new role," *The Ottawa Citizen*, December 26, 1992, p. B3. In the Hollywood movie *True Lies* (1995), an Arab terrorist group called "Crimson Jihad" planned to launch a nuclear attack on the United States from inside the country. It had obtained four war heads from Kazakhstan.

20. Tim Weiner, The New York Times, "U.S., Russia co-operate on spy network," *The Ottawa Citizen*, January 20, 1996, p. D10.

21. David Sapsted, The Daily Telegraph, "End of Cold War freezes out U.S. spies," *The Ottawa Citizen*, September 19, 1998, p. A10.

22. Reuters, "NATO chief warns of Islamic extremists: 'As dangerous as communism was,'" *The Globe and Mail*, March 20, 1995, p. A17.

23. A March 2, 1997 editorial in *Le Monde* (Paris), which was translated and reprinted in *The Guardian Weekly* (Manchester), stated in a discussion about NATO that the Mediterranean was "the region that has become the most strategically sensitive for Europe since the end of the cold war."

24. For example, Adel Safty, "Political Islam: the two sides of the coin," *The Globe and the Mail*, July 6, 1993, p. A23; Adrian Hastings, The Guardian, "Church Has Failed Bosnia," *The Ottawa Citizen*, July 10, 1993, p. C5; Almas Alam, "'Fundamentalist' label is used with curious selectivity," *The Toronto Star*, December 27, 1993, p. A33; and Martin van Creveld, New Perspectives Quarterly, "The monster terrorism breeds," *The Ottawa Citizen*, August 29, 1998, p. B7.

25. For example Gwynne Dyer, "Sinister Arab replacing 'Reds' as all-purpose foe," *The Toronto Star*, March 16, 1992, p. A17; Stanley K. Sheinbaum, "Just Think ...," *New Perspectives Quarterly* (Spr. 1992), p. 64; Editorial, "Islam Revisited," *The Globe and Mail*, February 6, 1995, p. A20); Elaine Sciolino, "Seeing Green: The Red Menace is Gone. But Here's Islam," *The New York Times*, January 21, 1996, pp. E4, E6; Jay Stone, "Billionaires, bombers and belly dancers," *The Ottawa Citizen*, March 17, 1996, p. C1; and Andrew Phillips and Barry Came, "The Prime Suspect," *Maclean's*, January 24, 2000, p. 27.

26. Jacques Ellul, *Propaganda: The Formation of Men's Attitudes*, translated by Konrad Kellen and Jean Lerner (New York: Alfred A. Knopf, 1969), p. 47.

27. In a slip of the tongue during a television interview, former British prime minister John Major referred to the actions "the West" was taking against Saddam Hussein before quickly catching himself and replacing the term with "the world community"—which itself is a euphemism for the international consensus often induced by Northern powers in their own favour. Huntington, "The Clash of Civilizations?" pp. 39-40.

28. Zuhair Kashmeri, *The Gulf Within: Canadian Arabs, Racism and the Gulf War* (Toronto: James Lorimer, 1991), back cover.

CHAPTER 8

RETURNING TO A MILLENNIAL STRUGGLE

Four Horsemen of the Apocalypse

The Gulf War was the first major conflict that Western powers engaged in after the end of the Cold War. It seemed to become an occasion for integration propagandists to construct a sweeping image of civilization in apocalyptical struggle with barbarism, of two long-standing foes engaging in millennial conflict. Apart from the continual barrage in the daily media, the Gulf War was the subject of longer "think pieces" in American magazines published in the period from Iraq's invasion of Kuwait in August 1990 to the end of the Gulf War in February 1991. They painted a picture in which Muslims and the West were separated by fundamental differences. Among such write-ups were those by four influential Western ideologues, Bernard Lewis, Daniel Pipes, V.S. Naipaul, and William Pfaff, in *The Atlantic*, *The National Review*, *The New York Review of Books*, and *The New Yorker*, respectively. Although these four U.S. periodicals do not have as large circulations as *Time* and *Newsweek* (or *Maclean's* in Canada), their readerships would seem to include opinion-leaders such as journalists.

While criticizing the general mass media coverage of the Gulf War in his February 28, 1991 column in *The Globe and Mail*, Ray Conlogue stated:

> The thoughtful American journals, fortunately, have been analysing the racism and historical contempt for Islam that lies behind this campaign. William Pfaff's admirable Reflections: Islam and the West in the Jan. 28 issue of New Yorker, together with Bernard Lewis's The Roots of Muslim Rage in the September issue of Atlantic magazine are among the best.

The February 11 cover story of *Maclean's* on "Islam and the Gulf War" by D'Arcy Jenish also referred to Bernard Lewis's article as a key source of information. The writers of the longer essays, whose own distortions of Islam remained invisible to such journalists, are considered "experts" on the subject and are frequently quoted by the mass media. Think pieces on Islam in high-profile periodicals seem to appear during critical events in Muslim societies, allowing their authors to make far-reaching generalizations that influence the conceptualization of these events. The four long articles written during the Gulf War all framed relations between Western and Muslim civilizations as essentially conflictual. They appeared to subscribe to what Benjamin Barber cites as the "exceptionalist thesis," according to which "Islam creates an exceptional set of circumstances that disqualify Islamic countries from becoming democratic and fates them to an eternal struggle against the Enlightenment and its liberal and democratic children."[1] Whereas other incidents such as "the Rushdie affair" had also precipitated similar constructions, integration propagandists seemed compelled to develop a grander ideological scenario in order to justify the marshalling of overwhelming military might against one developing, albeit heavily armed country.

Published in the month following Iraq's invasion of Kuwait, Bernard Lewis's "The Roots of Muslim Rage" was the September 1990 cover story in *The Atlantic*. Apparently stung by criticism of his previous work by the likes of Edward Said, Lewis seemed careful in couching his write-up within prefatory remarks that lauded the historical contributions of Muslims, and specified that the "Muslim world is far from unanimous in its rejection of the West." However, the general tenor of the article was to demonstrate an essential divergence between the Muslim and Northern civilizations. On the cover page of the monthly was a drawing styled in the manner of the official portraits of Ottoman sultans; but the bearded man in the turban scowled fiercely and in each eye had the image of an American flag—the object of his "Muslim rage." The Orientalist scholar placed the contemporary conflict within a millennial struggle between the two civilizations (without bothering to deal with the awkward questions of why Saddam Hussein had followed a rigorous program of modernization, promoted protective measures for Christian and Jewish minorities, and persecuted Muslim activists in Iraq):

> The struggle between the two rival systems has now lasted for some fourteen centuries. It began with the advent of Islam, in the seventh century, and has continued virtually to the present day. It has consisted of a long series of attacks and counterattacks, jihads and crusades, conquests and reconquests...For the past three hundred years, since the failure of the second Turkish siege of Vienna in 1683 and the rise of the European colonial empires in Asia and Africa, Islam has been on the defensive, and the Christian and post-Christian civilization of Europe and her daughters has brought the whole world, including Islam, within its orbit.

Centuries of history were collapsed together to support the notion that the two rival monoliths have been fighting the same war "for some fourteen centuries." This is typical of the tendencies of a number of Orientalists who favour sweeping generalizations about Muslims.[2]

Having painted the backdrop of the millennial conflict, Lewis then proceeded to expound upon the reasons why his undifferentiated, stereotypical Muslim was enraged at contemporary Christendom.

The Muslim has suffered successive stages of defeat. The first was his loss of domination in the world, to the advancing power of Russia and the West. The second was the undermining of his authority in his own country, through an invasion of foreign ideas and laws and ways of life and sometimes even foreign rulers and settlers, and the enfranchisement of native non-Muslim elements. The third—the last straw—was the challenge to his mastery in his own house, from emancipated women and rebellious children. It was too much to endure, and the outbreak of rage against these alien, infidel, and incomprehensible forces that had subverted his dominance, disrupted his society and finally violated the sanctuary of his home was inevitable. It was also natural that this rage should be directed primarily against the millennial enemy and should draw its strength from ancient beliefs and loyalties.

In Lewis's view, even though the Muslim lived in the twentieth century he had medieval sensibilities and hatreds: whereas his feelings of resentment at being defeated and colonized may be understandable, his perceived rage at the supposed emancipation of his women and children was not. Thus, our heroic invasion and bombing of the Iraqi's territory could be justified in the interests of safeguarding the human rights of his female and infant victims, within the dramaturgy of the larger, millennial struggle offered by this historian. Lewis wrote further that Muslims were not upset about imperialism *per se*, in which Western powers were "merely following the common practice of mankind through the millennia of recorded history," but were incensed with the colonization of Muslims by "infidels": "This may help us to understand the current troubles in such diverse places as Ethiopian Eritrea, Indian Kashmir, Chinese Sinkiang, and Yugoslavian Kossovo, in all of which Muslim populations are ruled by non-Muslim governments." The particularity of political, economic, and historical causes of rebellions against central governments by peoples who happened to be Muslim were negated because all followers of Islam were always motivated by medieval religious impulses. (Lewis said nothing about the involvement of Christian Eritreans in the war against the Ethiopian government, the role of churches in political and military movements in places such as Poland, the Baltic republics, and Latin America, or the influence of religious Jews in Israeli politics.)

Lewis asserted that it was not in anti-colonialism, anti-Zionism, Nazism, or Marxism in which the fundamental "roots of Muslim rage" against the West were to be found. The real source was much more elemental—it was the fear of Western capitalism and democracy "which provide an authentic and attractive alternative to traditional ways of thought and life." In contrast to fascists or communists, Muslims were opposed to the entire project of modernity. Unlike scholars like Fatima Mernissi, who has attempted to carry out an historical and social psychological inquiry about the ambivalence of the political elites of Muslim countries towards democracy, on the one hand, and the democratic aspirations of the citizens, on the other[3], Lewis offered a unidimensional view of Muslims having cultures completely antithetical to those of the West.

> It should by now be clear that we are facing a mood and a movement far transcending the level of issues and policies and the governments that pursue them. This is no less than a clash of civilizations—the perhaps irrational but surely historic reaction of an ancient rival against our Judeo-Christian heritage, our secular present, and the worldwide expansion of both.

This was not just a military conflict but one of historical, even apocalyptic proportions: "a clash of civilizations," "our Judeo-Christian heritage" against "Islam"—good versus evil. (Samuel Huntington adopted from Lewis the notion of the "clash of civilizations" to formulate the basis of his controversial thesis on international relations.) The thrust of the message was: we have to support the war against Iraq because it is part of a larger challenge to our heritage and to our future.

Daniel Pipes, another Orientalist who also frequently appears as an "expert" on Islam in the mass media, published the lead article titled "The Muslims are Coming! The Muslims are Coming!" in the November 19, 1990 issue of the bi-weekly *National Review*. The heading echoed the legendary alarm raised by Paul Revere during the American Revolutionary War: "The British are coming! The British are coming!" On the cover of the magazine was a photograph of a group of men in traditional Arab garments riding camels full gallop directly at the camera; a promotional card attached to the magazine cover read, "MANY WESTERNERS FEEL MORE THREATENED BY THEIR MUSLIM IMMIGRANT NEIGHBOURS THAN BY SADDAM HUSSEIN." The focus here shifted towards Muslims living in Western countries, who were presented as a fifth column in the global struggle between Islam and the West.

> All immigrants bring exotic customs and attitudes, but Muslim customs are more troublesome than most. Also, Muslims appear most resistant to assimilation. Elements among the Pakistanis in Britain, Algerians in France, and Turks in Germany seek to turn the host into an Islamic society by compelling it to adapt their way of life.

What effect such constructions of immigrant Muslim communities may have had during the war against Iraq is difficult to assess accurately; however, there were numerous reports of attacks, ranging from verbal abuse to destruction of property and physical assaults, against people of Arab and Muslim backgrounds in various Western countries.[4]

Although Pipes stated that all Muslims could not be seen as the "paramount enemy" and that only "dyed-in-the-wool fundamentalists" hated the West, he went on to develop an image of a fearsome threat from Muslim societies. Like Lewis he constructed an image of Muslims as being very different from Westerners. In this scenario, the Iraqi regime against whom Western powers were preparing to go to war, was presented as a "Muslim government":

Today, many Muslim governments dispose of large arsenals; the Iraqi army, for example, has more tanks than does the German, and the nuclear missiles banned from Europe by the Intermediate Nuclear Force treaty can be found in the Middle East. Middle Eastern states have turned to terrorism into a tool of statecraft. About a dozen Muslim states have chemical and biological war capabilities. Impressive capacities to manufacture a wide range of matériel have been established in Egypt, Iraq, Iran, Pakistan, and Indonesia. Before long, several of these states are likely to deploy atomic bombs.

Muslim countries have the most terrorists and the fewest democracies in the world. Only Turkey (and sometimes Pakistan) is fully democratic, and even there the system is frail. Everywhere else, the head of the government got to power through force—his own or someone else's. The result is endemic instability plus a great deal of aggression.

Pipes did not discuss the role of Western powers in sustaining aggressive capabilities and instability in Muslim-majority and other countries around the world, nor did he touch upon the proliferation of armaments in states such as Israel, India, or Brazil—to say nothing of the five elite powers. (His oblique reference to the presence of nuclear missiles in the Middle East seems to have studiously avoided mentioning Israel, the only country known to have nuclear capability in that region.) Only the acquisitiveness of the Muslim-majority governments in obtaining the tools of violence is highlighted.

What strategies should the West adopt in the face of such alarming developments? Pipes surveyed various "imaginative" and "provocative" proposals regarding the response Western states should take in face of the peril from Muslim societies. He constructed a scenario of a world war, pitting industrial democracies/Christendom against a global "fundamentalist Islamic wedge":

Some say the key is building cooperation among Western states. On the mundane level, industrial democracies should band together and preserve the liberal traditions of freedom of speech, freedom of religion, and the like; and they should cooperate against terrorism and other acts of violence. NATO should be extended outside the European theater. SDI [Strategic Defence Initiative, i.e., "Star Wars"] should be developed for use against Iraqi or Libyan missiles.

More imaginative are those who would reach out to the Christian portions of the Soviet empire as an ally against the Muslims. As the three Slavic republics, the three Baltic republics, and Moldavia, Georgia, and Armenia return to their historic allegiances, they can extend the reach of Europe eastward. The more provocative notion involves building a military alliance with these peoples, especially the Russians. The London *Sunday Times* calls on the West and the Soviet Union jointly to "prepare for the prospect of an enormous and fundamentalist Islamic wedge" stretching from Morocco to China. William Lind has suggested that "Russia's role as part of the West takes on special importance in the light of potential Islamic revival…The Soviet Union holds the West's right flank, stretching from the Black Sea to Vladivostock."

We see here the strengthening of the idea of a Christian North in the post-Cold War era. The internecine European war that had lasted most of the twentieth century was over, and it was time once again to face the real enemy in the South. Pipes quoted the historian Walter McDougall, who also presented Russia as

> …holding the frontier of Christendom against its common enemy. Should the Russian empire in Central Asia threaten to collapse, a full-scale religious war fought with nuclear, chemical, and biological weapons is not impossible. The Iraqis and Iranis [sic] have already proven themselves capable of it, and the desperate and frustrated Russians certainly possess the means. Even more than Israel/Palestine, the old caravan routes may contain the site of the next Sarajevo.

Secular governments in countries such as Iraq and those in Central Asia became "Muslim" and those in Western Europe and the former Soviet Union "Christian" in these constructions of the new post-Cold War global order. Missiles targeted at each other by NATO and the Warsaw Pact are to be re-directed southwards against the Muslim hordes. (One can imagine the frenzied rearming of "Christian" and "Muslim" governments and minorities by the Northern military-industrial complexes, which would gleefully respond to this global re-alignment of loyalties.[5]) For Pipes these ideas "are a great improvement over the supine policies that many Western states, especially European ones, have adopted in recent years." He seems to suggest that, in light of the larger clash of civilizations, Northern integration propagandists should be able to lie about the real capabilities of the Muslim enemy: "It is better to exaggerate the danger of Libyan thuggery than to lick Qaddafi's boots—as too many Westerners have done since the oil boom of 1973-74."[6] Pipes' article, which was published at the time when Western governments' were seeking to present Iraq as a massively armed state that could only be defeated by enormous military strength, probably aided in creating a general frame of mind that saw the trasnational media uncritically adopt a sharp "us versus them" approach to reporting the conflict.

On January 31, 1991, as UN Coalition forces were bombing Iraq, *The New York Review of Books* published an address that V.S. Naipaul made to the Manhattan Institute in New York. An acclaimed writer who lives in London, Naipaul was born in Trinidad and is of Indian descent. His novels and non-fiction publications have frequently referred to Muslims, mostly in negative contexts: "For Naipaul and his readers, 'Islam' somehow is made to cover everything that one most disapproves of from the standpoint of civilized, and Western, rationality."[7] In 1981, he published a political travelogue that narrated his whirlwind tour of Iran, Pakistan, and Malaysia. It was in writing this book, Naipaul disclosed, that he "formulated the idea of universal civilization."[8] He based his remarks to the Manhattan Institute on this notion. However, his universal civilization did not include Muslim societies; instead in the latter, "the faith was the complete way, filled everything, left no spare corner of the mind or will or soul, [compared] to the other world where it was necessary to be an individual and responsible; where people developed vocations, and were stirred by ambition and achievement, and believed in perfectibility." This manichean scheme, through which he contrasted the light of the universal civilization with the darkness of "Islam," was presented as a response to the request of a senior fellow of the institute who had asked him to address "Why is Islam held in opposition to Western values?"

Naipaul's construct ideologically supported the emerging notion of a global conflict between Western civilization and Muslims at the particular time when the West was going to war against Iraq. This highly skilled propagandist was able to weave into his narrative the historical place of Iraq in "a terrible story of plunder and killing...[written in the] Arab or Muslim imperial genre." This story was drawn from a thirteenth-century Persian account of the eighth-century Arab conquest of the Hindu region of Sindh, located in what is now Pakistan. Naipaul expressed astonishment at the adulation of contemporary (Muslim) Sindhis for the Arab conquerors of their ancestors. This was used to illustrate how the "doubly-colonized" non-Arab Muslims "had been stripped by their faith of all that expanding intellectual life, all the varied life of the mind and the senses, the expanding cultural and historical knowledge of the world." His presentation attempted to demonstrate the mind-numbing servility that he perceived among Muslims in Iran, Pakistan, and Malaysia, who were beholden to an alien Arab religion. Naipaul depicted the adherence to Islam as a far worse colonization than that by European powers. The message here was that it was the duty of the bearers of the universal civilization to liberate non-Arab Muslims from Islamic ideas, which "in the end [will] blow away." In this way he skilfully managed to link current events in the contemporary state of Iraq, in the guise of the global Other, to the origins of regressive "Islam." On the other hand, Naipaul found "the Christian precept, Do unto others as you would have others do unto you" to be one of the bases of the universal civilization. Therefore, whereas Islam and even his own ancestral Hinduism were cast away as entirely unfit for the modern age, he presented aspects of Christianity as still relevant. This was akin to Lewis's linking of contemporary Western civilization to "our Judeo-Christian heritage."

William Pfaff's "Reflections" on "Islam and the West" appeared in *The New Yorker* in the same week as Naipaul's *New York Review of Books* article. Like the former, the syndicated, Paris-based American columnist on international affairs, argued that it was Islam that was holding Muslims back from becoming modern. Exhibiting an understanding of Muslim history that was a little broader than Naipaul's, Pfaff, however, often appeared contradictory—listing the scientific achievements of Muslim civilization while at the same time portraying it as essentially lacking in intellectual creativity. He stereotypically characterized Islam as "a religion of nomads," thus disregarding the complexity and diversity of urban Muslim cultures as well as the fact that Muhammad himself was a city-dweller. "The scientific and technological failure of Islamic civilization reflects the fact that nomadic technology, on the whole, is fixed; it lacks a capacity for development because, except in the military sphere, it has no need for it." Like Lewis and Naipaul, Pfaff saw the source of modern Western civilization in the West's religious heritage. While insisting that Islam was responsible for the Muslim failure to modernize, he located the roots of Western technological progress in the Bible and in the intellectual endeavours of Christian theologians such as Thomas Aquinas. Pfaff built his image of two essentially different worlds by emphasizing what he viewed as the absence of speculative theology in the Muslim civilization and its inability to respond to historical change in contrast to the "culturally and economically aggressive modern West."

The columnist wrote that the failure of contemporary Muslim states was due to their reluctance to embrace wholeheartedly Western ideologies and Western ways of life. Attempts at seeking a "synthesis of civilizations" were "likely to lack authenticity" since the Muslim world view did not have the intellectual tools to develop a practical program "for ordinary people in an integrally religious society." The only option that remained therefore was the complete Muslim surrender to Western ideas, which presumably would provide the means for such people to become authentically modern. Even as the article weakly argued against Western intervention in Iraq, it pointed out that the real war was long-term and ideological.

What has happened in Iraq, and happened before that in Iran, and the terrible traumas that have been produced by the struggle between the Palestinians and the Israelis all arise from the provisional defeat of a people and a religion by a rival, yet related, civilization. This is what the crisis in the Middle East is fundamentally about. The grievances (and grief) of modern Islam, its paranoia and defiance come from that.

Reducing territorial conflicts such as that between Israelis and Palestinians as arising from religious defeat, the author set the stage for another millennial struggle between Islam and Northern Christendom, which had been briefly diverted by the fratricidal Cold War. Pfaff's scenario, in adherence to dominant discourses, had rendered Palestinian, Iraqi, and other Middle Eastern Christians nonentities.

These four articles are examples of how the war with Iraq became an opportunity for Western ideologues to develop the model of a global conflict of historical proportions between the North and Muslims. The attention created among the public by the Gulf War enabled integration propagandists such as these to put forward elaborate schemes that provided cultural and moral frameworks for going to war against a country with a Muslim majority. Their essays, which attempted to paint the bigger picture, could dwell on the "roots," "fundamentals," and "universals" of the millennial conflict between an essentially irreconcilable pair of antagonists, and provided the framework for the media reports on the war. With the decline of the atheist Soviet Union, Northern propagandists could once again talk about a Christendom in conflict with Muslims all over the world including former Soviet Central Asia. The revival of the Muslim as a primary Other was not difficult to achieve since the memory of the long struggle between Christian Europe and the Muslim East could be invoked by using cognitive models extant even in the secular North's literary and artistic corpus. Additionally, the specific conflicts of Northern powers against countries with Muslim majorities could also be portrayed as belonging to the same age-old struggle. Whereas the Oriental Other includes the "yellow peril" from the Far East (witness the occasional bouts of criticism against China and Japan by North American and European ideologues) and other threatening images derived from Asia, Africa, and Latin America, the most persistent presentation of danger has been focused on Islam. The exploitation of Islamic symbols by the religious and secularist leaders of Muslim states in their anti-Northern rhetoric facilitates the task of the Northern propagandists. All this seems to have encouraged the rise of the image of a (post-Christian) North re-engaging in its millennial confrontation with Islam.

A Global Media Narrative

Whereas the major news networks had previously glossed over Saddam Hussein's brutal repression of certain sections of the Iraqi population, mainstream journalists covering the Gulf War vied with each other to uncover his slightest misdemeanour. The mass media reportage of the conflict manifested a global narrative. This is confirmed by the findings of a large number of studies about the coverage in Canada, the United States, Britain, Ireland, India, Malaysia, Japan, Turkey, Iran, Jordan, Egypt, Brazil, Spain/Catalonia, Soviet Union, Finland, Norway, and Sweden.[9] Reporting on the war was constrained by the structural nature of news production and the hegemony of Western news networks, particularly the Atlanta-based Cable News Network which became a transnational purveyor of "live" television coverage. With a few exceptions, most of the 1,400 foreign journalists covering the Gulf War from Saudi Arabia and Israel abided by the military restrictions. The range of coverage was limited by the American-led UN Coalition forces' control of media access through news pools and the Iraqi, Saudi, and Israeli censoring of reporters' accounts. Even anti-US newspapers in countries such as Iran were largely dependent on Western news agencies as sources.[10] Among the most enthusiastic supporters of the news pool system, which was overwhelmingly dominated by American and British news organizations, was NBC's Canadian-born reporter, Arthur Kent—who came to be known as "the Scud Stud."

Canadian television networks, like television networks around the world, used CNN feeds to a large extent in their coverage of the Gulf War. Whereas there was less reliance on American sources in the print media in Canada, newspapers did print a substantial number of articles from American and British news services. And although a few journalists did challenge the information and justifications offered by Western politicians for carrying out the mainly one-sided war against a less developed country, most media seemed to have been reduced to the status of cheerleaders for the Coalition forces.[11] The murmurs of oppositional and alternative voices were drowned out by the torrent of reports and analyses couched in dominant discourses.

The few high profile attempts to get the other side of the story were severely criticized in Western countries. CNN's Peter Arnett, the only American television journalist to remain in Iraq after the bombing had begun, was widely lambasted for being an Iraqi sympathizer after interviewing Saddam Hussein and reporting that a factory producing baby milk formula had been destroyed by Coalition air attacks.[12] A *Toronto Sun* editorial on January 18, 1991 titled "TV terrorists" stated:

It was a Twilight Zone show. With much of civilization at war with Iraq, there was CNN yesterday giving a free ride to enemy propaganda.

Abdul Amir al-Anbari, Iraq's ambassador to the United Nations, blithely defended Saddam Hussein's frightening Scud missile attack on Israel. It was justified by years of Israeli aggression, he said.

The exchange crystallizes a key issue in every war. When do the media cross the line from being objective observers to giving aid and comfort to the enemy?

"Objectivity" has never meant simply turning on the microphone to everyone and anyone.

Journalistic objectivity, in this view, seemed to imply turning cameras and microphones only to authorized knowers. Some Conservative Party members of parliament in Britain dubbed the BBC the "Baghdad Broadcasting Corporation" for showing pictures of the civilian victims of an American air raid on the Iraqi capital.[13] Israeli censors took NBC's Martin Fletcher off the air "for reporting what were said to be too many details about a Scud attack on Tel Aviv."[14] Contrary to the findings of most researchers on the war's coverage by Western mass media organizations, the Vancouver-based National Media Archive—a branch of the right-wing Fraser Institute—found Canadian and US television networks to be "An Extension of 'Radio Iraq.'"[15] A similar assessment was made of the Canadian Broadcasting Corporation by a board member of the corporation, John Crispo.[16] There are therefore strong checks on any journalist who dares to present other than a consensual viewpoint on a matter of such importance as a war in which her country is involved.

The major tendencies of the Gulf War coverage were to demonize Iraq's president and its military forces and to de-emphasize or, alternatively, glamorize the violence carried out by Coalition forces. Saddam Hussein became the personification of the country which was being pulverized by Western warjets: since the primary coverage focused on him personally (it was "Saddam's" missiles, tanks, planes, and buildings that were targetted) the systemic destruction of the economic infrastructure of the country went largely unreported during the war. American sources generally described the continual bombing of Baghdad in celebratory terms, relating it to "the fireworks finale on the Fourth of July"; television audiences were enthralled by the pyrotechnic effects of the "smart bombs" and the wizardry of the state of the art technology. Even ABC's Peter Jennings, seen to be the least jingoistic of American network news anchors (a tendency he attributed to his Canadian origins), remarked in wonder at the "brilliance of laser-guided bombs."[17] Unlike the Vietnam War, there were few pictures of dead people—the Gulf War was mainly presented as a clean conflict in which mostly SCUD missiles and Iraqi military sites were destroyed with minimal "collateral damage" (i.e., human casualties).

The only people to be portrayed as victims in the early weeks of the war were Western pilots who had been captured by the Iraqi forces. On January 22, 1991, after the Baghdad government had indicated it would locate these prisoners of war in factories and schools, the front pages of many newspapers described them as "human targets" since they had become vulnerable to the Coalition's attacks. The implication was that the relentless bombing for a whole week by the United Nations Coalition forces had not hurt any human beings. This event reinforced the media's construction of the war as a morality play. In response to the Iraqi tactic, the British prime minister remarked about Hussein, "It is perfectly clear that this man is amoral."[18] The entire conflict was presented as a battle between good and evil, the civilized and the barbaric. The American president said about the involvement of the US in the war, "Our cause in just. Our cause is moral. Our cause is right."[19] Canada's prime minister was quoted by newspapers as stating that one of the main issues guiding its involvement in the Gulf War was "simple morality…a terrible wrong has been perpetrated in Kuwait by Saddam Hussein and the world community has a moral obligation to step in and stop it."[20]

Illustration 7: The Gulf War as a morality play

He characterized the first Iraqi missile attack on Israel as "a very evil act by a very diabolical man," and an opposition party member who had been against Canadian involvement in the war, described it as "barbarism on top of barbarism."[21] The German foreign minister compared Hussein's attack against Israel as an attempt at "genocide."[22]

The extreme demonization of the Iraqi president served to conceal the scale of violence being carried out by the UN forces. A *Jordanian Times* editorial stated,

When Saddam sends 38 Scud missiles into Israel he is a terrorist and when the American coalition makes over 90,000 sorties in one month and throws more than 100 thousand tonnes of explosives, mostly over Iraqi and Kuwaiti civilian targets, they are champions of justice.[23]

(Jordan's government supported Iraq in the war, although it was not militarily involved.) Whereas Western journalists exaggerated the effect of SCUD missiles "raining" on Israel and Saudi Arabia, they had largely disregarded the horror caused by some two hundred Iraqi SCUDs landing on Iranian cities between 1987 and 1988 during the Iran-Iraq War.[24] Many Western journalists covering the Gulf War speculated that SCUD missile warheads would carry poison gas. On January 17, in reporting the first SCUD against Israel, a Canadian Broadcasting Corporation radio news bulletin actually declared that a mustard gas attack was under way. "In fact, the Americans were the only ones to use chemical warfare, in the form of napalm...[but this] was buried in the war coverage."[25]

One Saudi Arabian civilian, thirteen Israeli civilians, and twenty-eight American soldiers were killed as a result of Iraqi SCUD attacks during the Gulf War. On the other hand, US military and CIA estimates of Iraqi dead in the war ranged between 100,000 and 250,000. These figures included those killed by Coalition missiles launched from the air, land, and sea, as well as by other methods such as the burying alive by American forces of Iraqi troops *en masse* in their trenches and the annihilation of an Iraqi military column retreating from Kuwait on what came to be known as "the highway of death." A Harvard University medical team's survey of Iraq estimated in May 1991 that, due to the deliberate Coalition bombing of civilian installations including electricity generating stations across the country, 170,000 more Iraqi children would die in that year alone.[26] Yet, during the war Western mass media largely portrayed "violence" as being carried out by the Iraqi military and not by the United Nations Coalition's forces. The host of ABC's *Nightline* program declared nearly a week into the almost continual bombing of Iraqi cities, "Aside from the Scud missile that landed in Tel Aviv earlier, it's been a quiet night in the Middle East."[27] It was as if mainstream Western journalists had become completely oblivious to the massive violence that their governments were carrying out.

Before, during, and after the war, there was a steady stream of negative journalistic descriptions of the Iraqi president as the cause of all the problems not only in the region but in the entire world. In the run up to the hostilities, a

January 13 editorial in *The Montreal Gazette* stated that the Gulf War "is the war of every country which values international law and order and the containment of aggression." And at the start of the Coalition's bombing *The Ottawa Sun* declared on January 17: "Now that the fighting has begun, the goal must be a speedy allied victory: The liberation of Kuwait, the return of Iraq to the community of civilized countries and, at long last, the establishment of peace and stability throughout the Middle East." Hussein was responsible for dashing the hope of global peace in the post-Cold War era. An *Ottawa Citizen* editorial of February 16 said: "Half a year ago, many people in the democratic and newly democratising world had begun to hope that war had become obsolete, a shameful anachronism. That was before Aug. 2, when Saddam Hussein's army shot its way into Kuwait." And the daily explained in the February 23 issue why George Bush, as leader of the "free world," felt compelled to go to war to restore global order. He said, "It is a big idea: a new world order, where diverse nations are drawn together in common cause to achieve the universal aspirations of mankind: peace and security, freedom and the rule of law."

Illustration 8: Seeking peace through war

The just war had to be fought in order to (re)instate peace—another war to end all wars, following which utopia would be established. "Smart bombs" would carry out "surgical strikes" to eliminate diseased tissue from body of the Middle East and make it whole again. Even Richard Gwyn, a *Toronto Star* columnist played to the same tune of peace through war on January 16: "Once our bombs and missiles have completed their mission—as they will—we are going to have to start listening to the voice of the Middle East." Before we "start listening to the voice of the Middle East" we have to pulverize it with our weapons. As many times before in human history, peace was sought through violence.

Dehumanization and Demonization

There was a very clear tendency among Western propagandists to dehumanize the Iraqi forces, as often occurs in cultural constructions of the military enemy. *The Globe and Mail* quoted General Norman Schwarzkopf, the operational head of the Coalition forces, in a February 28, 1991 article saying that the Iraqi invaders of Kuwait were not part of "the same human race as we are." An American pilot returning from destroying Iraqi tanks in a night mission said on television, "It's almost like you flipped on the light in the kitchen at night and the cockroaches started scurrying and we're killing them."[28] This particular type of comparison of Iraqis with insects was quite common. An army surplus store in Saskatoon, Saskatchewan, printed up T-shirts with a mock advertisement for a bogus "Iraqnophobia" movie, parodying the 1990 film *Arachnophobia* (the fear of spiders).[29] Iraqis were also likened to wild game:

> During the brief land war launched by Washington, the allies shot thousands of fleeing Iraqi soldiers and civilians in the back. The shooting was described as being like "a giant hunt." The Iraqis were driven ahead, "like animals," by the allied air and land attacks. U.S. pilots were said to have likened their attack on the convoy to "shooting fish in a barrel." The retreating Iraqis were said to have presented a "bounty of targets." "We hit the jackpot," one pilot said. "It was like a turkey shoot."[30]

The term "turkey shoot," says Noam Chomsky, was used at the turn of the century during the US troops' slaughter of Filipinos: "one of those deeply rooted themes of the culture that surfaces as if by reflex at appropriate moments."[31]

Much of the dehumanization of Iraqis was focused on Saddam Hussein, who had come to embody the country that was being bombed. A few days after Iraq invaded Kuwait, a *Washington Post* columnist wrote an essay with the headline "Bush and the Beast of Baghdad."[32]

> Two weeks into the Gulf War, the *New York Times* published an unusually large cartoon across the top of the op-ed page. Titled "The Descent of Man," it showed from left to right a Clark Gable-like man in a suit and tie, a gorilla, a monkey, a venomous snake, and finally Saddam Hussein, depicted as small and filthy with a cloud of flies surrounding his head. This grotesque caricature was reminiscent of Nazi propaganda that presented Jews as subhuman, and Ku Klux Klan literature comparing African-Americans to apes.[33]

Hussein was also described as a "monster," "devil," "Satan," and "the Antichrist." He was often portrayed as acting out stereotypically Arab tendencies. In this, Western propagandists were adhering to the cognitive scripts according to which Arabs and Muslims supposedly act. An *Ottawa Citizen* journalist described the Iraqi leader in a February 4, 1991 article as "no more than a very proficient Arab terrorist," who would use chemical weapons in the war. A few days before the war began, Jean-V. Allard, a retired Canadian brigadier-general, was reported by Montreal's *La Presse* as saying, "C'est un fanatique; comme les autres Arabes, et il ne mérite pas d'être membre des Nations Unies et d'autres organismes du genre: ça n'a plus de sens. Les Arabes, ce sont des bandits." An NBC backgrounder, rebroadcast by CBC's Newsworld service on January 20, traced what it viewed as the inherent nature of contemporary Iraq's violent tendencies to the medieval Muslim civilization and all the way back to the Sumerians. An article reprinted from *The San Francisco Examiner* in *The Ottawa Citizen* of January 17, claimed to uncover the socio-psychological reasons for a seemingly inexplicable strategy that the Iraqi president had adopted: "The answer lies in the mind of Saddam and in the profound forces of Middle East history, culture and thinking that have nurtured the nihilistic side of the Arab mind." Another piece from *The Financial Times* of London published in the Insight section of the Toronto-based *Financial Post* on January 23 stated that "the Palestinian question is so deeply embedded in the psyche of the whole Arab world that every problem in the region is tainted by it." The "Arab psyche" was used to explain Saddam Hussein's actions: he was the manifestation of millennia of Arab history and cultural (mal)development that had produced congenital nihilism, barbarism, and propensity towards violence.

Descriptions of other non-Iraqi Arabs prior to the Coalition's offensive were also couched within negative frames. A *Los Angeles Times* report, used by *The Ottawa Citizen* on August 11, 1990, related the Arab League's deliberations on the Iraqi invasion of Kuwait in this manner: "While the international community has demonstrated unprecedented unity in trying to force President Hussein to retreat, the 22-member Arab bloc is in confused disarray." The "international community"—a euphemism for countries led and dominated by Western powers—was thus distinguished from the "Arab bloc." Another article in the same issue of the Ottawa daily reprinted from *The New York Times* stated that the disagreement in the Arab League "essentially pitted pro-western states, particularly the oil-rich against the radicals." Thus, Syria—a longtime pariah for Americans and on the U.S. State Department's list of "terrorist states"—was no longer a radical since it had sided with the West against Iraq. (No mention was made of Libya, which was both oil-rich and on the same State Department list; it had not joined the UN Coalition nor did it support Iraq militarily.)

Even after some Arab governments decided to become part of the Coalition, there were frequent references to their lack of resolve and to their potential treachery towards the "international community." Three days after the UN attack began the publisher of *The Ottawa Citizen* wrote an editorial titled, "A necessary and just war" stating that "The volatility of the quite remarkable international coalition, particularly the Arab component, and of its collective will to act against Hussein and his dreams of regional domination and continuing holy wars demanded action sooner rather than later." Thus, the "volatility...of the Arab component" of the Coalition became the reason for not letting economic sanctions and negotiations take their course, which many voices in the West and elsewhere were urging. Even in the third week of the war, a columnist for the paper wrote, "Under pressure from their own anti-Israeli publics, they [Arab members of the Coalition] might swivel their missile launchers toward Israel—or just quit the war altogether." On February 6, a *Globe and Mail* write-up suggested that if "support for the war were to flag seriously in the West and the military campaign lose steam" then Syria's president Hafez "Assad will be the first to jump ship, get out of the coalition." (As it turned out, the UN Coalition remained intact to the end of the war.)

Judging from the focus on Muslims in the Western mass media's Gulf War coverage, it would appear that "Arab" or "Iraqi" exclusively connoted "Muslim." The substantial Iraqi Christian minority was virtually ignored. Tariq Aziz, the Iraqi foreign minister who was ubiquitous in the Western coverage of the Baghdad government, was rarely identified as a Christian; on the other hand, Saddam Hussein's own parading of his newly-found "Islamic" credentials were given a high profile. A *San Francisco Examiner* backgrounder on "How [the] Iraqi president looks at the situation," reprinted in *The Ottawa Citizen* on January 17, stated, "Saddam's preference for martyrdom in battle is an honored form of demise in Arab history, one that goes back to the 7th century death of Ali [sic] in the battle of Karbala. It is also a style of death that the Moslem religion rewards with an assured place in paradise, no matter what sins one may have committed." The daily also published an article on January 15 from the London-based *Independent* which carried the lead: "The most powerful armies in Christendom are now poised to fight the largest military force in the Muslim world." A cover story on "Islam and the Gulf War" in *Maclean's* edition of February 11 linked the Muslim supporters of Saddam Hussein to the "rise of fundamentalism [which] has underscored the underlying differences between the Christian and Moslem worlds." A columnist for *La Presse* stated on January 17: "Ou l'Irak est rapidement écrasé: le monde alors devra composer avec le ressentiment et l'humiliation arabes, et la montée du fanatisme islamique." Many mass media reports speculated in this way on the defeat of Iraq and the growth of "Islamic fanaticism" as a threat to the (Christian) world. Reiterating the theme outlined by "experts" like Bernard Lewis, Daniel Pipes, V.S. Naipaul, and William Pfaff, the Gulf War was presented as an apocalyptic conflict between the two world religions whose adherents had engaged in wars against each other over the last millennium.

Journalists were also not above using biblical references to describe the conflict. An *Ottawa Citizen* journalist likened the combat between the American Patriot missile and the Iraqi SCUD to that between David and Goliath in a January 23 article: "Combined with its [the Patriot's] advanced guidance system, it renders the relatively stupid, slow Scud into a Goliath facing David—except David has a laser-guided exploding stone." The ABC suppertime news broadcast on January 19, 1991 showed "an American airman in Saudi Arabia writing a message on a bomb being put in place, and then read it loud for the audience: 'If Allah doesn't answer, ask for Jesus.' "[34] In case anyone had missed the broad hints about the Gulf War being a battle between good and evil, a reporter for *The Independent* described the bombardment of Iraqi troops, in a report republished in *The Ottawa Citizen* on February 7, in this manner: "The night raids began at 7:15, barely an hour after dark, but already four huge red glows appeared in the northeast horizon like a scene from *Gotterdamerung*." An apocalyptic battle from the Wagnerian opera was used to underline that, following weeks of aerial assault, the twilight of the conflict approached with the imminent land battle.

Another article in the *Citizen* had a large headline on February 23 stating, "HIGH NOON FOR BUSH: U.S. offering one of two certainties—withdrawal from Kuwait or ground war." An accompanying drawing portrayed Bush in the guise of Gary Cooper from the movie *High Noon* (1952), wearing a sheriff's badge and carrying a gun in holster, as he strode alone and purposefully towards the reader. The Canadian newspaper and its readership shared this cognitive model with others in the world where Hollywood imagery has become part of the global cultural narrative: "Toward the end of the Gulf war when Bush issued an ultimatum to Saddam, which would expire at midday on 23 February 1991, many American and British newspapers that morning carried the headline 'High Noon.' "[35] From the Bible to Wagner to Hollywood, journalists drew on the mythic to portray the Gulf War as a personal combat between the American president as the global personification of good and his Iraqi counterpart as that of evil. In a discussion on a CBS *Sunday Morning* program, a senior reporter said that Bush had rejected the most recent proposals for peace agreed to by Iraq because without the ground war the American president would not have been able "to humiliate Saddam Hussein. He really wanted to go mano-a-mano with Hussein."[36] Global media narratives constructed the war as a combat between the protaganist, who represented Christian temperance, modern rationality and technological prowess, and the antagonist, who embodied Islamic fanaticism, medieval barbarism and mindless violence. The green Muslim monster had replaced the red communist bogeyman as the West's primary nemesis.

NOTES

1. Barber, Benjamin R. *Jihad vs. McWorld* (New York: Times Books/Random House, 1985), pp. 207-208.

2. Big picture views about what Said identifies as the "timeless Orient" are also to be found in Lewis's more recent publication titled *The Middle East: A Brief History of the Last 2,000 Years* (New York: Scribner, 1996).

3. Mernissi, Fatima, *Islam and Democracy: Fear of the Modern World*, translated by Mary Jo Lakeland (New York: Addison Wesley, 1992), pp. 42-59.

4. See Zuhair Kashmeri, *The Gulf Within: Canadian Arabs, Racism and the Gulf War* (Toronto: James Lorimer, 1991); Abu-Laban, Baha and Sharon McIrvin Abu-Laban , "The Gulf War and Its Impact on Canadians of Arab and Muslim Heritage," in Baha Abu-Laban and M. Ibrahim Alladin, eds., *Beyond the Gulf War* (Edmonton: MRF Publishers, 1991), pp. 119-42; American-Arab Anti-Discrimination Committee, *1991 Report on Anti-Arab Hate Crimes: Political and Hate Violence Against Arab-Americans* (Washington: American-Arab Anti-Discrimination Committee, 1992); and Committee to Advise the Attorney-General on Racial Vilification, *Racial Vilification in Victoria* (Melbourne, Government of Victoria: 1992). According to Hanny Hassan of the Council of the Muslim Community in Canada, even as late as 1995 some Muslim children in the country were suffering from psychological trauma resulting from harassment experienced during the Gulf War. Hanny Hassan, "Muslim Reportage in North America and Europe," presentation to The Media and Ethnicity: An International Symposium, Mississauga, Ontario, April 17, 1995. Mistreatment of Arabs and Muslims in the U.S. was also reported following the bombing of a federal building in Oklahoma City in April 1995 due to intense speculation in the mass media that this act had been carried out by "Islamic fundamentalists," until the arrest of right-wing suspects with links to white supremacist groups. According to the Council on American-Islamic Relations, 216 incidents of harassment of various degrees were carried out against Muslims across the U.S. following the bombing. "U.S. Muslims the target of discrimination, violence," *The Ottawa Citizen*, April 27, 1996, p. C7.

ISLAMIC PERIL

5. David Cortright noted about the addition of new members to NATO from Eastern Europe, in his February 26, 1997 column in *The Nation*: "Military spending in Central and Eastern European countries is already spiralling out of control. Hungary has announced a 22 percent increase in military spending for 1997, and Poland is projecting a doubling of its military budget by 2002. Much of this spending will go for the purchase of weapons from the United States and other NATO countries, providing a bonanza to arms traffickers." In a more cheerful vein, a June 19, 1997 headline in *The Ottawa Citizen* announced "NATO expansion may benefit Canadian military suppliers: Hungary, Poland and Czech Republic expected to upgrade Soviet-era inventories."

6. This is particularly noteworthy given that the Reagan administration admitted to using "disinformation" (which was published by the mass media) in its attempt to convince other Western countries like France to join its efforts to undermine the Libyan leader Muammar Qadhafi. See Bernard Weinraub, "White House and Its News: Disclosures on Libya Raise Credibility Issue," *The New York Times*, October 3, 1986, pp. A1-A2.

7. Edward W. Said, *Covering Islam: How the Media and the Experts Determine How We See the Rest of the World* (New York: Pantheon Books, 1981), p. 7.

8. V.S. Naipaul, *Among the Believers: An Islamic Journey* (London: Andre Deutsch, 1981), p. 23. He also published a sequel in 1998 titled, *Beyond Belief: Islamic Excursions Among the Converted Peoples*.

9. James Winter, *Common Cents: Media Portrayal of the Gulf War and Other Events* (Montreal: Black Rose Books, 1992) pp. 1-66; Mason Harris, "The Language of Dwarf-Killing: Orwell and Victory in the Gulf," in Mordecai Briemberg, ed., *It Was, It Was Not: Essays and Art on the War Against Iraq* (Vancouver: New Star Books, 1992), pp. 62-76; Douglas Kellner, *The Persian Gulf TV War* (Boulder, Colo.: Westview, 1992); Hamid Mowlana, George Gerbner and Herbert I. Schiller, eds., *Triumph of the Image: The Media's War in the Persian Gulf—A Global Perspective* (Boulder, Colo.: Westview, 1992); Mashoed Bailie and David A. Frank, "An Occidental Construction of the Orient: Media, Madness, and the Muslim World," in Janet Wasco and Vincent Mosco, eds., *Democratic Communications in the Information Age* (Toronto: Garamond Press, 1992), pp. 75-86; John R. MacArthur, *Second Front: Censorship and Propaganda in the Gulf War* (Berkeley, Calif.: University of California Press, 1993); Taisto Hujanen, "The Textuality of the Gulf War in TV News Compared: Big and Small Operators Play a Different Game," *Nordcom Review of Nordic Mass Communication Research* 2 (1992), pp. 101-110; Knut Sogstad, "The Gulf War: As Reality and Fiction," *Nordcom Review of Nordic Mass Communication Research* 2 (1992), pp. 19-30; and Håkan Hvitfelt, "The Dramaturgy of War: Notes on the Gulf War," *Nordcom Review of Nordic Mass Communication Research* 2 (1992), pp. 47-60.

10. Kazem Motamed-Nejad, Naiim Badii, and Mehdi Mohsenian-Rad, "The Iranian Press and the Persian Gulf War: The Impact of Western News Agencies," in Hamid Mowlana, George Gerbner and Herbert I. Schiller, eds., *Triumph of the Image: The Media's War in the Persian Gulf—A Global Perspective* (Boulder, Colo.: Westview, 1992), pp. 99-103.

11. See James Winter, *Common Cents* and Mason Harris, "The Language of Dwarf-Killing." However, Ann L. Hibbard and T.A. Keenleyside, disagree with this view. See their "The Press and the Persian Gulf Crisis: The Canadian Angle," *Canadian Journal of Communication*, 20:2 (Spr. 1995), pp. 255-66. Their study uses traditional quantitative methodology, which fails to take into account the significance of dominant discourses in determining the overall message of media coverage. Walter C. Soderlund demonstrates how, although American print coverage of another foreign news story was quantitatively larger, its qualitative differences with Canadian coverage were minimal. See his "A Comparison of Press Coverage in Canada and the United States of the 1982 and 1984 Salvadoran Elections," *Canadian Journal of Political Science*, 23:1 (Mar. 1990), pp. 59-72.

12. Douglas Kellner, *The Persian Gulf TV War*, pp. 293-97.

13. Martin Shaw and Roy Carr-Hill, "Public Opinion and Media War Coverage in Britain," in Hamid Mowlana, George Gerbner and Herbert I. Schiller, eds., *Triumph of the Image: The Media's War in the Persian Gulf—A Global Perspective* (Boulder: Westview, 1992), p. 145.

14. John R. MacArthur, *Second Front*, p. 110.

15. National Media Archive, "Canadian and American Network Coverage of the Gulf War: An Extension of 'Radio Iraq'?" *On Balance* 4:6 (June 1991), p. 1.

16. Nash, Knowlton, *The Mircophone Wars: A History of Triumph and Betrayal at the CBC* (Toronto: McClelland and Stewart, 1994), p. 50.

17. MacArthur, *Second Front*, pp. 110-111.

18. "Brits keep stiff upper lip in face of war," *The Ottawa Citizen*, January 23, 1991, p. A2.

19. George Bush, "State of the Union," *Vital Speeches of the Day* 57:9 (Feb. 15, 1991), p. 261.

20. "War morally justified, PM tells Commons," *The Toronto Star*, January 18, 1991, A19.

21. " 'A very evil act by a very diabolical man': PM," *Montreal Gazette*, January 18, 1991, B1.

22. "Iraqi missile hits Tel Aviv homes," *The Globe and Mail*, February 4, 1991, p. A3.

23. Hamid Mowlana, Danielle Vierling and Amy Tully , "A Sampling of Editorial Responses from the Middle Eastern Press on the Persian Gulf Crisis," in Hamid Mowlana, George Gerbner and Herbert I. Schiller, eds., *Triumph of the Image: The Media's War in the Persian Gulf—A Global Perspective* (Boulder, Colo.: Westview, 1992), p. 171.

24. Hamid Mowlana, "Roots of War: The Long Road of Intervention," in Hamid Mowlana, George Gerbner and Herbert I. Schiller, eds., *Triumph of the Image: The Media's War in the Persian Gulf—A Global Perspective* (Boulder, Colo.: Westview, 1992), p. 33.

25. James Winter, *Common Cents*, p. 30.

26. Ibid, pp. 34-36.

27. Martin A. Lee and Norman Solomon, *Unreliable Sources: A Guide to Detecting Bias in the Media* (New York: Lyle Stuart, 1991), p. xix.

28. P. Sainath, "The New World *Odour*: The Indian Experience," in Hamid Mowlana, George Gerbner and Herbert I. Schiller, eds., *Triumph of the Image: The Media's War in the Persian Gulf—A Global Perspective* (Boulder, Colo.: Westview, 1992), p. 67.

29. A bar in Winnipeg also planned an "Iraq-no-phobia" dance, billed as an "End of the World Dance," which was cancelled due to complaints from city residents. *The Saskatoon Star*, to its credit, published an editorial on January 16, 1991 criticizing the plan. This image is a recurring one, however; seven years after the Gulf War, the May 1998 cover of the *World Press Review*, a U.S. monthly, portrayed a drawing of Saddam Hussein's head attached to the body of a large spider under the title "Saddam's Trap: How Can the World Deal with Him?"

30. Asu Aksoy and Kevin Robins, "Exterminating Angels: Morality, Violence, and Technology in the Gulf War," in Hamid Mowlana, George Gerbner and Herbert I. Schiller, eds., *Triumph of the Image: The Media's War in the Persian Gulf—A Global Perspective* (Boulder, Colo.: Westview, 1992), p. 209.

31. Noam Chomsky, "The Media and the War: What War?" in Hamid Mowlana, George Gerbner and Herbert I. Schiller, eds., *Triumph of the Image: The Media's War in the Persian Gulf—A Global Perspective* (Boulder, Colo.: Westview, 1992), p. 52.

32. James Winter, *Common Cents*, p. 27.

33. Martin A. Lee and Norman Solomon, *Unreliable Sources*, p. xxi.

34. John Law, "Media Myopia: The Cultural Gap," *The Washington Report on Middle East Affairs* 9:11 (Apr. 1991), p. 61. There is a tendency in dominant discourses to present "Allah" as being distinct from "God." For example, a *Calgary Herald* article on January 13 about people of various religious backgrounds praying for a peaceful resolution of the Gulf conflict related that while Christians and Jews were praying to "God," "Calgary's Muslim groups have been bowing in prayer to Mecca asking Allah for peace."

35. Akbar S. Ahmed, *Postmodernism and Islam: Predicament and Promise* (London: Routledge, 1992), p. 232. Using a well-known phrase from *Dirty Harry* (1971), another Hollywood film, George Bush dared Saddam Hussein to "make my day." Such "sentences are made immortal through the media, a cultural gift to the entire world. They are quoted, parodied, copied and are constantly in print," states Ahmed. Indeed, they serve as buttresses for global narratives.

36. James Winter, *Common Cents*, p. 33.

CHAPTER 9

The Jihad Model of Journalism

Dominant discourses view the modern state as the most rational way to organize polities—it is not moved to action by what are often considered to be irrational religious notions. But even though the entire world has been divided into sovereign states, the narratives of transnational media make implicit distinctions about the orientation of Northern and Southern countries. Whereas power struggles in the North are usually seen as ideological or political, most conflicts in the Southern parts of the world are to be attributed to ancient tribal, religious, or ethnic hatreds. Particular struggles which have complex economic or social causes are often reduced to "Christian-Muslim," "Muslim-Jewish," "Hindu-Muslim," and "Shia-Sunni" conflicts in dominant discourses.[1] This does not require much ideological labour due to the primacy in the North of the core image of Muslims as a people generally prone to fanatical impulses. Mainstream journalists seem to view the religious conflict script as self-evident, not requiring explanations of why a particular war should be considered religious. When engaged in conflict, contemporary Muslims are generally seen as driven by an irrational hatred as opposed to the scientific rationality that is the mark of modern Northern civilization. Technological society promotes the idea that truth—and ultimately, utopia—is to be achieved through scientific progress. According to the March 1, 1989 edition of the influential Toronto-based *John Kettle's FutureLetter*, a periodical that forecasts socio-economic trends: "Science has taken on much of the role of religion, offering a different kind of truth, truth that is open to proof rather than faith. In the west it is a noble pursuit to challenge existing truth, whereas in Islam and other fundamental [sic] religions it is blasphemy to challenge dogma or revealed truth." Whereas this publication did state that scientific truth was open to challenge, it failed to point out that the fundamental premises of technological society are rarely questioned in dominant discourses.

In a media analysis of the use of religious language during the Gulf War, published in the February 2, 1991 issue of the *Spectator* newsmagazine, Ian

Buruma surmised that "Our own world is not as secular as we might think." Whereas the "Islamic" symbolism of the secular-minded Saddam Hussein unabashedly exploited the religious sentiments of Muslims, similar appeals to the divine were also made by Northern leaders during the war. This form of rhetoric has a venerable tradition, wrote Buruma:

> One might think back to the spirit of the Great War, which was soaked in religious imagery. The actual aims of that war were fuzzy at best. But the noble sacrifices made for King and Country were likened by poets and journalists to the sacrifice of Christ. *Pilgrim's Progress* was often invoked: 'The King...commanded the...Shinning Ones to go out and take Ignorance, and bind him hand and foot, and have him away.' And just as Saddam Hussein tried to whip the Shia Muslims into a rage by accusing infidel bombers of destroying holy sites, the Germans [during World War II] were rumoured to have desecrated such sacred idols as the holy Virgin of Albert. This is almost echoed by the CNN reporter in the Pentagon who called the Iraqi attack on Israel 'blasphemy', because it took place on the Sabbath.

Such an accusation of "blasphemy" by Northern propagandists is generally considered an acceptable use of language in such circumstances, and is not viewed in dominant discourses as fanatical or even irrational.

The religious strife script, which highlights the religious elements of certain conflicts, gives rise to a cognitive macrostructure that portrays peoples of various backgrounds engaging in religious conflict with each other. The jihad model is the specific cognitive macrostructure which presents the conflicts involving Muslims as caused by their religion. Dominant constructions of conflicts between Christian and Muslim groups by the ostensibly secularist transnational mass media has generally involved the portrayal of the Christian as the victim and the Muslim as the victimizer. In the cases where the facts clearly indicate that the reverse is true, that is when Muslims are victims and Christians are victimizers, the religious conflict script either completely disappears or is mitigated. Therefore, when "Muslims" were viewed as the primary victims in the war in Bosnia-Herzegovina during the 1990s, "Serbs"—not "Christians"—were the villains; on the other hand, when Lebanese "Christians" carried out the 1982 massacres in the Sabra and Shatila refugee camps in Beirut, "Palestinians"—not "Muslims"—were the victims. The religious strife script has also been dropped when larger ideological purposes appear to be at stake, as when covering the Central Asian involvement of Turkey, a country with a largely Muslim population but which is also a member of NATO.

However, dominant media discourses *did* use the jihad model in reporting an uprising in the mostly Muslim Chechnya, a small southern republic in the Russian federation. One newsreader on the Newsworld channel of the Canadian Broadcasting Corporation stated that it was "the rebellious religion of Islam"[2] that was opposing Moscow. The Chechens had become part of the Muslim Other in the aftermath of the Cold War. It is also worth noting that the dominant coverage of the conflict between Chechnya and the Moscow government stressed the "Islamic" zeal of Chechens in December 1994 and January 1995, when the latter were preparing for war.[3] However, references to religion almost completely vanished subsequent to the brutal invasion of the republic by Russian troops and the clear emergence of Chechens as victims. Similarly, they were systematically called "Islamic militants" and "Islamic extremists" by Moscow-based correspondents when Russia launched its second campaign in September 1999.[4] (The Russian government had obtained tacit approval from Western governments for their offensive by framing it as part of the international war against Islamic terrorism.[5]) However, by mid-October, when Western leaders began to express their protests against the bombing of civilian centres, the Islamic appellation disappeared once again from Western media accounts.

A massacre in the mountains

The jihad model is most likely to be in use in cases where the interests that a Muslim group is challenging are Northern and/or Christian, and where the former appears to be acting in the role of the villain and the latter that of the victim. Even when political, historical, ethnic, or territorial problems are largely at issue, the focus is placed on the religious distinctions between combatants. A primary example of such cultural constructions was the coverage of the Azeri-Armenian war from the mid-1980s to the early 1990s in the Caucasus region of the Russian federation. This conflict, which had broken out as the Soviet Union was collapsing, was over Nagorno-Karabakh, a territory inside Azerbaijan with a majority of ethnic Armenian inhabitants. In a study of the coverage by five American newspapers of this conflict from February through August 1988, Levon Chorbajian found that:

> The religious strife model [sic] was the most commonly used framework for reader understanding. References to Christian Armenians and Moslem Azerbaijanis appeared in 20% of the articles (47 out of 230). Ethnic conflict and nationalism were nearly as common. References to democracy and self determination appeared only rarely.

> Couching events and issues in these terms…allowed the media to conceal the real conflict nexus which was Armenian-Turkish and not Armenian-Moslem. By doing so the media could conveniently avoid calling attention to NATO ally Turkey. Turkey and Turkic appeared in only 6% of the articles (14 out of 230). In most cases it was simply mentioned in passing that Azerbaijanis were a Turkic or Turkic speaking people.[6]

Most articles published in Canadian newspapers about the war between Azeris and Armenians were filed either from American or other transnational news sources such as the British-based Reuters news agency, whose correspondents were based in Moscow. Their coverage was generally characterized by the tendencies outlined by Chorbajian. This seemed to indicate the (re)emergence of the Muslim Other in eastern Europe at the collapse of Soviet Union.

Typical of news stories about the conflict is the following first paragraph of a February 29, 1992 *Ottawa Citizen* article, attributed primarily to the Washington Post news service:

Troops of the former Soviet army were ordered Friday to withdraw from the war-torn enclave of Nagorno-Karabakh in a move that seems likely to lead to an escalation in the fighting between *Muslim Azerbaijan* and *Christian Armenia* (emphasis inserted).

Such references to the religions of the Azeris and Armenians that did not explain how they related to the strife between them, seemed to imply that the war was a religious one involving a theological struggle and perhaps a battle for converts. Another example of this tendency is found in a February 24, 1992 article in *The Montreal Gazette* about an aerial Azerbaijani bombing of Armenia, which stated: "Yesterday morning, Sukhoi-25 jets raided residential areas of Stepanakert and dropped bombs near an Armenian church, Christ the Savior, in nearby Shusha at the precise moment the divine liturgy was being said." It was as if the bombing by Azerbaijani planes was timed exactly to coincide with the sacred Christian ritual. Readers inundated with reports about the militant march of Islamism would have been led to believe that this was yet another manifestation of that phenomenon.

The religious strife script appears to operate within the bounds of dramaturgical parameters where the villainous portrayal of the Muslim is favoured over that of seeing her as a hero or even as a victim. However, the jihad model, deriving from the religious strife script, almost completely disappeared during the reportage in March 1992 of a massacre of Azeris by Armenians, and reappeared clearly only after the coverage had peaked. This massacre occurred in March in Khojaly, an Azeri village in Nagorno-Karabakh. Figures for the number of deaths ran from as low as "dozens" up to a high of 1,000. This story seemed to upset the neat journalistic scheme in which the Christian Armenians of Nagorno-Karabakh were completely surrounded and oppressed by Muslim Azeris, who occupied the rest of the country. Specific damage control tactics were apparently adopted to mitigate the dissonant facts emerging from the coverage of the event in which Muslims were victims and Christians their victimizers.

The manners in which the story was reported in morning editions of *The Montreal Gazette*, *The Globe and Mail*, *The Toronto Star* and *The Ottawa Citizen* between March 2 and 7, 1992 is tracked below. Several trends can be identified in the coverage of the killings:

- the massacre itself was treated as a secondary issue, usually at the ends of articles;
- prominence was given to Armenian denials, and Azeri "allegations" were characterized as "gross exaggeration";
- difficulties were cited in verifying the exact number of deaths due to the inaccessibility of the area, despite the display of bodies on Azerbaijani television;

- the scale of deaths in the Khojaly massacre was downplayed by placing them within the general loss of life in the war at large;

- when the facts of an Armenian massacre of Azeri villagers became irrefutable, indications of religious identity completely disappeared as did photographs of the bodies and mourners;

- even though all the newspapers under study were largely using the same news wire material, the narrative in one daily began returning to systematic references about religion earlier than those in the others; and

- there was a complete absence of comment on the massacre either in editorials or in opinion columns.

The news on the Khojaly massacre first broke on Monday March 2, 1992 in *The Montreal Gazette* with the headline "CIS moves to pull out troops: Azeri refugees accuse Armenians of killing hundreds." The main subject of the article by Reuters, datelined Agdam, Azerbaijan (a town close to Khojaly), was the troop pull-out by the Russian-led Commonwealth of Independent States; of the eight paragraphs in the write-up, only three (beginning with the fifth) dealt with claims of the massacre. An accompanying AFP photograph showed an elderly Azeri man weeping "as a body of a child is brought into makeshift morgue in Agdam." In contrast to the usual reporting of the conflict, there was no reference to the religious affiliation of the Azeris or the Armenians. None of the other three dailies mentioned the event that day.

On the following day, Tuesday March 3, all four newspapers cited "allegations" about the massacre. The piece which referred to the killings most clearly was a Reuters story and photo filed from Agdam published in *The Toronto Star*. There was a sole, indirect allusion to religion in the caption of the picture: "An Azeri woman cries out for her dead father yesterday as his body lies in a mosque with those of other victims"; the religion of Armenians was not identified. *The Montreal Gazette* carried a write-up with a Moscow dateline by the Los Angeles Times news service, squeezed in between reports of troubles in other parts of the former Soviet Union. It had an AFP picture in which an "Azeri policeman removes the body of a girl near Khojaly, which Armenian militants attacked last week"; the surrounding field was strewn with bodies. No religion was mentioned. *The Globe and Mail*'s article on the event used Associated Press and Reuters stories, also filed from Moscow. Only three (beginning with the ninth) of the fourteen paragraphs dealt with the killings; no photo was used. There were not any indications of religious affiliations. *The Ottawa Citizen* was the only paper to carry a Canadian wire service's article on the massacre, filed from Moscow by Southam News. Here too, the focus was on the Russian "troop exit" rather than the killings. "Christian Armenians" were mentioned in the context of a political settlement, not that of the deaths of Azeris—whose creed was not identified.

	March 2	March 3	March 4	March 5	March 6	March 7
Montreal Gazette	No	No	No	Yes	No	Yes
Globe and Mail	(Story not covered)	No	No	No	Yes	No
Toronto Star	(Story not covered)	No	No	No	(Story not covered)	No
Ottawa Citizen	(Story not covered)	No	No	(Story not covered)	(Story not covered)	No

Table 2: Use of the jihad model in coverage of the 1992 Khojaly massacre

It is noteworthy that all four Canadian papers using material from four different media institutions based in the U.S., the UK, and Canada stated the reported numbers of casualties in the middle or end of the respective articles. The *Globe*'s headline was, "CIS sends general to oversee pullout: Azerbaijani official says 50 killed as violence intensifies in enclave," with the figure of 1,000 deaths from Azeri sources not appearing until the tenth paragraph. The *Star*'s headline read, "Azeris mourn victims of alleged massacre"; the lead referred to "dozens of bodies" but again, the figure of 1,000 was not cited until the ninth paragraph. Neither *The Montreal Gazette* nor The Ottawa Citizen's headlines alluded to the massacre, with references to 1,000 not appearing until the middle of the articles.

In contrast to this tendency, figures of deaths were generally given prominence when Armenians were the victims in the ongoing conflict. A March 12, 1988 write-up in *The Ottawa Citizen* headlined "Armenian massacre reported" had placed the higher estimate of deaths in the lead paragraph and the lower one in the middle of the article. The first paragraph stated:

> Witnesses to the violence in the Azerbaijani city of Sumgait spoke of a "horrifying pogrom" and the killing of "at least" 350 people, a man who visited the city Wednesday said here yesterday.

And halfway down the report:

> The [police] officer said that reports of Azerbaijanis storming the houses of Armenians were true and that about 300 people had been injured and 37 were dead.

The religious strife angle was also emphasized here:

> Shikov said that the violence in Sumgait was one-sided, with Azerbaijani

Moslems killing Armenian Christians. "This was no ethnic conflict," he said. "It was a genuine pogrom."

The use of the term "pogrom," which is most frequently used to describe attacks on Jews in the late 19th and early 20th-century Russia, thus linked a Muslim group in a former Soviet republic to a form of anti-Semitic violence. The word was never used in the four dailies under study to describe the Armenian killings of Azeris in their coverage of the Khojaly massacre.

On Wednesday March 4, as evidence of large scale killings of Azeris in Khojaly grew, the four Canadian newspapers prominently carried denials by the Armenian officials. There were no photographs in any of the publications. *The Montreal Gazette* had an article from the Los Angeles Times News Service datelined Moscow and an editorial on the Azeri-Armenian conflict, although the latter dealt with the CIS pull-out and did not mention the killings. (This was the only editorial on the war in the four journals during the entire week of the coverage of the massacre.) *The Globe and Mail* printed a write-up filed from Agdam, with joint AP and Reuters credits. *The Toronto Star* used an AP article, also with an Agdam dateline, and *The Ottawa Citizen* had an AP story from Moscow. There was not a single mention of religion in any of the four papers. Thus, at the height of the ongoing discovery of the massacre, even indirect references to the religious backgrounds of the victims or the villains had disappeared as had pictures of the bodies or of people in mourning. Conversely, reporting on the denials of the large scale of Azeri deaths had increased.

On Thursday March 5, the *Citizen* did not have coverage of the Azeri-Armenian conflict. The *Star*'s story from the Los Angeles Times News Service, datelined Moscow, described how "Azeri TV shows piles of bodies." But again there was no accompanying picture and no mention of religion. However, the *Gazette* carried an AP article with a photo of an Azeri woman weeping at a gravesite, and *did* have three references to religious affiliations:

> Wails of mourning mixed with gunfire yesterday as fighting edged closer to this city bordering the disputed region of Nagorno-Karabakh and Azerbaijanis buried more dead from last week's Armenian attack.

> Azerbaijan's government called on the United Nations to send peacekeeping troops to patrol the mostly *Muslim* country's border with *Christian Armenia* and prevent further bloodshed in Nagorno-Karabakh.

> The government condemned the assault on the town of Khojaly as deliberate genocide and accused former Soviet troops of complicity. A spokesman for the troops, now under the command of the Commonwealth of Independent States, flatly denied any involvement.

> Presidents Boris Yeltsin of Russia and Nursultan Nazarbayev of Kazakhstan made urgent new appeals for a ceasefire in the bloodiest ethnic conflict in the former Soviet Union. Nazarbayev, a *Muslim*, said he was "especially stunned" by the storming of Khojaly [emphasis inserted].

The *Globe*'s front page had the same AP picture as the *Gazette*, with a write-up from AP and Reuters on an inside page. The initial paragraphs were largely similar to those in the Montreal paper; however, unlike the article in the *Gazette*, indications of religion were completely absent. Compare this paragraph in the *Globe*'s article with the one quoted above from the *Gazette*:

> Wails of mourning mixed with gunfire yesterday as Azerbaijanis buried their dead and fighting edged closer to this city bordering on the disputed region of Nagorno-Karabakh.

> Azerbaijan's government condemned last week's Armenian assault on the town of Khojaly as "deliberate genocide" and charged complicity by troops of the Commonwealth of Independent States. Commonwealth armed forces denied involvement.

> Presidents Boris Yeltsin of Russia and Nursultan Nazarbayev of Kazakstan made urgent appeals for a ceasefire in the bloodiest ethnic conflict in the former Soviet Union. Nazarbayev said he was "especially stunned" by the storming of Khojaly.

Without access to the original wire copy from AP and Reuters we cannot assume either that the *Globe*'s editor systematically edited out all indications of religious affiliation or that the *Gazette*'s inserted them.

On Friday March 6, the *Globe*'s article on the Azeri-Armenian war did make references to religion, albeit in the second-last paragraph:

> Mr. Mutalibov [president of Azerbaijan] accused Russia of being behind the recent upsurge of fighting and success by Christian Armenians in Nagorno-Karabakh, which is predominantly Armenian but lies within Muslim Azerbaijan.

In the "inverted pyramid" arrangement of the write-up, based on AP and Reuters stories from Baku (the capital of Azerbaijan), the most important facts seemed to be that two former Soviet republics, Azerbaijan and Moldova, were accusing Russia of escalating ethnic strife within their respective borders. It was only at the eleventh paragraph that references to the Khojaly massacre began, with religious affiliations appearing in the fifteenth. The *Gazette* had a shorter version of the AP/Reuters story and an AP photo of family members weeping at the "coffin of Nagorno-Karabakh fighting" (not used by the *Globe*). The Montreal paper had only eleven paragraphs, which did not include the one in the *Globe* that mentioned religion since the bottom of the inverted triangle was omitted. Neither the *Star* nor the *Citizen* reported on the conflict in their March 6 editions.

On Saturday March 7, the four dailies had articles about the resignation of the president of Azerbaijan. The *Gazette*'s report was by the Canadian Press (CP) with a Moscow dateline. The tenth paragraph made references to religion:

> Nagorno-Karabakh is a predominantly Christian Armenian enclave inside mostly Muslim Azerbaijan where more than 1,000 people have been killed

in four years of ethnic violence. It's the longest-running and most violent of the many ethnic disputes in the former Soviet Union.

The write-up then went on to give brief accounts of recent casualties and of "Azerbaijani claims" of an Armenian "massacre" without giving any numbers. The story in the *Citizen* was credited primarily to Southam News with "files from CP and Washington Post." It is clear that the file from CP was the same as that used by the *Gazette*, since two paragraphs—including the one quoted above—were almost identical in both the articles. However, the references to religion made by the *Gazette* were absent in the Ottawa publication. Therefore, one can assume here that there was a conscious editorial decision either by the *Gazette* to insert religious affiliations or by the *Citizen* to remove them.

Interestingly, that day's issue of the *Citizen* had another article from CP on the same page on the Azeri-Armenian conflict, which did refer to religious loyalties but not to the Khojaly massacre. This was a story on Canadian medical aid, also filed from Moscow; it was placed next to the one on the resignation of the Azerbaijani president. The sixth paragraph read:

> Nagorno-Karabakh is a predominantly Christian Armenian enclave inside mostly Muslim Azerbaijan where more than 1,000 people have been killed in four years of ethnic violence. But a new level of fighting flared recently in the isolated mountainous region.

No direct allusions were made to recent reports of the Khojaly massacre even though a spokesman for the International Committee of the Red Cross was quoted saying that "the Red Cross used part of the money to purchase 1,000 'body bags' to remove the bodies of recent fighting." Although the article mentioned "1,000" as being *all* the deaths during the previous four years, this was the same number of deaths attributed by Azeri sources to the Khojaly massacre. Whereas the urgent shipment of Canadian medical aid apparently seemed to have been prompted by the recent massacre, the write-up did not clearly identify the event. It appears that the paper was having trouble placing reports that identified Armenians as Christians and Azeris as Muslims in stories where the former appeared to be the villains and the latter their victims.

The same seemed to be the case in that day's *Globe and Mail*, which also had two articles on the same page about the Azeri-Armenian situation. A Reuters piece from Baku reported on the stepping-down of the Azerbaijani president, stating that "The public outcry that led to Mr. Mutalibov's resignation was sparked by serious Azeri losses during Armenia's capture of the town of Khojaly last week. More than 100 bodies, many mutilated, were found in surrounding hills and Azeri officials said at least 1,000 people had been killed." No mention was made of religious backgrounds which, however, did appear in the adjoining feature article written by the newspaper's Moscow bureau chief and datelined Yerevan (Armenia's capital). As in the case with the *Citizen*, there was no allusion to the massacre in the latter article that did describe Armenians as Christians and Azeris as Muslims. The *Star*'s piece on the Azerbaijani president's resignation, filed from Moscow by the Washington Post news service, related that "Azerbaijani militiamen have sworn to avenge an alleged massacre by Armenian forces last week in Khojaly, an Azerbaijani town in Karabakh." There were two Reuters photos related to the president's downfall but, again, no mention was made of the creeds of the Azeris or Armenians. However, immediately below this story was the continuation of a front-page feature story by the paper's Moscow bureau chief, Stephen Handleman[7], on the growth of "Islam's political appeal" in other former Soviet republics of Uzbekistan and Tajikistan.

Therefore, from March 2 to March 7 the four newspapers' coverage of the massacre in Khojaly had consistently tended to downplay the event's significance. The claims of Azeris were described as "exaggerations" and the lower numbers of deaths were given prominence over the higher ones, even though in previous cases when Armenians had been killed the figures appeared in reverse order. There was no editorial comment condemning or even lamenting the loss of life in any of the four papers. But most remarkable was the almost complete disappearance of references to religion at the peak of massacre's coverage. The newspapers seemed extremely reluctant to allude to the facts that the killers in this case happened to be Christians and their victims Muslims; whereas religious affiliations tended gratuitously to be stated in the general reporting of the conflict, the Khojaly massacre did not seem to fit the dominant model in which the Muslim Other was threatening Christendom.

In subsequent coverage of the Azeri-Armenian war the Khojaly massacre had become insignificant and the reportage went back to routinely identifying people according to their religious backgrounds. For example, a write-up in the March 11, 1992 issue of the *Globe*, credited to AP and Reuters and datelined Brussels (since it was written within the context of the Conference on Security and Co-operation in Europe's discussions), stated:

> The mostly *Christian* Armenian enclave, with about 200,000 people, has been controlled by predominantly *Muslim* Azerbaijan since 1929 [emphasis inserted].

Compare this with the following which had appeared on March 4, at the height of the reportage of the massacre, when both *The Toronto Star* and *The Ottawa Citizen* had used AP stories:

> Nagorno-Karabakh's population of about 200,000 is mainly Armenian. But it is surrounded by Azerbaijan, which has administered the territory since 1929.

At that time it had apparently seemed inappropriate to refer to religions. Although the March 11 *Globe* story was accompanied by a picture of Azeri mourners at Agdam, it made no mention of the Khojaly massacre but referred instead to the "ancient accusations" of Armenia and Azerbaijan against each other. Thus, ideological closure was effected over the event (which had resulted in the highest death toll of any single encounter in the war) by relegating it to the catalogue of "ancient accusations."[8]

A March 14 feature article in *The Star* by a staff writer, who seemed to be working in the same manner, juxtaposed the Armenian "massacre" against "Azeri pogroms." He went on to broaden the jihad model to place the Azeri-Armenian struggle within the "ancient rivalry" of "Islamic powers" such as Turkey, Iran, Iraq, and Egypt:

> But the South Caucasus situation is only part of a much wider conflict.
>
> Today, a struggle is going on for the leadership of the Islamic world.
>
> It is the same struggle that had been waged for centuries before the Western empires, with their overwhelming military technology, forced much of the Islamic world into a straitjacket.
>
> It is not a question of Sunni Muslims versus Shias, although that is part of it. Throughout history there have been East-West struggles in the region —between Greece and Persia, between Rome and Persia, between the Arabs and the Persians, between the Ottomans and the Persians.
>
> The increasing modernization of the Islamic world—and the fall of Communist Russia—has revived that struggle.

Through some remarkable contortions of logic the writer attempted to show that the very modernization of the Muslim people was making them revert increasingly to their ancient ways. Moscow's domination of the South Caucasus was also a good thing because it kept a lid on religious irrationality. The implication was that if the Northern powers do not again force Muslim countries into a neocolonial "straitjacket" the region would become a hotbed of "Islamic" militancy.

It is ironic that even when Muslims are massacred in large numbers by non-Muslims, the blame can be directed towards Islam. According to Jacques Ellul, the integration propagandist can count on the inexhaustible capacity of "current-events man" to forget the details of daily reporting:

> ...such a man is highly sensitive to the influence of present-day currents; lacking landmarks, he follows all currents. He is unstable because he runs after what happened today; he relates to the event, and therefore cannot resist any impulse coming from that event. Because he is immersed in current affairs, this man has a psychological weakness that puts him at the mercy of the propagandist. No confrontation ever occurs between the event and the truth; no relationship ever exists between the event and the person. Real information never concerns such a person.[9]

Although such a complete divorce from the "truth" probably does not occur all the time, the continual output of the mass media overwhelms the person absorbed primarily with immediate happenings. A newspaper reader usually dose not refer to the details of previous reports to notice inconsistencies and contradictions; she merely retains an overall impression that conforms to the basic myths and cognitive models concerning the particular issue. In the coverage of the Azeri-Armenian conflict the lasting impression is that of Islam destabilizing the global post-Cold War global order.

Georgia, Bosnia-Herzegovina

Whereas the jihad model was only occasionally dropped as a frame for the Azeri-Armenian war, it has been almost completely avoided in the dominant reporting of conflicts where Muslims are normatively identified as victims. An AP feature article on former Central Asian Soviet republics in the June 15, 1992 issues of *The Ottawa Citizen* and *The Globe and Mail*, which referred to the struggle between "Christian Armenians" and "Muslim Azeris," preferred to describe a conflict in "South Ossetia, a separatist region of Georgia" as "ethnic" even though the warring parties there also happened to be Christian and Muslim. The occasional backgrounder like that on the various "ethnic tensions" in the disintegrating Soviet Union in the December 26, 1991 issue of *The Ottawa Citizen* from *The Chicago Tribune*, while citing the differing religious affiliations, expressly stated that the problem was "territorial." This write-up distinguished between the respective struggles of various peoples in Nagorno-Karabakh and Georgia:

> Nagorno-Karabakh, a kind of Soviet version of Northern Ireland, is controlled by Shiite Muslims from Azerbaijan but populated mainly by Christian Armenians. It has witnessed hundreds of deaths as the Azeris asserted their control over the local Armenians.

> An almost identical situation exists in the northern part of Georgia, where wealthier and better educated Georgians control an area known as southern Ossetia, which is populated by poorer Persian-descended people.

> While there are religious elements involved—the Georgians are Christian, the Ossetians Muslim—the real distinction is over land and the desire of the Ossetians to be part of Russia, not Georgia.

> Territorial disputes are also at the root of ethnic clashes between Muslim Abkhazians and Christian Georgians around the Black Sea coastal city Sukhumi. The area is the traditional homeland for Abkhazians, who reject the Georgians' domination.

According to this narrative, whereas the Armenians were the victims in Azerbaijan, the Ossetians and Abkhazians had this role in Georgia: Armenians in Nagorno-Karabakh were "controlled by Shiite Muslims from Azerbaijan" and there had been "hundreds of deaths as the Azeris asserted their control over the local Armenians," while the "wealthier and better-educated Georgians control an area known as southern Ossetia, which is populated by poorer Persian-descended people" and the Abkhazians "reject the Georgians' domination" over their "traditional homeland."

This conforms to what Robert L. Ivie has identified as one of the classic ways of portraying victimage: "The usual strategy is to construct the image indirectly through contrasting references to the adversary's coercive, irrational, and aggressive attempts to subjugate a freedom-loving, rational, and pacific victim."[10] "Control" and "domination" were ascribed to the Azeris and Georgians, whereas the victims (the Armenians, the "poorer" Ossetians and the Abkhazians) strove to assert their own sovereignty over areas where they were in majority and that were their "traditional homelands." It is also interesting to note the manners in which relationships with the Muslim bogeyman Iran are constructed: while the Azeris were identified as Shi'ite Muslims (the majority branch of Muslims in Iran) the Ossetians were described as "Persian-descended people." (Following the establishment of the *ulama*-led government in Tehran, the use of "Persia" and "Persians" has become a common discursive tactic for creating distance from Iran, which was historically referred to as Persia.[11])

Thus, when the Christian was the victim the conflict was constructed as being primarily religious and in the case where the Muslim was disadvantaged it was constructed as being "territorial," even though territory was clearly the major problem in all these wars. No explanation was given for depicting the conflict in Nagorno-Karabakh as religious except for implications arising from it being "a kind of Soviet version of Northern Ireland" and the Azeris being Shi'ite Muslims. (As the conflict in Northern Ireland has been between people who are of Catholic and Protestant backgrounds it is generally scripted as being religious, notwithstanding the general absence of theological argumentation and propaganda that would be expected to be an overt feature of a religious war.) And since "Shi'ite Iran" is generally viewed as wanting to export its revolution, the Shi'ite Azeris must also be working for the domination of Islam over Nagorno-Karabakh. One file photo used by the *Citizen* to illustrate the June 15, 1992 article showed an Azeri with a raised, clenched fist carrying a flag with a crescent and a star, considered to be an Islamic symbol.

The villainous characterization of the Georgian government was at its height in the dominant Northern discourses' depiction of the struggle between the supporters of the former president Zviad Gamsakhurdia, who was toppled from power in January 1992, and those Georgians who resented his authoritarian rule. During that time, the Ossetians, who were being suppressed by Gamsakhurdia's government, emerged as victims in the coverage of this conflict by transnational news agencies' correspondents based in Moscow. Georgia's image had also suffered in the reporting of its relations with Moscow, from which it was one of the earliest to secede. As specific "nationalities" within the Soviet Union began to agitate for autonomy or independence in the late 1980s and early 1990s, the Gorbachev and Yeltsin governments were generally portrayed as holding on course the progressive programs of reform in the face of conservative communist reaction. There seemed to be apprehension among Western "experts" and Moscow-based journalists such as *The Los Angeles Times'* correspondent who wrote in an article reprinted in *The Montreal Gazette* on November 6, 1987 that "Such conflicts would provide conservatives with their most convincing argument—that democratization within the Soviet empire is impossible, and in fact suicidal." Even though there were a number of differences between the respective discourses of the West and the disintegrating Soviet Union, they seemed to converge on this issue. Since the conflict between the Georgians and the Ossetians, a tiny ethnic minority that has traditionally been loyal to Moscow, was placed within the larger one between the Georgian and the Soviet governments, Northern journalists did not seem to feel the need to couch the issue in religious terms.

The religious conflict script was also largely avoided in the war involving Christian and Muslim antagonists in Bosnia-Herzegovina. Since 1968, Slavs of Muslim cultural backgrounds in the former Yugoslav region have been permitted to register officially as belonging to a "Muslim nationality." "Muslims" in the former Yugoslavia are distinguished from "Serbs," "Croats" and other "nationalities" despite sharing common ethnic origins with these groups. The Serbs emerged as the villains in their conflict with Croatians during 1991 and early 1992. When the focus moved to Bosnia-Herzegovina, the Serbs, having been cast in the role of the victimizers, remained the villains and Bosnia's Muslims and Croats became the new victims. Following the large-scale atrocities by the Serbs against the Muslims, the latter came to be entrenched as victims in dominant media discourses by mid-1992. (Since newspaper accounts covering the war did not explain that Bosnian Muslims were identified as such because that was their official designation as a "nationality" in the former Yugoslavia, the readership most likely saw this only as a religious identity rather than a religio-cultural one.) However, it seems remarkable that even though members of a religious group were named as primary victims, the dominant coverage of this conflict resisted framing it as a religious war. Whereas there occasionally was coverage of Croats and Serbs going to church during ceasefires and of Muslim burial ceremonies, the war was not described as "Christian-Muslim." The religious affiliations of the Serbs were either not identified within the context of the brutal conflict or their Eastern Orthodox beliefs were emphasized, underlining the distinctions between the Western and the Eastern Churches. Even in reports which indicated that both Serb and Croat nationalists were working together to take advantage of the Muslims' vulnerability to enlarge their respective territories, the conflict was not portrayed as a "Christian-Muslim" one. For example, this May 15, 1993 *Citizen* headline: "Croats, Serbs plot to isolate Muslims."

The reluctance of Northern journalists in casting the Bosnian conflict as a religious one contrasted markedly with such characterizations of other wars between peoples of Christian and Muslim background. Statements by "Muslim fundamentalists" are usually taken at face value when they indicate that the reasons for their violent activities are "Islamic." But declarations by some "Serbs" that they were fighting for Christendom were largely treated with scepticism. For example, a Reuters article in *The Toronto Star* issue of April 14, 1992 stated:

Bosnia's Serbs, condemned internationally as the aggressors in a savage war, want to be seen as Christian crusaders saving Europe from Islam.

"This is religious war," said orthodox Bishop Vasil from the northeast Bosnian city of Tuzla. "The West does not understand."

But skeptics say Orthodox churches in the area are poorly attended, and that the faith is being used as a cloak for purely political ends.

"This is a war for land and money. Religion is an excuse," said a Catholic priest, one of the scared Croatian minority still living in Banja Luka.

Muslim charity workers in the city agreed, saying relations with the orthodox Church were good before the war began.

One rarely finds similar examples in the transnational media that discuss how Islam may have been used "as a cloak for purely political ends." The "religious" motives of "Muslim fundamentalists" seem beyond doubt because in dominant Northern scripts that is how Muslims are supposed to act; true Christians, on the other hand, are not expected to engage in savage warfare.

Occasional television interviews of Bosnian Muslims depicted them making references to Serb snipers as "terrorists." But Western journalists who reported that the Serbs were motivated in their attacks on Muslims by fears of perceived threats to the Eastern Orthodox Church in Bosnia-Herzegovina did not refer to the former as "Christian terrorists" or "Christian extremists." And although the Bosnian Serbs were fighting against the internationally-recognized government of Bosnia-Herzegovina, they were rarely described as "rebels." In a letter published by *The Globe and Mail* on July 5, 1995, Wilfred Cantwell Smith, a noted Orientalist, wrote:

The headline of your article Muslim Forces Threaten Canadians (June 21) is a flagrant illustration of a general anti-Islamic bias shared by most Westerners and fuelled by most Western media, especially in North America.

On the same page as the above article about threats, you speak in a longer article of "the beleaguered Bosnian government," Western "support of the Bosnian government," "the Bosnian government's dream of a pluralistic democracy," and so on, and never once mention that they are Muslim—for in that article they appear in a sympathetic light. Once there is a matter of their making an anti-UN move, however, this other article speaks of "the Muslim-led Bosnian government," and the headline refers only to their being Muslim.

I have not failed to notice that your reporting on the former Yugoslavia has throughout spoken of "the Serbs" and "the Croats." We never read, this past while, that the "Christians" took all those UN hostages, including Canadians, although the Serbs are just as much Orthodox...and the Croats just as much Roman Catholic, as the Bosnian government and its supporters are Muslim.

That this letter by a prominent Orientalist criticizing dominant discourses was published by *The Globe and Mail*, with the headline "Anti-Islamic bias shows," indicates that alternative discourses are not completely absent from mainstream Northern media nor from Orientalism.

Journalists appear to find the religious strife script a convenient way to explain conflicts whose historical and sociological roots they do not understand. It seems that once a war has been defined as a religious conflict between Muslims and Christians this is accepted as a given in dominant media discourses. There do also tend to be in operation cultural dynamics that emphasize the role of the Muslim as villain. Mainstream Northern journalists appear to be comfortable with this construction since they share in a historical memory that holds Islam to be a primary Other. On the other hand, even though the Northern mass media ostensibly have no religious affiliations, they are reluctant to identify Christians as villains, especially when have victimized Muslims. At the end of the ideological war with Moscow, the jihad model seems to have become a means to depict the rise of the Muslim monster from the grave of the communist ogre.

NOTES

1. For example, Western journalists had divided Beirut during the Lebanese civil war into "Christian East Beirut" and "Muslim West Beirut." G.H. Jansen, discussing an incident in which the forces of a [Catholic] Maronite general were shelling parts of the city, indicates how the overlapping of religious communities within the various factions and geographical areas was distorted by the simplistic dichotomy: "The target for Aoun's gunners, many of whom are themselves Muslims, has been what is usually called 'predominantly Muslim West Beirut,' but at present there are almost as many Christians as Muslims in West Beirut." G.H. Jansen, "The Papal attack on Syria: Unfounded and unwise," *Middle East International*, September 8, 1989, p. 57.

2. Lorne Saxberg, *CBC Newsworld*, November 9, 1991, 13:00 news bulletin.

3. Andrew Higgins, The Independent, "Fanaticism rooted in Stalin-era repression," *The Ottawa Citizen*, December 20, 1994, p. A6; Reuters photo, "Answering Call: Muslims from the village of Sernovodsk pray in a local mosque Friday after religious and political leaders called for a holy war against advancing Russian troops," *The Ottawa Citizen*, December 24, 1994, p. G5; Michael Specter, The New York Times, "Religion and the defence of Chechnya," *The Globe and Mail*, January 17, 1995, p. A17.

4. Amelia Gentleman, "Russia names Chechen as bomb plotter," *The Observer*, September 19, 1999, p. 22; Geoffrey York, "Russia escalates two-week bombing assault on Chechnya," *The Globe and Mail*, September 25, 1999, p. A12; Ruslan Masayev, Associated Press, "Air attack kills dozens, Chechens claim," October 9, 1999, p. E17; Associated Press, "Thousands held in Russia as police hunt bombers," *The Ottawa Citizen*, September 18, 1999, p. A16.

5. Mike Trickey, "Axworthy slams offensive in Chechnya," *The Ottawa Citizen*, October 23, 1999, p. E7.

6. Levon Chorbajian, "Nagorno Karabakh: A Study in Mythmaking," unpublished paper presented at the Media and Crisis conference, Laval University, Quebec, Oct. 1990, pp. 6-7.

7. This journalist had been criticized for his tendency to support speculation about the "Islamic dimension" of the disturbances in Central Asian republics in a letter by Amyn Sajoo to the editor of the *Peace & Security* magazine. Sajoo wrote about Handleman's article in a previous issue of the magazine: "Somehow the nationalism of Estonians, Latvians and Armenians against Moscow's over-reaching authority is deemed perfectly reasonable, but that of Uzbeks, Tadzhiks or Kazakhs is portrayed as some dark

fundamentalist prospect. Never mind that the churches have played a prominent role in rallying nationalist sentiment from the Baltic to the Caucasus. The slightest hint of Muslim fervour conjures up images of militancy on the march. For Handleman, even 'afternoon prayers in Bukhara contain an ominous message for Moscow itself.'" Amyn B. Sajoo, "Rampant Orientalist Stereotypes," *Peace and Security* 4:2 (Sum. 1989), p. 19.

8. An Associated Press story on the Armenian capture of a town in Nagorno-Karabakh carried by *The Montreal Gazette* on June 29, 1993, whose lead described the exodus of Azeri refugees from the region, once again dropped religious references.

9. Jacques Ellul, *Propaganda: The Formation of Men's Attitudes*, translated by Konrad Kellen and Jean Lerner (New York: Alfred A. Knopf, 1969), p. 47.

10. Robert L. Ivie, "Images of Savagery in American Justifications for War," *Communications Monographs* 47 (Nov. 1980), p. 284.

11. However, it is noteworthy that the use of "Iranian" had predominated during the reign of pro-Western Shah Mohammed Reza Pahlevi, who was overthrown in 1979. A pertinent example is this description of the Ossetians in a book about West Asian peoples: "The Ossetians are an Islamic people who speak a language that is related to Iranian (Persian)." Herman Wouters, *Peoples and Customs of the World: West Asia* (Geneva: Ferni, 1979), p. 43.

CHAPTER 10

TOWARDS INFORMED AND CONSCIENTIOUS REPORTING

Self-Knowledge By the Way of the Other

This book has sought to show how the spectre of "Islamic peril" is portrayed in the mass media's reporting of international relations. Mainstream journalists usually adhere to the dominant discourses on violence. These discourses accord an implicit primacy to nation-states, particularly to elite nations such as the American superpower, the permanent members of the United Nations Security Council, and the members of the Group of Seven/Eight. At the bottom of the hierarchy of nations are pariahs like Iran, Iraq, Libya, Syria, Afghanistan, Sudan, Cuba, and North Korea. The wholesale violence carried out by elite nations, on the global, and by all states on the domestic scale, is generally invisible in the mass media; on the other hand, the retail violence of sub-national groups is highlighted. Also unseen is structural violence, which is omnipresent at the international and domestic levels, and which indirectly but inexorably leads to the maiming and death of people.

The transnational media, headquartered in the U.S. and Europe, also adhere to the dominant Northern discourses on Islam. Centuries-old primary stereotypes, particularly that of "the violent Muslim," continue to influence contemporary perceptions. Critical examination of the motivations and social conditions of people claiming to act in the cause of Islam is seldom conducted, and deviant activity by people who happen to be Muslim is often attributed to their religion. Significant differences among Muslims and among Islamists are usually glossed over. The image of the "Islamic terrorist" has become a staple in coverage of Muslim societies. Whereas terrorism perpetrated by certain Muslim groups should indeed be of concern, similar depictions of Christians, Jews, or followers of other religions carrying out violence in the names of their respective faiths are rarely carried out. Describing a war as a jihad—whose definition is contested among Muslims themselves—becomes a way for Northern propagandists to discredit the motives of the Muslim combatants who are considered hostile to Northern interests. Even when conflicts involving Muslims result primarily from political, economic, or cultural causes, they are frequently framed as religious wars. The term "Muslim extremists" is often used to describe even those who use non-violent means of opposition to Northern hegemony.

Confrontations are often presented in polarized frameworks by the mass media as "Christian versus Muslim," "Islam versus the West," "Sunni versus Shia"—this is usually due to a journalism that seeks pat answers for complex situations. The current struggles in Muslim societies to deal with centuries of decay and exploitation—both domestic and colonial—and the attempts to confront these problems with indigenous religio-cultural approaches are usually reduced to conflicts between "fundamentalists" and "modernists." This tendency dovetails with discursive constructions of the post-Cold War order, in which the "Evil Empire" of the communist East is often replaced with the Muslim East as a primary Other. The resilience of the topoi of violence, lust, greed and barbarism, which have become integral to global media narratives, facilitates this process. Not only are these age-old images used as frames to interpret current events, but when Muslim groups are in conflict with a Northern power the reporting tends inevitably to favour the latter.

While some Northern discourses do attempt to impart alternative views on Muslim societies, much of the mainstream reporting is laden with formulaic references. "Islam" becomes a composite entity, with little distinction made between its diverse followers and their respective beliefs, cultures, and actions. Since setting off a bomb in a skyscraper is portrayed as being "Islamic," then the act of the Islamic prayer becomes evidence of radical militancy. Time and space lose all meaning when talking about this "Islam"—ideological genealogies of "Islamic terrorists" going all the way back to the time of Muhammad are drawn up by Orientalists and reproduced by the mass media. Indeed, the Islamic prophet has become the epitome of the core images that have recurred for centuries in Northern imaginaries about Muslims. Such essentialist views of the religion's adherents reinforce the idea that they are inherently unable to rise above their supposedly savage state.

Crisis situations in Muslim societies appear to cause propagandists to fill their narratives with stereotypical depictions of Islam. The hijacking of an American airliner by a group of Lebanese Muslims became "*Islamic* terrorism," the kidnapping of several Western men in Beirut came to define the entire historical phenomenon of hostage-taking, the territorial war between Azeris and Armenians was framed as "Islam versus Christianity," the guilt of the Nazi Holocaust against European Jewry was transposed onto the Arabs in conflict with Israel, Saddam Hussein in the guise of the Muslim despot became the contemporary Hitler waging war against "the Allies," and the object of containment shifted from the communist East to the Muslim East. Our just wars are based on "Judeo-Christian" ethical/moral principles and abide by international law, but their jihad is an expression of barbarism. The dominant image of Muslims as villains who habitually victimize Christians and Jews seems to have had concrete behavioural effects. Apart from prompting systemic ill-treatment of Muslims, this image probably helped determine the reluctant response of Northern public opinion and governments to the Israeli repression of Palestinians, the large-scale rape and massacres by Serb rebels of Bosnian Muslims, and the massive Russian bombing of Chechen homes and marketplaces.

As they echoed George Bush's call for a "New World Order," mainstream journalists reaffirmed the image of universal just war led by America against evil. Implicit in this quest for global utopia was a promise of world peace bringing with it freedom, democracy, and equality for all humanity. But that was an illusion. In their failure to deconstruct the propaganda of their own governments and those of repressive Southern regimes, the North-based transnational media become complicit in entrenching the global *status quo*. The research done on the Gulf War's coverage in several countries—whose media remain dependent on global news networks—provides us with a clear indication of the emergence of an globally dominant media narrative. The major news agencies and the global broadcasting networks such as CNN and BBC operate on the fundamental premise that they are largely objective and report "world news" in a generally unbiased fashion, akin to social science methodology. The modern scientific method, a universalized discourse derived from the North, is supposed to provide as clear as possible a picture of the truth. This view belies the reality of information-gathering (journalism in this case) as a *cultural* practice which is necessarily influenced by collective memories embedded in the myths, legends, classic pieces of literature, and socialization experiences that shape our world views.

The self-awareness of one's own cognitive processes is the first step towards the production of less ethnocentric and more authentic accounts of events. Indeed, Edward Said, Rana Kabbani, and Thierry Hentsch, among others, have attempted to demonstrate that the portrayal of the Muslim East has served to project the less-attractive Northern qualities of the Self onto the nearest Other. Since the Northern gaze into the Orient has turned "as in a convex mirror, to reflect the Occident that had produced it"[1], Northern "*self-knowledge must lead by way of the Other.*"[2] Transnational mass media, which seemed so eager to support the "just war" should be equally willing to foster democracy in Muslim societies in order to create a better global society: "These problems are interwoven, binding Muslims and non-Muslims together. There can be no just and viable world order—let alone a 'New World Order'—if these wrongs are not redressed."[3] Not only are there discursive links between violence and the media, but also technological ones. Fatima Mernissi draws attention to the relationship between the Northern media and the Northern military: the global hegemony of both has transgressed the borders of Muslims societies.

The enemy is no longer just on the earth; he occupies the heavens and stars [with satellites] and rules over time [with the Christian calender and Universal Coordinated Time]. He seduces one's wife, veiled or not, entering through the skylight of television. Bombs are only an incidental accessory for the new masters. Cruise missiles are for great occasions and the inevitable sacrifices. In normal times they nourish us with "software": advertising messages, teenage songs, everyday technical information, courses for earning diplomas, languages and codes to master.[4]

The North decides whether satellites will be used for education, propaganda, or missiles. It has hitherto mainly used this technology to create global consensus in its own favour, failing which it has resorted to coercion.

Northern powers generally continue to pursue an ethnocentric agenda at international fora, developing a political, economic, and socio-cultural infrastructure that reflects Northern values and strengthens Northern positions vis-à-vis the South. This bolsters the structures put in place during and after the colonial era. Contemporary international law broadly replicates the values of the Christian international law on which it is based, and world trade agreements reinforce the economic hegemony of Northern industry and agriculture. The preferential arrangements within the European Union simultaneously raise barricades against Muslim, Christian, and Jewish neighbours, with whom they have had long trading and cultural relationships, as well as against non-white minorities within.

Despite their self-assumed universalist posture (bearing "the white man's burden"), Northern societies remain tribal at a very fundamental level. Citing from Joseph Campbell, Mernissi remarks that even such a momentous and technologically significant event as the first human landing on the moon was not bereft of primitive ritual.[5] The universalizing nature of Neil Armstrong's resounding statement "one small step for man, one giant leap for mankind" notwithstanding, he proceeded to install a tribal totem onto the moonscape and then treated his attentive, transnational, earthbound audience with a quotation from his religion's scripture. Whereas most Americans may not view the planting of their national flag and recitation from the Bible as contrary to the universalist ethos, using the political symbols of a Muslim-majority country and a Koranic verse in a similar situation would most likely be condemned as signs of chauvinism and religious fundamentalism.

Although this study has not dealt with the stereotypes that Muslims have about others, there seems to exist an almost reciprocal level of misunderstanding and derision in a number of Muslim discourses about the North. However, the latter is economically, technologically, and militarily more powerful and has hegemony over global discourses; on the other hand, Muslim societies generally lack the communications hardware or knowhow to have a material effect on a transnational basis. Nevertheless, while Muslims have long become familiar with the intrusions from the North, Northern societies are beginning to acknowledge that they have to come to terms with the adherents of Islam who constitute one-fifth of humanity. Muslim populations continue to increase at a significant pace because of their comparatively high birth and conversion rates. Islam is well on its way to becoming the second most-popular faith after Christianity in many Northern countries largely as a result of immigration patterns and the numbers of native-born North Americans and Europeans becoming adherents. The Muslim

Other who used to be far away across the oceans is now more likely to be a next-door neighbour. As Homi Bhabha has suggested, the postcolonial Other, whether inside or outside the Northern nation, is to be accounted for within the "enunciative 'present' of modernity"[6]—the Self is finding it increasingly difficult to completely distinguish itself from the Other. Polarized frameworks of "us versus them" are becoming even more invalid than ever.

What role does journalism have in responding to this situation? The answer obviously does not lie in promoting coverage that overlooks the ills and problems in Muslims societies, but perhaps is to be found in encouraging an informed and conscientious journalism that places events and processes within their contexts. (I have deliberately avoided using the terms "objectivity"—a human impossibility; "accuracy"—an ideal more suited to mathematics, not journalism; "balance"—often reduced to ritually supplying just two points of view that may not be essentially different; or "fair"—the "Fairness Doctrine" in American journalism has been primarily interpreted as the requirement to have "balance.") We are dealing here with issues that speak to the professionalism as well as the ethics of the craft. Many Northern journalists have already been genuinely adapting their methods to take into account the increasing ethnic, cultural, and religious diversity of their societies. However, even though there have been some efforts to understand Muslims better, the older discourses on Islam continue largely to provide the frameworks for their portrayal. Assuming that Northern news organizations are interested in producing informed coverage, what can be done to allow for journalists to have a better comprehension and provide such reportage about Muslims? A conscientious journalism would require going beyond the dominant cognitive scripts and models that govern traditional reporting of the subject matter, avoiding the use of generalizations and stereotypes, and seeking diverse viewpoints on "positive" and "negative" aspects of the story. Bad journalism is replete with speculation, false dichotomies, and absolutes (e.g., clichés such as "the gulf between Islam and the West can never be bridged").

The traditional approaches of media activities such as assignment decisions, newsgathering techniques, editing methods, and the ever-present tyranny of the deadline structurally impede the construction of an informed report. Therefore the challenge that the journalist faces in enhancing the professionalism of her craft and of the mass media institution is to be shared by the technical, managerial, and executive ranks of news organizations as well as by those who train journalists. A comprehensive review on journalism curriculum by Everett Dennis, former director of the Gannett Center for Media Studies at Columbia University and a much-discussed article on the same topic by Stuart Adam, former director of Carleton University's School of Journalism and Communication, both urge the integration of theory drawn from academic disciplines into the professional aspects of journalism training.[7] Such an approach would help to move journalism schools away from being industry-oriented trade schools to training men and women with a broader base of knowledge about the world. It would help to inculcate a more informed and critical perspective on events and issues that would resist slippage into formulaic and clichéd forms of reporting, especially about foreign cultures.

Demystifying Muslim Societies

A significant part of the responsibility for the failure of Northern mass media to provide informed coverage of Muslim societies lies with Muslims themselves. They have not been able to explain clearly the ethical and humanistic content of Islam; they have also, by default, often allowed militant Islamists to become the spokespersons for all Muslims. Underpinning the issue of miscommunication between Muslims and their Northern observers are a number of serious problems among the former. Many Muslim societies have had shortcomings in developing effective political leaderships, genuinely democratic and self-sufficient communities, dynamic civil societies, and workable mechanisms for conflict resolution among Muslims and with non-Muslims. They have also been slow to implement creative strategies for harnessing human and material resources, independent infrastructures for scientific research, or contemporary methodologies to study indigenous intellectual heritages. The results have been war, social instability, poverty, hopelessness, and a lack of confidence that makes individuals susceptible to the simplistic solutions offered by Islamists and political extremists. Overemphasis on material values by the dominant discourses of development, which have been adopted by most governments of Muslim-majority countries, have also increased the appeal of the solutions based on narrow interpretations of scripture.

Among the other key problems of Muslim societies has been the failure to understand the North, and particularly the West. The ideas of liberalism were introduced into Muslim lands in the nineteenth century, but an appreciation of concepts such as the freedom of expression seems frequently absent among governments. Even though the formal rights and freedoms of individuals in democratic societies are usually modulated by structures of power, they remain integral to the self-image of most Western societies. These contradictions appear confusing to many Muslims, who also find it hard to reconcile the West's secular ethos with its ethical and moral values. They often stand bewildered at the North's kaleidoscopically-shifting media images and plethora of consumer products, which they themselves consume without comprehending either their cultural origins or long-term effects. Western support for Israeli governments which have dispossessed Palestinians of their lands and property have brought into doubt Western commitment to the ideals of universal justice. In a reversal of a long historical tradition of inter-communal tolerance, anti-Israeli feelings have mutated for a number of Muslims into anti-Jewish sentiments. This in turn has led dominant Northern discourses to view the religion of Islam as being anti-Judaic.

When Salman Rushdie offended the sensibilities of Muslims, some were goaded by self-serving demagogues into reacting through violence. This reaction in the name of Islam was interpreted as barbarism by those Northern observers who encoded the conflict "as Freedom of Speech versus Terrorism,"[8] despite Rushdie's own declaration that "I have never seen this controversy as a struggle between Western freedoms and Eastern unfreedom."[9] There seemed to be no grey space, no occasion for second thought. Muslims who seriously attempted to grapple with the "Rushdie Affair" and expressed reservations about the content of The Satanic Verses (1988) tended to be lumped in with the militant Islamists by certain self-appointed guardians of Western freedom, some of whom had not even bothered to read the book. The latter demanded no less than a complete acceptance of the tome: "many liberal intellectuals sounded like Inquisition priests in their shrill and blanket condemnations."[10] Needless to say, they were astonished at Rushdie's own (albeit short-lived) return to the fold of Islam. The misunderstandings on the parts of Northern and Muslim societies seem to feed on each other to generate an increasing number of distortions.

There are, however, some genuine attempts on both sides to learn about the Other. A significant proportion of the work currently emerging from Orientalist institutions seeks to be more cognizant of indigenous Muslim values. In October 1990, as Northern integration propagandists were drawing a dark picture of the "Islamic" Iraqi enemy, one gathering of Muslim and non-Muslim scholars meeting in Indonesia was engaged in discussion about the interface of Muslim and Northern societies. Discourse at the transnational seminar on the "Expressions of Islam in Buildings" ranged on issues such as the meanings of modernity, tradition, secularism, and humanism. Some participants noted that although modernists among Muslims have rushed to embrace Northern education and consumer goods as well as industrial, electronic and military hardware, there has been little impetus to develop "intellectual modernity."[11]

The status of women as well as of ethnic, cultural, and religious (including Muslim) minorities in a number of Muslim societies has failed to conform to the Universal Declaration on Human Rights. Afghanistan's Taliban government's treatment of women is held up as the worst example of gender-based repression in the world. Several other Muslim-majority governments have imposed restrictions on minorities and sometimes even turned a blind eye to physical attacks upon them. Apart from discrediting the Islamic concept of the harmonious Muslim community (ummah), such actions make a mockery of the status of dhimmi, protected peoples, which gives Jews and Christians freedoms to practice their religions and run their own institutions. Much work needs to be done to enhance human rights in Muslims societies; but it is intellectually dishonest to expect stringent application of standards developed primarily according to dominant Northern discourses, and which are subject to political manipulation even in the democratic West.

The Muslim ummah, currently in its 15th century, is undergoing a period of collective soul-searching reminiscent of Western Christendom during the late Middle Ages. However, the crisis for Muslims is rendered even more acute because contemporary technological discourses are culturally alien to them, whereas the Renaissance and the Reformation were indigenous European developments. Whereas journalists need necessarily to continue reporting on corruption and human rights abuses wherever they exist, a knowledgeable approach requires that they be aware of the historical and socio-cultural backgrounds of the societies they cover as well as the nature of their own relationships with them. The status of the Muslim female is a case in point. She remains under the constant threat of having her limited privileges revoked by conservative regimes. But Fatima Mernissi points out that, ironically, it is the unremitting panoptic gaze of the Northern powers that is one of the strongest argument of Muslim conservatives against the establishment of greater freedoms for the individual, women, and minority groups: "when the enemy satellites are keeping watch, it is not the moment to wallow in one's individuality."[12] This is the same collective enemy that brutally colonized Muslim lands and still launches attacks against them. Intense feelings of vulnerability, indeed nakedness, in the face of Northern cultural, economic, and military intrusions are a factor in the frequent unwillingness even to explore the issue of rights. The wagons also remain circled against the relentless attacks in the transnational media; what is perceived as the latter's siege against Muslims gives the elites of conservative regimes the excuse to sustain and even strengthen societal restrictions. Northern observers are generally oblivious to, or perhaps choose to ignore, the consequences of their constant, collective gaze upon the Muslim object—a gaze which, despite its omnipresence, serves to mystify rather than enlighten.

The generalization and polarization of all Muslims as "fundamentalists" and "moderates," "traditionalists" and "modernists," "fanatics" and "secularists" serves to distort communication. It tends to make the Muslims who are interested in constructive dialogue with non-Muslims defensive about their beliefs or, contrarily, disdainful about any interaction. The outside observer needs to understand, first of all, that beyond the agreement on the fundamentals of Islam, there is vast diversity among its one billion adherents living not only in their ancestral lands from Senegal to Mindanao, but also as immigrants in Northern societies from California to Sweden to New Zealand. Even among Islamists there is a wide divergence of opinion about the parameters of "true Islam" and the ways of adhering to it.

The Northern mass media have the tendency to declare manifestations of Muslim belief such as the call for decency in films, wearing the *hijab*, or even performing the Muslim prayer as certain signs of "Islamic fundamentalism," when petitions for the reduction of violence in children's television programs, the wearing of Christian religious apparel, or attending Church are generally not considered out of the ordinary in the North.[13] John Esposito urges that we should

> ...move beyond facile stereotypes and ready-made images and answers. Just as simply perceiving the Soviet Union and Eastern Europe through the prism of the "evil empire" had its costs, so too the tendency of American

administrations and the media to equate Islam and Islamic activism with Qadhafi/Khomeini and thus with radicalism, terrorism and anti-Americanism has seriously hampered our understanding and conditioned our responses...The challenge today is to appreciate the diversity of Islamic actors and movements, to ascertain the reasons behind confrontations and conflicts, and thus to react to specific events and situations with informed, reasoned responses rather than pre-determined presumptions and reactions.[14]

Whereas certain elements among Muslims do indeed pose a threat to Northern interests, to see all practising Muslims as constituting a collective peril makes the locus of the actual danger difficult to locate. It also inhibits the development of a genuine dialogue between Northern and Muslim societies.

Other Ways of Telling

Just as it seemed that the world would be organized under a unitary New World Order, there has emerged a profusion of challenges. The postfeminist, postmodernist, postcolonial, and other dissenting movements of the marginalized in the South and the North, speaking against the hegemony of dominant discourses, have inspired the search for alternative perspectives. Several suggestions have been made for more informed and more authentic ways of depicting the Other. Representations that have reduced a multitude of life experiences to stereotypical portrayals of "immigrant," "Third World," "Black," "Oriental," "Arab," "Muslim," or "Islamic radical" can be liberated through open-ended, multidimensional narratives that do not ascribe essentialist characteristics to any group. Postcolonial writers are attempting to develop "other ways of telling."[15] Their polyvalent discourses allow for the understanding of human beings as operating in multiple fields at the same time. The challenge for journalism is to explore these new forms of narrative.

Unfortunately, most journalists generally remain quite unprepared to cope with such tasks. Stuart Adam, who proposes greater emphasis on "the moral, the literary, and the philosophical faces of journalism education," laments that the standard style manuals for journalists "rarely speak of the power of metaphor and other literary devices to convey meaning."[16] The focus on the imparting of professional skills in most journalism schools and the minimal exposure to the humanities or even the social sciences leaves students with limited intellectual tools to understand the world. The problem is multiplied when the graduates of such schools are given foreign reporting assignments. Frequently, events in other countries are interpreted through narrow perspectives that are unable to understand the subtleties of situations arising from unfamiliar cultural and historical backgrounds.

How does one carry out interpretations of events in another culture to produce a coherent account for the reader at home, without lapsing either into a ethnocentric narrative or losing oneself completely in the Other's discourse? An answer may be found in Abdul JanMohamed's identification of "the specular border intellectual," who must disengage personally from allegiances to any one culture, nation, group, institution, etc. "to the extent that these are defined in monologic, essentialist terms."[17] The specular border intellectual "caught between two cultures...subjects the cultures to analytic scrutiny rather than combining them."[18] Instead of becoming disoriented and out of place, she uses the vantage point that she occupies to view horizons difficult for others to envision. The Reverend Benjamin Weir, who was held in captivity by a militant Islamist group in Lebanon, seems to have became such an individual in seeking to understand his captors, despite his suffering at their hands:

> I reflect on their self- and group-perception neither to justify nor to approve, but to describe. In fact, I deeply resented what they were doing to me. They prevented my freedom. They were a physical and psychological threat to me. They caused distress to my family. They caused fear to my colleagues. They upset the scheme of life, and they shook the foundations of what social order was still left in Beirut. Their violence had already caused, before my capture, great loss of life and severe destruction at the U.S. Embassy and the Marine base. None of this could I excuse. Obviously I could not trust them. But still it was important to me to try to understand them. That understanding came to me very slowly, bit by bit, over sixteen months of my captivity.[19]

It appears that under such circumstances the task of the border specular intellectual is little short of heroic, but apparently not impossible. The foreign correspondent, by learning to question the essentialist bases of her own socialization could genuinely begin to understand the people she is covering (but, as Weir indicates, understanding does not necessarily mean agreeing with them). The ideal of a specular border journalism has the potential for providing genuinely global narratives that are not monolithic but pluralist, in which cultures are not arranged hierarchically. Such discourses become all the more crucial as people in different locations on the planet seek to develop a world-wide civil society.

One of the most significant barriers facing the development of informed reportage about Islam is the lack of knowledge and unease among many Northern journalists about religion in general. Henry A. Grunwald, a former editor-in-chief of *Time*, arguing for the need for a "new journalism" in the post-Cold War era, noted:

> Crucial among the newer topics journalism must address are tribalism and ethnic self-assertion, phenomena about which social scientists, let alone reporters, know little; likewise with religion, a subject most journalists have found unsettling ever since it wandered from the Sunday religion pages to the front page. Religious wars, large and small, seem increasingly likely in the decades ahead. *Time* magazine recently tied together in one cover package the bombing of the World Trade Center in New York City by Muslim fundamentalists, the seige in Texas of a group of cultists whose leader apparently thought he was a messiah, and the conflict between

Muslims and Christians in Bosnia. This link was legitimate but frail, because these were very different manifestations of "religion." Not every Muslim fundamentalist wants to blow up New York City, and few Christian fundamentalists belong to cults ready for Armageddon. The press must discuss such distinctions knowledgeably and conscientiously.[20]

Unfortunately, such journalistic hindsight about "religious wars" seems to occur usually after considerable damage has already been done by traditional media discourses. Deviant faith frequently becomes the focus for reporters not familiar with issues of spirituality. NBC's former bureau chief in Cairo, S. Abdullah Schleifer, remarks that peaceful religious events are usually disregarded by the foreign press: "Somehow religion only comes alive as a story when somebody is getting insulted or killed."[21] Most Northern journalists covering Muslim societies are largely unfamiliar not only with the subtleties of the contemporary religious debates but also with the primary beliefs and practices of their members. The practice of sufism, popular in virtually all Muslims societies and which emphasizes Islam's humanistic side in its aspirations for universal fellowship, goes almost unacknowledged in the mass media.

The failure of Northern observers to realize the impending fall of the Shah of Iran in 1979 was largely due to their ignorance about the extent of the populist outrage against the monarch, that had been harnessed by the religious leadership for its own purposes. State-run mass media, which had largely lost credibility among the public, were circumvented by traditional means of communication linked to religious institutions.[22] This remarkable underground network was virtually invisible to Western journalists who were enamoured with the Shah's much-touted modernization policies, that in reality had left large numbers of Iranians dispossessed and alienated. In a study on the American mass media's coverage of the Iranian hostage situation, Hamid Mowlana considers alternative modes of reporting in a conflict situation.[23] He suggests that journalists should have attempted to assist in the resolution of the Iranian hostage crisis rather than inflame passions on both sides with their reporting. Instead of contributing to a crisis mood, the Northern media could help to create non-conflictual attitudes in periods of moderate stress. An exploration of "universal concepts of religious, ideological, or traditional values should be used to bridge the existing cultural communication gap. The common aspects of life that unite rather than divide could be emphasized."[24]

Beyond the economic, cultural, and military humiliations suffered by the Muslim at the hands of dominant Northern powers, one has to acknowledge the violence done to her spirit. The extreme reactions of some dispossessed Muslims towards Northern interests cannot be explored without taking into account the spiritual dimensions of the conflict. Such an analysis is attempted of the Iranian hostage-takings (1979-81) by Robin Woodsworth Carlsen:

If we considered some of these points: the context within which the Iranian action has taken place, the perception they have of the foundation of our policies, the interpretation they must give to the kind of reaction we have had to this confrontation, we might realize another level of approach, another level of understanding, one that would enable us to transcend the disastrously narrow basis of our present attitude... the Iranians would believe they would be doing an injustice to *us* if they gave in to our demands, i.e. released the hostages under the terms the U.S. has demanded. For the Iranians believe the world is caught in the most tragic spiritual condition, that is, through this drama that the potency, the beauty, the resoluteness of the religious consciousness will be revealed, [and] the bankruptcy—morally, spiritually—of the purely secular, realpolitik conditioned view of the world will be exposed.[25]

The intrusions of the values and commodities emanating from a secularist and consumerist culture have affected the world views of Muslims in profound manners. While many do not understand the bewilderment they experience, they do sense a threat to their fundamental senses of right and wrong. Observers of these tragedies cannot divorce the subsequent reactions—some of which are violent—from their causes. Carlsen's approach, in attempting to communicate at the level of the human spirit and of universally acknowledged values, brings to light a plea for justice on the part of the Iranian dispossessed. He also carries out moral, political, psychological, and aesthetic analyses in his study. Such a multi-faceted scrutiny should not excuse or justify atrocities carried out by Muslim militants, but it helps bring to light some underlying causes.

Despite Edward Said's own disposition in favour of "secular criticism"[26] he is appreciative of the "science of compassion" adopted by Louis Massignon in his extended study of Muslim societies. A devout Catholic and scholar of religion (and a specular border intellectual by JanMohamed's definition), he strived to understand the spiritual universals that underlay the faith and practices of Christians and Muslims. Said notes in Massignon's work the notion of distance that kept Christianity and Islam distinct, without the attempt to assert the dominance of one's own religious or cultural background: "the religion [Islam] attracted and yet resisted the Christian in him, although—and here is the man's extraordinary stroke of genius—he conceived his own philological work as a science of compassion, as providing a place for Islam and Christianity to approach and substitute for each other, yet always remaining apart, one always substituting for the other."[27] For Massignon, "language is both a 'pilgrimage' and 'spiritual displacement' "[28] which enabled his non-hegemonic narrative. Despite some shortcomings of Massignon's approach,[29] journalists would do well to learn from it.

Contemporary approaches of conflict resolution suggest the importance of understanding symbols and symbolic behaviour (rituals) on the part of disputing parties. More than statistics or descriptions of events, the symbolic subtexts of human interactions should be among the primary foci of interest for observers. Symbols and rituals help establish power, and are key to interpreting gestures of peace-making, forgiveness, and harmonious co-existence.[30] Underlying symbols and rituals is myth; it is vital for journalists as observers of the human condition to be cognizant of the place of myth and symbols. The mythical significance of Jerusalem, for example, is key to understanding the contemporary relations not only between Palestinians and Israelis but also among Muslims, Christians, and Jews. Uniform media references to "the Temple Mount" rather than "Haram al-Shareef" privilege the Jewish perspective and history over the Muslim. Mohammed Arkoun has argued for a better appreciation of "the *radical imaginary* common to the societies of the Book/books,"[31] namely, Jews, Christians and Muslims. The radical imaginary is viewed here as the common Abrahamic root of these believers' respective sets of symbols, which could be tapped to understand the true universals shared by these communities for the development of dynamic national and transnational civil societies. (Indeed, there is a larger need to extend understanding of human universals to engender a genuinely global civil society.)

The secularist[32] outlook militates against a full understanding of human impulses. Jacques Ellul has argued that it is the fundamental human attraction to totalizing world views, which seek to provide answers to all questions, that makes the secular individual responsive to the universal myths couched even in the technological state's propaganda.[33] There appears to remain a primary affinity to the spiritual import of communication even among those inured to the technique-dominated ethos of contemporary society. Aziz Esmail proposes a wider humanistic discourse that would integrate an understanding of the material and the spiritual aspects of life.

This means transcending our present compartmentalization of knowledge into discrete techniques and disciplines. Let me emphasize here that I am arguing for something deeper, something more basic, than what is nowadays called an "interdisciplinary" approach. The task is not simply to make the "disciplines" blend together into what would merely be an intellectual cocktail mixture. It is, rather, to explore the human foundations in their unity, in a state logically prior to, and transcending, the division of the human project into separate arts, crafts, and sciences. The ultimate aim, in this as in other areas, should be to reconnect knowledge to the human person, for man stands at the point of intersection between technique and spirituality.[34]

In this, Esmail envisions the disintegration of the dichotomies that have separated religion from humanism and tradition from modernity. Technique, rather than alienating the individual through its obeisance to rationalism, can thus be vitalized by responding to the innermost aspirations of human beings.

The dominant discourses of journalism are rationalistic; they tend to undervalue those actions and events that cannot be explained by "the logic of the concrete"[35] which derives from mainstream political or socio-economic theories. Media narratives therefore generally disregard the non-rationalist expressions of the human spirit. Quite apart from religious motivations, all human beings carry out actions whose causes have little to do with the rational faculty. Astute journalists have long recognized that compassion, love, devotion, faith, loyalty, honour, pride, ambition, guilt, jealousy, fear, anger, hate, and revenge are among the most powerful "positive" and "negative" impulses, driving people to behave in manners that rationalism fails to inspire. Those who do not understand these fundamental workings of human communication fail to comprehend the non-rationalism of much of social, political, and economic behaviour as well as the roots of truly universal values. As a result they tend to attribute the actions which they do not understand to "the bizarre," "the strange," "barbarism," "fanaticism," or "fundamentalism." They also fail to comprehend the direct, physical violence which is a reaction to the structural violence of the rationalist discourses that deny what Johann Galtung calls the "higher needs" of human beings. Understanding the dynamics of power and violence in the relationship between Northern and Muslim societies necessarily involves an appreciation of the continual assault by the dominant technological discourses on the spiritual as well as the rational sensibilities of people in these societies.

If Northern journalists wish to produce informed reporting on Muslims they will find it necessary to reorient their modes of operation. First of all, one has to understand the basis one's own conceptualization about the Other. Collective cultural memories play a large part in our views about Islam, as do our society's fundamental myths. It is also important to acknowledge the importance that religious beliefs hold for significant numbers of people; they cannot be dismissed as superstitions, bizarre, or quaint but as forming a vital part of many individuals' existence. The human spirit is the source of universal values; rather than dwell on superficial differences, the recognition of the truly universal can help the observer of foreign cultures to understand the basis of their members' actions. Symbols and rituals embedded in daily life constitute a language that is a truer guide to deeply-held attitudes than political and diplomatic discourses. The journalists who understand the value of these fundamental forms of communication are able to decipher the reality that underlies words and gestures. Those who are mired in stereotypical images of groups and individuals produce hackneyed reports that do not go beyond conflictual scenarios. The institutional response of the mass media to a conflict situation is usually to react first, using clichés and stereotypes in almost unrestrained manners, and then to reflect upon the matter. Journalism as a craft has to explore more seriously the ways of rising above those of its institutional structures that inhibit informed and conscientious reporting. Whereas structural constraints, like the deadline, the world view of the gatekeeper, and the desire to see one's work used by media outlets mould adherence to formulaic models of particular situations, the practice of informed journalism by significant numbers of reporters can conceivably produce a critical mass of more authentic coverage.

The Northern media have increasingly been in dialogue with Muslims regarding the coverage of Islam. Individual Muslims and organizations have used a variety of means such as writing letters to editors, holding meetings with the staff of media organizations, and publishing reports about coverage. Religious leaders such as Shaykh Hisham Kabbani, founder of the Islamic Supreme Council of America, Shaykh Faisal Abdur Razak, director of the Islamic Forum of Canada, the Aga Khan, Imam of Nizari Ismailis, and Rexhap Boja, Grand Mufti of Kosovo have sought to explain aspects of Islam and to project the plurality of Muslims through various communication strategies. Several Muslim journalists working in Northern media have also attempted to present alternatives discourses. Newspapers occasionally print opinion pieces by Muslim readers on the portrayal of Islam. The Washington-based Council for American-Islamic Relations (CAIR) runs an active campaign, largely through electronic mailing lists and the World Wide Web, to counter negative stereotyping. It frequently organizes lobbying campaigns, encouraging subscribers to register their comments with the media institution in question; recipients of its "action alerts" are reminded to be "FIRM but POLITE. Hostility is counterproductive."[36] The Ontario-based Canadian Islamic Congress analyses coverage of Muslims by Canadian press. It summarizes its findings in an annual report titled *Anti-Islam in the Media*, which has received attention from journalists.[37] The congress also disseminates an on-line weekly newsletter to an inter-continental readership.

Some Hollywood producers have attempted to forestall controversy by screening the rough cuts of their films for representatives of Muslim as well as other religious institutions.[38] A few media organizations have also apologized for running offending items. For example, a complaint by CAIR led to an apology from the producers of *The Royal Canadian Air Farce*, a comedy program on the Canadian Broadcasting Corporation in which a character appeared in Arab clothing, spoke in a mock Arabic accent, and read an advertisement for a fictitious store called "Terrorist Depot." CRFB, a Toronto radio station, recanted for the failure of a open-line talk show host to challenge a caller who said, "Nero burned the wrong people—he should have burned the Muslims."[39] The transnational credit card company Mastercard withdrew a French television advertisement that ran in Quebec after protests from Muslim organizations: it was set in a fictitious Muslim location and appeared to make fun of the word "Allah."[40] Another set of complaints led GeoCities, a major provider of free personal web page services, to remove a website which contained deflamatory statements like: "Islam imposes a threat to the whole world which is far worse than deforestation, nuclear destruction or AIDS. It is an insidious, devilish disease creeping into the veins of the world."[41]

There is a stream of articles about Muslims in mainstream newspapers whose frames do not conform to dominant discourses. These appear to be more frequent in times of low tension between Northern and Muslim societies. The front of *The New York Times*' Week in Review section highlighted the portrayal of Muslim societies on January 21, 1996. "Seeing Green: The Red Menace is Gone. But Here's Islam" by Elaine Sciolino reviewed the threats posed by groups of militant Islamists in their specific contexts, showing the absence of an overall, coherent danger posed by a monolithic Islamic peril. This feature article described the alarmist tendencies in the post-Cold War era, especially among those who seek to reduce the complexities of transnational politics and conflicts to the spectre of the "green menace" (green is the colour usually related to Islam in Muslim narratives). Another piece in *The New York Times* on January 28, 1996, written by an Israeli journalist who had travelled extensively in the Caucasus, sought sympathetically to understand the causes and depth of Chechen nationalism.

The Ottawa Citizen's film critic, Jay Stone, titled his Sunday column of March 17, 1996, "Billionaires, bombers and belly dancers." It looked at the consistent tendency of Hollywood movies to present Arabs and Muslims according the core stereotypes of greed, violence, and lust. "Where are the movie Arabs and Muslims who are just ordinary people?" he asked. "It is time for Hollywood to end this undeclared war." An opinion piece in *The Observer* on April 21, 1996 by William Dalrymple briefly scanned Islamophobic coverage of Muslims in the British press. He surmised that "Anti-Muslim racism seems in many ways to be replacing anti-Semitism as the principal Western expression of bigotry against 'the other.'" An Associated Press article in the June 1, 1996 issue of *The Ottawa Citizen*, written by Haroun Hassan and datelined Mogadishu, Somalia, related how shariah-based rulings of local judges had helped reinstate order to part of the war-torn capital. Its headline, "Islamic court returns order to lawless city," was one of the rare occasions when "Islamic" was used positively in a political story. Another AP article published in *The Globe and Mail* on October 16, 1996 was about the complaint of the Iranian delegate at the World Conference on Women and Sport in Lausanne, Switzerland, regarding the lack of consideration given by the International Olympic Committee to the needs of Muslim women. The November 1996 issue of the *World Press Review* reprinted an article *The Economist* on "The Silent Black Muslim Majority" in the U.S.:

> Their journey pursues the true spirit of what Muslims call *jihad bil nafr*—the greater *jihad*—striving within the self to improve, to become more spiritual. (*Jihad fi sabil Allah*—the lesser *jihad*—is the much misrepresented striving in the path of God, only a small part of which concerns holy war.)

Andrew Cohen, a member of the editorial board of *The Globe and Mail* published an article on November 9, 1996 on the editorial page narrating his experience of visiting Hebron in the West Bank:

> As we walk the streets, eyes peer from narrow doorways. We are as obvious as Caucasians in Calcutta, but there is no hostility. A smile and a few words in Arabic are received warmly.

> For all that, though, my anxiety remains. It is less the Palestinians—though Hebron bears witness to their capacity to kill—than those pistol-packing settlers. It is the Star of David they've scrawled on the market walls, as arresting here as the swastika elsewhere. It is the swagger of their walk and the confidence of their beliefs, oblivious as they are to consequences.

A write-up by Marda Dunsky in *The Washington Post* and reprinted in *The Guardian Weekly* on February 7, 1997, was another rare indictment of Jewish settlers in the Occupied Territories. It contextualized the high-profile violent incidents like the assassination of former Israeli prime minister Yitzhak Rabin and the massacre of Muslim worshippers in Hebron's Ibrahimi mosque by highlighting the continual violence that the settlers carried out in the West Bank.

> The perception of Israel's moral superiority is so entrenched, at least in the United States, that comparing the violent settlers with bus bombers of Hamas may seem unthinkable to some. But the history of settler violence shows that the fears of Arab Hebronites for their safety in the mosque and the marketplace are as legitimate as those of Jewish bus riders in Tel Aviv and Jerusalem.

Such alternative narratives are almost non-existent in mainstream North American media, and are all the more remarkable when they do appear.

There has been a tendency in recent reporting on conflict involving Muslims to indicate that not all Muslims adhere to terrorism. In many such cases, which seem to be prompted by complaints by Muslims regarding poor coverage, this caveat becomes just another media ritual as the journalist then goes on to adopt the familiar decontextualized and stereotypical approach. Informed and conscientious journalism would take the trouble to explore various sides of the story, interviewing not only the familiar coterie of terrorism experts but also those Muslim religious and scholarly sources who have a knowledgeable understanding of the issue at hand. Such views should then be presented not as the essential representation of monolithic Muslim opinion, as is frequently done, but that of the individual or institution concerned.

Occasionally, media content will directly attack attempts to bring critical perspectives to bear on reporting about Muslims. For example, Steven Emerson, a writer and film-maker on "Islamic fundamentalist networks," published a long opinion piece in *The Montreal Gazette* of November 1, 1999 challenging those who labelled the critics of militant Muslims as anti-Muslim. It was written in response to a previous op-ed article by a Salam Elmenyawi of the Islamic Centre of Quebec, who had complained about the consistently negative portrayal of Muslims by Emerson. The latter attacked Elmenyawi for implying that there was a conspiracy against Islam among Emerson and two other journalists publishing in the *Gazette*, and constructed his article, titled "Imaginary conspiracies," upon this reading of Elmenyawi's write-up. In effect, Emerson used Elmenyawi as a strawman to generalize about "Islamic fundamentalists," to exaggerate the reluctance of Islamist militants to claim responsibility for their terrorism, to disregard the structural and direct violence carried out by Northern powers, and to polarize the West and Muslims. The article opened with: "Today, Islamic fundamentalists have found a new language to propagate their radical views. Through a combination of misinformation, doublespeak and pressing politically correct buzzwords, they continue to promote their agenda while trying to hide

under the veneer of being victims." In this Emerson apparently failed to notice
the irony of his own attempt to silence criticism of his work from Muslims by
labelling them "Islamic fundamentalists."[42]

It should be stated, however, that those who insist that there exist active
media conspiracies against Muslims are making claims which are difficult to
prove. Most media organs in liberal democracies are the sites of contestation for
competing discourses. Dominant, oppositional, alternative, and other
perspectives interact with varying intensity in different media institutions.
However, dominant discourses, being ubiquitous and forceful, usually manage to
overwhelm competing narratives. The denial of the violence and oppression
carried out by specific Muslim groups is intellectually dishonest and morally
repugnant. Sources that produce apologias for the terrorism of Islamist militants
and repressive governments in Muslim-majority countries fail to appear credible.
The contextualization of terrorist incidents within the framework of violence in
human society and in global relations instead helps us to understand better the
relationship between Islamist militants and Northern powers. It is in the broader
interests of journalists and their readers to comprehend the fundamental sources
of human behaviour and the historical relations between various peoples; this
knowledge enables them to uncover the political underpinnings of dominant
discourses.

Coda: Thinking the Unthinkable

Dominant Northern discourses have named Islam as a source of global instability.
In this it is reduced to the interpretation favoured by the most militant of its
followers. Self-serving regimes in Muslim societies have generally tended to
exploit Islamic symbols to buttress their own power bases, thus further alienating
those among the dispossessed who are vulnerable to the propaganda of militant
Islamists. There has been little initiative among the latter to come genuinely to
terms with the issues of modernity within indigenous Muslim contexts, or to go
beyond a closed-minded dogmatism by broaching what Mohammed Arkoun has
termed the "unthinkable." While some Northern governments have made
isolated attempts to understand Muslims better, this has often been prompted by
the desire to control what is seen as a source of conflict and terrorism. There
appears to be a sustained trend among certain Northern integration
propagandists to institutionalize the view of Islam as one of the most disruptive
forces in the contemporary world. This discourse dehistoricizes the relationships
between Northern and Muslim societies, erasing the memory of the colonial era
in which indigenous socio-economic structures were destroyed and replaced with
a global system that favours the North.

Bernard Lewis and Samuel Huntington's "clash of civilizations" thesis
posits Muslims as a major threat to the North. Instead of searching for ways to
resolve this perceived conflict it incites Northern governments to adopt a more
aggressive stance towards Muslim countries. Overtures by the U.S. government
towards some "rogue states" notwithstanding, the dominant American discourses

on international relations remain generally irreconcilable towards Muslim entities that challenge the superpower's hegemony. Like a self-fulfilling prophecy, the clash between the two becomes more likely as their respective agendas are influenced by the militant elements amongst them. As the dispossessed among Muslim (and other Southern) populations come increasingly to suffer under the structural violence of Northern-dominated global structures, the possibility that they will respond with direct violence grows. And as this "Islamic peril" begins to threaten Northern structures of power, there will be greater restrictions placed on the freedom of Muslim communities in the North. There will also be increased deployment of Northern military power in Muslim societies and arming of client regimes. The outcome in Iran of such a process during the 1970s was the overthrow of the Shah—a favourite of Washington—and the ascendency of a mullah-led government. Several other Muslim-majority countries are facing various levels of militancy from Islamist groups and may be headed towards similar futures. The likelihood of these tendencies will probably be enhanced by Northern provocations arising from Bible-based predictions of Armageddon-like confrontations in the new millennium.

Dominant media discourses appear to be echoing rather than challenging the "clash of civilizations" thesis and the belligerency it proposes. The influence of Northern-based transnational media in global image and decision-making is well-established. Their world-wide reach and the dependence of media institutions in virtually all countries on them for foreign news coverage ensures that their stereotypes about Muslims are disseminated much more extensively and intensively around the world than the stereotypes that Muslims have about Northerners. However, certain journalists have genuinely attempted to provide more responsible coverage. Some Northern-based mass media have also been instrumental in uncovering corruption and human rights abuses in Muslim societies. But the generally negative and sometimes ideologically hostile approach of Northern discourses makes it easy for perpetrators of these crimes to dismiss this type of coverage as more anti-Muslim propaganda. An enhanced reputation for informed and ethical journalism in the transnational media would make such reporting more difficult to dismiss.

Some Northern journalists are coming to agree that they can play a role in defusing tense situations or at least in not contributing to their exacerbation. The call by the former editor-in-chief of *Time* magazine for a knowledgeable and conscientious journalism is an admission that reporters have often been neither. But it is also a recognition that the media have a place in not only acting as mediators of messages but also in the process of improving international, inter-cultural communication. The role of the growing number of Southern journalists who work for Northern-based media can be vital in this respect. Structural changes such as increased collaboration between media institutions in the North and the South could also be beneficial to both. Amending newsgathering procedures to ensure that getting it right is more important than getting it first would also improve the quality of reportage. However, as long as newsworkers assume that the "current affairs man" is too occupied with the urgency of today's news to notice the inaccuracies of yesterday's reporting, the craft will not rise above its formulaic style of coverage. Those media institutions in which there remains a general absence of intellectual honesty and of respect for the news consumer will not feel the need to contemplate structural changes.

Conscientious journalism comes from the acknowledgement by media professionals of the effects of their work on society. News workers cannot pretend that their claim to objectivity innoculates them from human subjectivity. Whereas it is humanly impossible to be completely objective, one can attempt to recognize the personal and cultural biases for or against the people one reports about. The media professional who seeks to be genuinely informed necessarily starts with the self. Through an initial inquiry into what the collective Self knows about the Other and also how this knowledge was acquired, one begins to free oneself from the constraints of hackneyed constructions and to produce more authentic coverage. Such reporting recognizes the ideological outcomes of media rituals, seeks to transcend the received scripts and models, and shuns the temptation to cast individuals and groups in the unidimensional roles of heroes, villains, and victims. Beyond just understanding the bases of the "facts" at hand, informed reporting requires the deconstruction of fundamental issues such as violence, peace, democracy, science etc.,—dominant assumptions about which have become naturalized in dominant discourses. Cognizance of the continual dialectic between different points of view that challenge each other enables the journalist to avoid entrapment into hegemonic interpretations. However, this process does not restrict itself to just *two* opposing points of view but leaves her reporting open to a multi-faceted reality. It does not dismiss alternative discourses but introduces them as legitimate expressions of the people who are the objects of news coverage. The rational, the emotional, and the spiritual all enrich this form of reporting, to which the journalist brings her own intellect, experience, instinct, and conscience. It is this kind of revitalized journalism that will help us better comprehend the nature of truly universal values and of contemporary issues such as "the Islamic peril."

NOTES

1. Rana Kabbani, *Europe's Myths of the Orient* (Bloomington: Indiana University Press, 1986), p. 85.

2. Thierry Hentsch, *Imagining the Middle East*, translated by Fred A. Reed (Montreal: Black Rose, 1992), p. 204.

3. Akbar S. Ahmed, *Postmodernism and Islam: Predicament and Promise* (London: Routledge, 1992), p. 265.

4. Fatima Mernissi, *Islam and Democracy: Fear of the Modern World*, translated by Mary Jo Lakeland (New York: Addison Wesley, 1992), p. 9.

5. Ibid, pp. 145-146.

6. Homi Bhabha, *The Location of Culture* (London: Routledge, 1994), p. 250.

7. *Planning for Curricular Change: A Report of the Project on the Future of Journalism and Mass Communication Education* (Eugene, Oregon: School of Journalism University of

Oregon, 1984) and Stuart Adam, "Thinking journalism," *Content*, July/August 1988, pp. 4-11.

8. Gayatri C. Spivak, "Reading *The Satanic Verses*," *Third Text* 11 (Sum. 1990), p. 57.

9. Salman Rushdie, *Imaginary Homelands: Essays and Criticism 1981-1991* (New York: Penguin Books, 1991), p. 396.

10. Akbar S. Ahmed, *Postmodernism and Islam*, pp. 261-62; also see Simon Cottle, "Reporting the Rushdie Affair: A Case Study in the Orchestration of Public Opinion," *Race and Class*, 32:4 (1991), pp. 45-64.

11. According to Azim Nanji, "Intellectual modernity...ought not to be seen as a totalizing discourse, but as a perspective, as a set of tools of comprehension which unlock creativity and release the potential for a constructive dialogue with the community in its contemporary environment." Azim Nanji, "Contemporary Expression of Islam in Buildings: What Have We Learned?" in Hayat Salam, *Expressions of Islam in Buildings* (Geneva: Aga Khan Trust for Culture, 1991) p. 220.

12. Fatima Mernissi, *Islam and Democracy*, p. 91.

13. For example, the July 8, 1995 edition of *The Toronto Star* had a story on the front page of its Life section about the conflict in Egypt between cinema owners who displayed sexually provocative billboards and those who objected to them; the latter were placed in the "fundamentalist" camp. This contrasted with the ways in which ethical, moral, and religious concerns of some North Americans were dealt with in the rest of the section. Page 3 had an advice column at the top of the broadsheet with the headline "Why does filthy language have to pollute our air?" The reader was complaining about the tendency of swearing in daily conversation. "Miss Manners" gave tips on how to deal with the problem, without marginalizing the concern. The headline at the top of the ninth page read, "Marketing distorts society, book says." The article was about the commercialization of North American society through the proliferation of advertising messages; this was also treated as a legitimate concern by the staff reporter. The longest article on page 14, the Religion page, was headlined, "Getting into the spirit of God" and was about the popularity of the Airport Vineyard Christian Church in Toronto. Page 16 carried a short story titled "Crime Doesn't Pay."

14. John L. Esposito, *The Islamic Threat: Myth or Reality?* (New York: Oxford University Press, 1992), p. 169.

15. John Berger's phrase; quoted in Edward W. Said, "Representing the Colonized: Anthropology's Interlocuters," *Critical Inquiry* 15:2 (1989), p. 225.

16. Stuart Adam, "Thinking journalism," pp. 8, 9.

17. Abdul R. JanMohamed, "Wordliness-without-World, Homelessness-as-Home: Toward a Definition of the Specular Border Intellectual," in Michael Sprinker, *Edward Said: A Critical Reader* (Oxford: Blackwell Publishers, 1992), p. 117.

18. Ibid, p. 97.

19. Benjamin M. Weir, "Reflections of a Former Hostage on Causes of Terrorism," *Arab Studies Quarterly* 9 (1987), p. 155.

20. Henry A. Grunwald, "The Post-Cold War Press: A New World Needs a New Journalism," *Foreign Affairs* (Sum. 1993), pp. 14-15.

21. S. Abdullah Schleifer, "Media Secularism Taints Appraisal of Middle East," *The Middle East Times*, 9, July 7-14, 1985, p. 9.

22. Annabelle Sreberny-Mohammadi and Ali Mohammadi, *Small Media and Big Revolution* (Minneapolis, Minnesota: University of Minnesota, 1994) and Hamid Mowlana, "Technology versus Tradition: Communication in the Iranian Revolution," *Journal of Communication* 29:3 (Sum. 1979), pp. 107-112.

23. Hamid Mowlana, "The Role of the Media in U.S.-Iranian Conflict," in Andrew Arno and

Wimal Dissanyake, eds., *The News Media in National and International Conflict* (Boulder, Colo.: Westview, 1984), pp. 94-95.

24. Ibid, p. 94.

25. Robin Woodsworth Carlsen, *Crisis in Iran: A Microcosm of the Cosmic Play* (Vancouver: The Snow Man Press, 1979), p. 40.

26. Edward W. Said, *The World, the Text and the Critic* (Cambridge, Mass.: Harvard University Press, 1983), p. 29.

27. Ibid, p. 285.

28. Ibid, p. 286.

29. Thierry Hentsch, *Imagining the Middle East*, pp. 171-178.

30. Daniel L. Smith, "The Rewards of Allah," *Journal of Peace Research* 26:4 (Nov. 1989), pp. 385-398 and Stephen P. Cohen, and Harriet C. Arnone, "Conflict Resolution as the Alternative to Terrorism," *Journal of Social Issues* 44:2 (1988), pp. 175-89.

31. Mohammed Arkoun, *Rethinking Islam: Common Questions, Uncommon Answers*, translated by Robert D. Lee (Boulder, Colo.: Westview Press, 1994), p. 9.

32. "Secularism/secularist" is not meant here in the sense of the separation of Church and State, but what Aziz Esmail refers to as "the strong sense of the term" (he calls Church-State separation "secular thinking" as opposed to secularism). According to Esmail, "Secularism in the strong sense of the term has the characteristics of an ideology, treating religion as a rival to itself, and attempting to offer a total explanation of its own…" Hayat Salam, ed., *Expressions of Islam in Buildings* (Geneva: Aga Khan Trust for Culture, 1991), p. 24. For a useful list of secularism's meanings, see Michael Hill, *A Sociology of Religion* (New York: Basic Books, 1973), pp. 228-251.

33. Jacques Ellul, *Propaganda: The Formation of Men's Attitudes*, translated by Konrad Kellen and Jean Lerner (New York: Alfred A. Knopf, 1969), p. 251.

34. Hayat Salam, ed., *Expressions of Islam in Buildings,* p. 27.

35. Gaye Tuchman, *Making News: A Study in the Construction of Reality* (New York: Free Press, 1981), p. 90.

36. cair1@ix.netcom.com, "CAIR-NET: Reader's Digest Smears Muslims," *listserv*, July 24, 1997.

37. For example, Bob Harvey, "Media stir hatred of Muslims: group," *The Ottawa Citizen*, September 29, 1999, p. A8.

38. Jay Stone, "To advise and consent," *The Ottawa Citizen*, December 12, 1998, pp. E1, E2 and Val Ross, "Marketing Moses: The selling of The Prince of Egypt has taken on Biblical proportions," *The Globe and Mail*, December 12, 1998, pp. C1, C4.

39. Bob Harvey, "Air Farce apologizes for Muslim skit," *The Ottawa Citizen*, January 29, 2000, p. A8.

40. Aaron Derfel, "MasterCard pulls TV spot after protests: Muslim groups complained ad was offensive to their religion," *The Montreal Gazette*, October 15, 1996, p. A4.

41. cair1@ix.netcom.com, "CAIR-NET: GeoCities to Remove Hate-Filled Site," *listserv*, October 23, 1997.

42. Emerson has a record of alarmist reporting about the threat posed by Muslims in the US. He has produced a highly controversial televison documentary called "Jihad in America." CBS apologized for his use of unsourced and inaccurate information in 1994 on "News Eye on America" (following strong protests from Muslims). Immediately following the Oklahoma terrorist bombing on April 19, 1995, by what turned out to be non-Muslim Americans, he declared, "This was done with the intent to inflict as many casualties as possible. That is a Middle Eastern trait." cair1@ix.netcom.com, "Muslims Asked to Contact CBS on Biased Report," *listserv*, August 5, 1997.

AFTERWORD

Live pictures of an airplane crashing into a world famous skyscaper, which then crumbled to the ground, is not normal television fare. Scheduled live transmission of events tends to be well-planned and publicised, with events usually unfolding broadly within the parameters of a preconceived script. Rarely does the camera capture completely unforeseen incidents. Even in the cases where television crews arrive moments after terrorist bomb explosions, the only "action" available for videotaping usually consists of emergency personnel's hurried movements, smoke billowing from damaged buildings, sirens wailing, and people weeping or shouting in anger.

But on September 11, TV viewers watched the United Airlines Boeing 767 approach the South Tower of the World Trade Center and ram into it at 9:03 a.m. Cameras had been set up around the site following the crash of an American Airlines plane into the North Tower some 15 minutes earlier. Perhaps the only comparable live broadcasts had been the explosion of the space shuttle Challenger in 1986 on television, the on-camera shooting of accused presidential assassin Lee Harvey Oswald in 1963, and the explosion of the Hindenberg zeppelin in 1937 on radio.

Journalists are taken completely taken aback by such traumatic incidents and have to scramble to provide coherent commentary as the disaster unfolds in front of them. In contrast to the well-rehearsed and controlled coverage of a scheduled live event, an unforeseen occurrence leaves the reporter disoriented. The completely unexpected action of an airliner being deliberately flown into one of the world's tallest and most symbolic buildings, followed by the massive loss of life, shook journalists and viewers' cognitive foundations of reality. When faced with the unusual, journalists respond by falling back on set patterns of information gathering and reporting. The resort to routine involves carrying out a prescribed series of actions for accomplishing coverage, such as contacting institutions to obtain access to relevant sites and persons, interviewing, attending press conferences, and using certain kinds of documentary sources. The contingencies of the news format like meeting deadlines as well as the necessity of obtaining "facts," pictures, and quotations from specific categories of people (eyewitnesses, authority figures), ensure that the routines are followed in a systematic manner.

At the same time, attempts are made to place even the most atypical oc-currences within cognitive scripts and models of behaviour shaped by the experience and the narration of previous events. Dominant cultural and religious worldviews of society are critical in shaping these cognitive structures with which we make sense of ongoing events. Even though the events of September 11 were extraordinary, their reporting—following the initial period of disorientation—was eventually placed within frames that had been in place to cover such issues as violence, terrorism, and Islam. There has emerged over the last three decades a set of journalistic narratives on "Muslim terrorism," whose construction is dependent on basic cultural perceptions about the global system of nation-states, violence, and the relationship between Western and Muslim societies. The dominant discourses about these issues help shape the cognitive scripts for reporting the acts of terrorism carried out by people claiming to act in the name of Islam.

Few mass media organs addressed the existence of structural violence in relation to the death and destruction caused by terrorism on September 11. Some exceptions were found in periodicals. The British medical journal *The Lancet* published an editorial by Richard Horton, titled "Public Health: a neglected counterterrorist measure," in its October 6 issue:

> Medicine and public health have important if indirect parts to play in securing peace and stability for countries in collapse. Health could be the most valuable counterterrorist measure yet to be deployed. Attacking hunger, disease, poverty, and social exclusion might do more good than air marshals, asylum restrictions, and identity cards. Global security will be achieved only by building stable and strong societies. Health is an undervalued measure of our global security.[1]

Using the assumption that annual figures for deaths were evenly spread over the year, the November 2001 issue of the development-oriented periodical, *The New Internationalist*, provided the following information to contextualize the loss of life caused by the terrorist attacks:

- Number of people who died of hunger on 11 September 2001: 24,000
- Number of children killed by diarrhoea on 11 September 2001: 6,020
- Number of children killed by measles on 11 September 2001: 2,700[2]

Vincent Mosco notes that destruction on an enormous scale was conducted between 1959 and 1975 to make way for the redevelopment of lower Manhattan by government and corporate interests. This area had comprised adjoining neighbourhoods that provided for a thriving mixed economy and affordable housing. The project to extend New York's downtown, including the construction of the World Trade Center, required the razing of "over sixty acres of buildings, an area four times the site of the WTC attack...[and] eliminated 440,000 of 990,000 manufacturing jobs."[3] Historical assessment of the structural violence that went into building the towers was virtually absent in the dominant coverage of the September 11 attacks.

On September 11, 2001, there was only one story and generally one perspective on the multiple TV networks of North America. Most experts interviewed responded to security matters and did not seem interested in the larger political, social and economic causes of the attacks. The focus was primarily on the immediate reaction rather than on the larger issues. After some initial fumbling, the Bush administration was soon able to set the frames and the agendas for reporting the unfolding story. Indeed, most media—stunned by the events of the day—seemed all too willing to accept the government's lead. As the hunt began for the "Islamic terrorists," journalists' narratives failed to provide a nuanced and contextual understanding of Islam, Muslims, or the nature of the "Islamic peril."

There was a greater diversity of voices that participated in the discussions that followed the terrorist attacks. Karen Armstrong, who has written about religious militancy in Islam as well as in Christianity and Judaism, appeared on TV a number of times; however, her attempts at explaining the broader context of such conflicts were often brushed aside as interviewers sought confirmation for their perceptions about an endemically violent Islam. The dominant discourse's sheer ubiquity, omnipresence, and manoeuverability overshadows the presence of alternative perspectives.

The terrorist attacks of September 11, resulting in the deaths of some three thousand people, revealed an overwhelming failure by the United States government to ensure the security of its citizens. However, relatively few questions were asked by journalists about the multiple lapses of security that had permitted the network of terrorists to plan, prepare and execute the complex series of hijackings and attacks. The media spotlight was focussed mainly on the incidents themselves rather than their broader causes. Instead of exploring how the American government's own activities abroad may have possibly laid the groundwork for the resentment leading to attacks against Americans, the media generally echoed the Bush administration's polarized narrative frame of good versus evil. The series of relationships between the U.S. government and various Afghan groups, including the Taliban, over the preceding two decades also remained largely unprobed: for instance, Washington's support for the mujahideen forces fighting against the Soviet Union in the 1980s, followed by an almost complete withdrawal as the country faced social and economic chaos in the 1990s, was hardly ever mentioned in the media, which instead presented the U.S. as a saviour for the long suffering Afghans. America's role as superpower and its involvement in and attacks on other countries were generally overshadowed. Instead, the righteous and moral stance of the U.S. became a key component of the dominant journalistic script for reporting "the war against terrorism"—a label produced by the administration and accepted uncritically as the rubric for the coverage of the U.S.'s military actions in Afghanistan.

It is remarkable how widely the Assassins legend, discussed in Chapter 4, was used in post-September 11 coverage. Articles in the London-based *Financial Times*[4] and the Toronto-based *Globe and Mail*[5] sought to link the terrorist attack to the historical group. A senior reporter with the Canadian Broadcasting Corporation, Joe Schlesinger, drew on the tale in the "Foreign Assignment" program on October 28, 2001. It also appeared in a news backgrounder by Emily Yoffe[6] on MSN's online "Slate" magazine. Even a *New York Times* article

that apparently sought to provide a positive historical understanding about medieval Muslim science as a contrast to contemporary terrorism opened with the
lead, "Nasir al-Din al-Tusi was still a young man when the Assassins made him
an offer he couldn't refuse."[7] Nor was the script writer of the popular drama
series "West Wing" on the NBC network immune to "the Assassins" bug: an
episode titled "Isaac and Ishmael" aired on October 10, 2001 referred to the
legend.

Nevertheless, there have been some notable cases in which journalists
have sought to conduct conscientious reporting of the events following the September 11 atrocities. The following by Robert Fisk seems to show that even
though he was almost killed by Afghan refugees in December 2001, he attempted to seek the causes of the incident from their perspective:

> And—I realised—there were all the Afghan men and boys who had
> attacked me who should never have done so but whose brutality was
> entirely the product of others, of us—of we who had armed their struggle
> against the Russians and ignored their pain and laughed at their civil war
> and then armed and paid them again for the 'War for Civilisation' just a
> few miles away and then bombed their homes and ripped up their families
> and called them 'collateral damage'.
>
> So I thought I should write about what happened to us in this fearful,
> silly, bloody, tiny incident. I feared other versions would produce a different
> narrative, of how a British journalist was 'beaten up by a mob of Afghan
> refugees'. And of course, that's the point. The people who were assaulted
> were the Afghans, the scars inflicted by us—by B-52s, not by them. And I'll
> say it again. If I was an Afghan refugee in Kila Abdullah, I would have done
> just what they did. I would have attacked Robert Fisk. Or any other
> Westerner I could find.[8]

In this, Fisk acts as a "border specular journalist," a category which I have discussed in the previous chapter. It is more urgent than ever that commentators
on global affairs learn to provide reportage in such honest and conscientious
manners that serve to enlighten rather than obscure our understanding of human conflicts.

Notes

1. R. Horton, "Public Health: A Neglected Counterterrorist Measure," *The Lancet* 358
   (Oct. 6, 2001), pp. 1113.
2. "Two Terrors," *New Internationalist*, (Nov. 2001), 19.
3. Vincent Mosco, "9/11 for Urban Policy," paper presented at the Annual Meeting of the
   Urban Affairs Association, Boston, March 2002.
4. Tom Scott, "Grim lessons from a Legendary Muslim," *Financial Times Weekend* (Oct.
   6-7, 2001).
5. Salim Mansur, "The Father of All Assassins," *The Globe and Mail* (Oct. 11, 2001) .
6. Emily Yoffe, "Bernard Lewis: The Islam Scholar U.S. Politicians Listen To," posted
   Tuesday, November 13, 2001: http://slate.msn.com/?id=2058632
7. Dennis Overbye, "How Islam Won, and Lost, the Lead in Science," *New York Times*
   (Oct. 30, 2001) .
8. Robert Fisk, "My Beating by Refugees is a Symbol of the Hatred and Fury of this Filthy
   War," *The Independent* (Dec. 10, 2001).

INDEX

IMAGINING THE MIDDLE EAST

Thierry Hentsch, *translated by Fred A. Reed*
Recipient of the Governor General's Literary Award for Translation

Examines how Western perceptions of the Middle East were formed and how we have used them as a rationalization for setting policies and determining actions.

> *This is a book of such intellectual vitality that it merits attention now, years after its publication, and should continue to be studied for decades.* —Humanist in Canada

> *For readers who want to understand the world of plural identities.* —Montréal Gazette

> *A stimulating work.* —Journal of Palestine Studies

> *This remarkable book...could be seen as advancing our understanding beyond professor Edward Said's Orientalism.* —Crescent

> *A thorough and valuable account.* —Arab Studies Quarterly

> *An important mediation on the Western encounter with the nearer Orient over two millennia and more.* —Middle East Policy

> *In the best of worlds, no certification of 'expertise' on the Middle East would be granted to anyone who had failed to read and understand what Hentsch has to say. It should be required reading for all of us.* —Middle East Studies Association Bulletin

218 pages, index
Paperback ISBN: 1-895431-12-3 $19.99
Hardcover ISBN: 1-895431-13-1 $48.99

FATEFUL TRIANGLE

The United States, Israel and the Palestinians
Noam Chomsky, Foreword by Edward Said

Since its original publication in 1983, Chomsky's seminal tome on Mid-East politics has become a classic in the fields of political science and Mid-East affairs. For its tenth printing, Chomsky has written a new introduction, and added a foreword by Edward Said.

This new, updated edition highlights the book's lasting relevance, and should be a treasure for fans of the first edition, and an eye-opener for those new to the work. It is invaluable to anyone seeking to understand the Middle East.

> *Tough-minded analysis raises difficult, painful questions.* —Globe and Mail

> *Chomsky's unrelenting tone paints a frightening picture.* —Maclean's

> *A must read for anyone following today's Middle East.* —The Financial Post

> *A devastating collection.* —Library Journal

> *A monumental work.* —Choice

> *Powerful and thoroughly documented.* —The Progressive

> *This is a jeremiad in the prophetic tradition, an awesome work of latter-day forensic scholarship by a radical critic of America and Israel.* —The Boston Globe

485 pages
Paperback ISBN: 1-55164-160-7 $24.99
Hardcover ISBN: 1-55164-161-5 $53.99